The Seven-Day Total Cleanse

A Revolutionary Juice Fast and Yoga Plan to Purify Your Body and Clarify Your Mind

Mary McGuire-Wien

with Jill Parsons Stern

D0051324

New York   Chicago   San Francisco   Lisbon   London   Madrid   Mexico City
Milan   New Delhi   San Juan   Seoul   Singapore   Sydney   Toronto

Library of Congress Cataloging-in-Publication Data

McGuire-Wien, Mary.
    The 7-day total cleanse : a revolutionary juice fast and yoga plan to purify your body and clarify your mind / by Mary McGuire-Wien with Jill Parsons Stern.
        p.   cm.
    Includes bibliographical references and index.
    ISBN 978-0-07-162374-2 (alk. paper)
    1. Detoxification (Health).   2. Fruit juices.   3. Vegetable juices.   4. Yoga.
I. Stern, Jill (Jill Parsons).   II. Title.

RA784.5.M345   2009
613—dc22   2009027016

To my son,
Charles McGuire-Wien,
and
my daughter,
Harriet (McGuire-Wien) Halloway

Chocolate Mousse Pie recipe on page 244 first appeared in *The Candle Cafe Cookbook*. Copyright © 2003 Candle Cafe. Reprinted by permission.

1 2 3 4 5 6 7 8 9 10 11 12 13 14 15 16 17 18 19 20 21 22 23 24 25   FGR/FGR   0 9

ISBN 978-0-07-162374-2
MHID   0-07-162374-4

Interior design by Monica Baziuk

McGraw-Hill books are available at special quantity discounts to use as premiums and sales promotions or for use in corporate training programs. To contact a representative, please e-mail us at bulksales@mcgraw-hill.com.

Please use your own personal discretion and wisdom as you enjoy discovering the information found in this book. Information in this book, and in the author's newsletter and on her blogs and website, is provided with the sole intention and purpose of sharing information. This book is not meant to provide advice or medical recommendations or to substitute for the advice provided by any physician you may have. You should not use the information contained herein for diagnosing or treating health problems or disease, nor as a medication prescription.

Contents

Preface

I FIRST DISCOVERED THE power of juice fasting many years ago when my daughter, who is now twenty-three, was only a year old. Juice fasting was considered a very extreme thing to do at that time, but I felt tired and unattractive. I was sure that if I could only lose the last eight pounds of "baby fat," I would "get my shine back" and be happy and energetic again. I attended the only juice-fasting program I could find, knowing I needed to get out of my day-to-day routine in order to succeed.

It was my good fortune that my choice led me to noted holistic lifestyle coach Alison Shore Gaines at the world famous Kripalu Center for Yoga and Health in Lenox, Massachusetts. Alison's skilled guidance and the safe, compassionate environment of the Kripalu Center were the catalysts for my personal transformation and became the foundation for the American Yogini Juice Cleanse.

When I first arrived at Kripalu, I thought that fasting was a deprivation that forced your body to lose weight. When I left a week later, losing weight had become the least of my concerns. It had happened easily, but I hardly cared anymore because I had gained such life-changing insight and inspiration. It was my huge "aha" moment.

On a cellular level, the tissue cleansing that goes on during a juice fast had liberated my body. Yoga postures and positions that had always been a struggle for me suddenly felt easy and right. And even after I returned home, what I had learned and experienced stayed with me. It didn't matter what came at me; I knew how to manage my energy, when to focus, when to soften. I began to use a juice cleanse on an annual basis.

As I continued my practice of annual cleansing, other things began to change. My life moved through different phases. My kids grew, my relationships changed, I experienced losses and gains, easy times and hard times. But I realized that when I chose to do a cleansing fast during any time of transition, I gained incredible clarity. Before long, I noticed a simple yet stunning example of how the straightforward act of cleansing my body had changed me: I literally gained a sense of direction. I used to get habitually lost. Even in familiar places, I was incapable of finding my way from point A to point B without having to call my husband to ask which way to turn. It sounds crazy, but as I began to tune into my own self and the information that served me, I stopped getting lost. It was then that I began to appreciate the importance of what I was doing and realized that I needed to share the message of the transformative power of juice cleansing with others.

The Seven-Day Total Cleanse is not simply a "detox diet" or a "fast." It is a revolutionary seven-day program of renewal, reflection, and revitalization that will literally change your life. Unlike the prolific fad diets that allow you to quickly drop a few pounds only to gain them back the first day you return to solid food, the seven-day plan will not only jump-start weight loss, but, more important, it will teach you how to foster a mind-body connection that goes beyond the physical changes you experience when you stop eating.

I realized that by combining the ancient and sacred rituals of purification with modern yoga practice I could create new yet familiar rituals that would guide others to experience the same life-changing revelations I had had. In the pages that follow I offer you the same guidance and loving care I offer my students and the guests who stay with us at American Yogini. As you follow the daily schedules in this book, I hope that you will feel my presence supporting and encouraging you. By choosing to participate in the Seven-Day Total Cleanse you are offering your body, mind, and spirit a great gift—the opportunity to truly rebuild, renew, and revitalize.

Acknowledgments

I THINK WHENEVER A book, film, or work of art comes to fruition, magic has taken place. Almost like a sleight-of-hand trick, what looks to be the work of one is in fact created by a team behind the curtain, cocreating with a consolidated vision.

I would like to acknowledge the Kripalu Center, which was my healing refuge and safe learning space for many years, and where I was inspired to find my own creative way to share yoga and all my gifts with my students. I am also grateful to Alison Shore Gaines, my first juice-fasting guide, whose mastery and knowledge are the very foundation upon which my work with cleansing stands.

Thanks to Charles Wildbank for unconditional love, 24/7 inspiration, enthusiasm, support, and unfailing positivity. All of what I do here would be impossible without him by my side.

To Margarita Moreno, our devoted "juice master," who contributed information about the healing properties of Mexican fruits and plants.

My students and juice-cleanse retreat guests are an impressive bunch, and they have all contributed in more ways than they know. I am very grateful to each and every one of them.

To the can-do girls, Shawn Williams and Laura Rosenberg, for sharing some great recipes. Special gratitude goes to Shawn Williams, who encouraged me to create juices that could be delivered to our New York City clients—and then delivered them herself—so I could stay home to write.

To Kathy Zimnoski, my kitchen assistant, for her morning smiles and morning love, for juice making and overall cheerleading. She is often the first person I see in the morning, and her enthusiasm and love got me going for many an early morning during the year it took to complete this project.

Benay Vynerib, friend and manager of Candle Cafe and Candle 79 restaurants in New York, has been there for me on more than one occasion during the years since I began presenting this important information to my students and community. Her generosity of spirit and natural graciousness is humbling. The cuisine at "The Candles" is the best in New York, indeed the best in the world. Thank you once again to these masters of vegan cuisine for sharing outstanding recipes.

I want to acknowledge my agent, Joanne Wyckoff, whose confidence in me gave me confidence in myself. I love working with her and could not imagine what I would do without her counsel.

Thank you to Jill Parsons Stern, with whom I absolutely *love* working. Working with Jill on this book was just fun, like a great game of Ping-Pong, and our productivity seemed effortless. She has been not only cowriter but teacher and friend as well. I have never before worked as closely with anyone so easily and comfortably. Because of her intrinsically generous nature, I benefited from positive, cheerful work sessions even when the heat was on.

I would be remiss if I failed to acknowledge Emily Carleton, my editor, who has championed my concepts to the entire McGraw-Hill team while guiding me ever so gently along the critical steps necessary to bring this, my first book with McGraw-Hill, to full fruition.

Thanks to Stacy and the Red Zee team for the Internet keyword and marketing research that helped name this book—and for juice tasting!

I acknowledge also the sunshine of my children, Charles and Harriet, and of my granddaughter, Eleanore; the simple sound of their voices over the phone was essential to the energy I required for the completion of this book.

And last, but far from least, the sun. Every single day of this project, without fail, I watched the sun rise—whether through clouds, blue skies, rain, or snow—and drank it up daily in the form of juice. My bodymind greatly benefited from this daily, delicious, and unconditional infusion of love.

PART 1

Why the Seven-Day Total Cleanse Will Work for You

T HE SEVEN-DAY TOTAL CLEANSE combines the detoxifying benefits of a nutrient-rich, raw juice cleanse with the principles of a yogic lifestyle and dynamic healing techniques drawn from traditional Indian and holistic wellness beliefs. This unique fusion of yoga, Self care, systemic cleansing, and the targeted nutrients found in my raw juice recipes promotes a conscious change in mind-set and habits resulting in mental, physical, and emotional benefits that continue long after the seven-day cleanse is completed.

The daily exercises, juices, meditations, and rituals of the Seven-Day Total Cleanse focus on the renewal and rebalancing of the seven chakras—powerful energy centers that traditional Indian medicine believes are aligned along the center of the body, from the first chakra at the base of the tailbone to the seventh chakra at the top of the head. When these emotional energy storehouses become blocked or exaggerated, you experience shifts in your physical, mental, spiritual, and emotional states. The program in this book will consciously bring your mind, body, and spirit into a new balance. From there you will be empowered to choose how you wish to treat yourself. In just seven days you will put yourself on the path to clarity of thought, renewal of spirit, and a joyful connection with your body.

1

The Seven-Day Total Cleanse

More than "Just" a Fasting Plan

WHEN STUDENTS COME TO my American Yogini *Hohm* for a retreat, they have already made a decision to cleanse their bodies through fasting, or abstaining from solid foods. But as they fully engage in my program, it soon becomes clear that that surface motivation is rooted in a (spoken or unspoken) desire for deep change. Each individual's commitment to, and reasons for, choosing to cleanse by fasting is unique to that person. Students frequently tell me they want to fast in order to lose weight, to jump-start a diet, or, more ambitiously, to break their bad eating habits.

Dedicating a certain amount of time to cleansing and fasting is the greatest gift that one can give one's Self. A properly guided cleanse is *not* simply a fad diet or a chance to participate in the "detox" trend. In fact, the very word *detox* insinuates that you are somehow toxic—and that is quite far from the truth. Our bodies are all miracles of filtration and efficiency. We are building new healthy cells every day, replacing old and tired ones that have served us well for months or even years. The body wants to make us well; it is our trusted partner, here to create health so we can enjoy a purposeful life.

Fasting and cleansing have been an important part of the yogic tradition for thousands of years. Purification practices have always been used to facilitate liberation from earthly bounds and to free the flesh from anything not supporting the union of the body with the divine. In yoga, these traditional purification practices are referred to as *austerities*, and they are part of a fundamental practice of burning off impurities that hinder the union of our finite bodies with the infinite body of the divine. The austerity of fasting is called *tapas,* which is the Sanskrit word for *heat* or *burning fire.* Fire and burning represent destruction, but it is from ashes that new forests quickly grow. In fact in some cultures, cremation is thought to free the spirit to the divine after death so that it can be reborn.

In yoga, fasting is used to burn off the finite and ego-driven Self to reveal the infinite and limitless Self. *Tapas,* then, is the burning off of mental, physical, and spiritual impurities that hinder one's connection with universal consciousness. Historically, austerities such as fasting were practiced with the intention of causing suffering in order to "burn off" whatever occluded one's awareness and energy, leaving one in a state of pure essential energy. Gurus guided their followers through the intense internal fires of dismay, doubt, and self-conscious striving to a state of total transformation.

Many people come to yoga because they are suffering in some way. Perhaps you feel a sense of pain or dissatisfaction that is hard to articulate, something not quite definable or justifiable. The accumulation of emotional debris—stored emotion that has not been looked at, not yet burned off—can manifest as a sense of unease, a feeling that things are not quite right. You may feel as if there is something "wrong" about you—your body, your face, your job, or your relationships. You may be experiencing an emotional crisis, linked to work, family, or a relationship. Although you may decide to try yoga or fasting to achieve the physical benefits of toning or weight loss, you may also be hoping that the practice of yoga will quiet your mind.

It doesn't matter how you have arrived at your decision to practice this seven-day cleanse. What matters is that you have found this book. As you practice this cleanse, all the feelings of being "wrong" that you may have been carrying around in your body for years and years will dissolve and a real, authentic, and personal life—one that will be right for you—will emerge in only seven days.

The Seven-Day Total Cleanse comes from my deeply rooted belief that you do not have to *continue* to suffer in order to burn off the spiritual and bodily toxins that obscure your best and highest Self. I have created this program to help you gain the ability to feel complete safety, comfort, and love toward yourself. Giving yourself comfort and love enables you to safely observe your suffering, and in this "watching," you can finally release it. I want everyone who undertakes the honorable and sacred practice of the Seven-Day Total Cleanse to feel how noble and regal a practice this is. By taking away just one element of your daily life—eating solid foods—and replacing it with pampering and loving indulgences, as well as delicious and richly combined elixirs, you will feel safe and free to release the undigested emotions that are obscuring your personal clarity.

Know that when you embark on this practice, you are following in the footsteps of kings and queens, yogis and yoginis, who have been luminaries at the leading edge of creation for thousands of years.

Why a Juice Cleanse Works Best

Our bodies and spirits are amazing, resilient entities, and every day we are given another chance for renewal—fresh blood circulates through our system, skin cells slough off and are replaced, new ideas arise and are nurtured or forgotten. So with all these opportunities for a fresh start, why do we cling to habits that are unhealthy? Why aren't we all at our ideal weights, why doesn't our skin glow with health, what stops us from finding fulfilling jobs or relationships? In short, why is it so hard to parlay this natural cycle of revitalization into a conscious union of mind and body?

One reason is that our bodies are worn out from working overtime to metabolize a steady diet of processed food. On a cellular level, our bodies exhibit their exhaustion and confusion with a host of complaints: headaches, eczema, asthma, digestive disorders, autoimmune disorders, allergies, and inflammation. Our bodies have become so sensitized and overwhelmed by triggers associated with unhealthy environments and foods that they rebel.

Eliminating processed foods from your body and diet and replacing them with the cleansing, nourishing juices of the Seven-Day Total Cleanse lets your body begin to recover at a cellular level. One of the most critical aspects of this cellular cleansing is the consumption of "live" or "raw" foods during your entire cleanse. All of the juices and most of the recipes in this book use only "live" foods as their ingredients. Live foods are foods that are totally unprocessed and thus retain the vitality of the plants and soil that produced them. All of the enzymes, minerals, vitamins, and nutrients of the food remain intact. They are fully alive, with the energy of the sun surging through their cells, and they pass their vitality along to you when you consume them.

Live foods are also called "raw" foods because cooking is one of many forms of processing that destroys the vitality of foods. Nature provides every raw fruit and vegetable with the exact and perfect catalyst it needs to transfer its life force energy to us: enzymes. The enzymes contained in raw fruits and vegetables do the work that must be done in order for us to absorb the nutrients. Without enzymes, our bodies cannot access the nutrients contained in the food we are eating. However, whenever we consume anything that is not in its natural, raw state, our bodies are forced to produce their own enzymes. This requires energy from your body, and the energy used to create these enzymes will be put toward accessing the nutrients, not toward cellular renewal or physical activity. This is one of the reasons you may feel like you need a nap after eating a big cooked meal or indulging in junk food.

In addition, raw vegetables and fruits contain water that hydrates our systems and are full of fiber, which helps to move things along so our bodies can process waste quickly and efficiently like the good filters they are. This means that by eating raw fruits and vegetables, we are cleansing all the time, just as we are meant to. A healthy body will have an elimination after every meal. Think of a baby: feed the baby and within an hour, you will have to change a diaper. You were once that baby.

Raw juices offer all the benefits of raw foods minus the fiber. Without the fiber, we spend even less energy of our own in the digestion process and the nutrients we absorb are extremely concentrated. The living enzymes contained in raw juices offer huge amounts of energy that can be completely directed toward detoxifying the body and clearing old, weary cells that are dragging us down by making us feel thick, foggy, and tired. When you cleanse, you are allowing your body to access the cellular memory of youthful vitality.

Of course most people do not care to eat completely raw diets, and this is perfectly understandable. I offer some delicious cooked recipes at the end of this book and encourage you to approach healthy eating in whatever way feels right for you. However, there are certain habits that will help to reinforce the beneficial changes that this seven-day cleanse will inspire in your body. In her book *The Raw Food Detox Diet*, noted nutrition expert and author Natalia Rose points out the wisdom of eating "raw till dinner" or "light to heavy"—that is, beginning your day with juices and moving on to consuming fruits, then vegetables, nuts, and finally cooked food. This approach floods your body with vital cell-scrubbing enzymes from the moment you start your day. It encourages prompt elimination of any toxins that might have built up during the night and ongoing cleansing throughout the day. Following this approach will leave your body feeling lighter and more energetic during the most active parts of your day.

The Seven Chakras

Having more physical energy is, without a doubt, one of the benefits you will experience as a result of undertaking any kind of cleansing program. But I want to offer you so much more during the seven days that I will be guiding you. You undertook this cleanse because you were seeking some kind of *change* in your life—and more than physical energy is required to enact change.

Each juice recipe in this book was created to support and strengthen a unique aspect of your physical body; however, they were also formulated to attend to the energy of each of the seven chakras that influence your mind, spirit, and body. No other juicing or cleansing program focuses on the balancing of these powerful energy centers in the same way as the Seven-Day Total Cleanse does. For the seven days of your cleanse, each juice, each exercise, each meditation, and each activity is specifically chosen to balance and support the energy of your chakras.

The seven chakras function together, flowing from the center of your fourth (heart) chakra simultaneously down to the grounding first chakra and up to the seventh chakra of connection. When all are in harmony, mind and body, emotions and physicality, spirit and universe come into a beautiful balance to serve your highest purpose.

Let me tell you about each chakra:

➤ **The first chakra,** also known as base chakra, is attuned to the color red and is located at the perineum. Emotionally, it endows you with a sense of stability and security and is connected with grounding spiritual energies. Physically it is associated with the rectum, the lower colon, and the lower back.

➤ **The second chakra,** also known as the sacral chakra, has an affinity for the color orange and is located just between your pubic bone and your sacrum. It is associated with passion, creativity, enthusiasm, sexuality, and the reproductive system and is an important emotional center. It manifests physically in your hips and sex organs.

➤ **The third chakra,** also known as the solar plexus chakra, is represented by the color yellow and is located between your spine and your navel. It is connected to willpower, expansiveness, and independence. Physically it is associated with digestion.

➤ **The fourth chakra,** also known as the heart chakra, is signified by the color green and is located at the center of your chest under your sternum. It is connected to devotion and unconditional love as well as to the heart, blood, and circulation.

➤ **The fifth chakra,** also known as the throat chakra, is associated with bright blue. It governs emotions arising out of communication, expression, and fluid thought and influences the thyroid, the lungs, the nose, and the throat.

➤ **The sixth chakra,** also known as the brow chakra, has an affinity for deep blue or indigo and is associated with intuition and mental clarity. Physically it is linked to the front brain, the eyes, the ears, and the pineal gland.

➤ **The seventh chakra,** also known as the crown chakra, is represented by the color purple or violet and is located at the top of the head.

It corresponds to universal consciousness, "beingness," and the release of karma and influences the skull, the brain, and the glands in the back and top of the brain.

As you move through the seven days of this total cleanse, I want you to think of your body and mind as being wholly integrated rather than as separate entities. In this book I'll use the word *bodymind* to describe this concept, a word that lets you "feel" how connected the two should be; one should not be put ahead of, or able to overrule, the other.

Like the chakras, the body and the mind are actually not separate, but different aspects of the same entity. It is only in our mind, whose very purpose it is to separate things, that we must use words in order to understand each part before we can experience wholeness. But in our heart, whose purpose it is to feel, the reality of our finite bodies is brought together with the infinite possibilities born from the integration of body and mind. Using the new word *bodymind* will help you to begin forming an understanding of what is happening as you practice the seven days of this total cleanse. After all, the Seven-Day Total Cleanse is not solely a body cleanse nor is it solely a mind cleanse. It is a total cleanse for your bodymind. It is the same with the chakras: we will "cleanse" each of the seven chakras one by one, but in fact by day seven, it is the wholeness of all these emotions and energies that will be perceptibly cleansed.

Understanding the gifts of each chakra and how they affect your bodymind empowers you to consciously control how you are navigating through life. For instance, something may have happened in your life that made you feel unsafe. Perhaps you lost your job or marriage, or you are faced with losing something that you have always believed is essential to your survival, such as your financial security. The primal emotion that emerges is intense fear, perhaps even terror. When this happens your first chakra, or the energy center located at the base of your body, extending down into your legs and feet, will respond by closing down to avoid feeling the fear. Your physical body will react with pain in your lower back, loss of movement in the lower intestines, or possibly cramps in the legs or feet. It may feel as though your whole lower body is in "lockdown," and indeed, it is.

When fear for survival kicks in and a great suffering, both physical and mental, ensues, the Seven-Day Total Cleanse will help you integrate and safely filter out long-held emotions so you can regain a sense of security, safety, and stability. Each day you will be given specific meditations, journaling tasks, pampering rituals, and of course special juice recipes that will allow you to cleanse and integrate the emotions and heal the body following the connections of each of the seven chakras.

As we said before, each of your body's chakras has a particular color affinity. Fresh foods whose natural colors correspond to the colors of the chakras are thought to enhance the absorption of energy by each individual cell in our bodies. Learning to "listen to your body" when choosing what to eat allows you to tune in to the harmonic energies of your entire system, including the subtle energies of the chakras. The American Yogini Juice Cleanse focuses on teaching you to "listen" to your body in order to increase your energy, attain your optimal weight, achieve emotional balance, and access the self-knowledge that will allow you to act with clarity.

Reshape Your Body

I know the reason why many of you picked up this book. It's the same reason that I first sought out a juice fast, the same reason that many first-time students contact me, and the same reason that drives the $40-billion-per-year diet industry. You want to know how much weight you can lose. You probably understand by now that the purpose of a cleanse is not to lose weight but rather to promote *change*, and I can tell you that most people *change* their physical bodies by losing an average of a pound a day on a juice fast.

While I am sure that your body may be seven to ten pounds lighter at the end of this cleanse, what really excites me is seeing the lifelong results as my students commit to a much deeper change than just dropping a few pounds. I am constantly amazed and delighted by students who have returned to their cleansing practice year after year and whose lives, as a result, have manifested great things as they have shared their best with the world each day.

There are many issues, large and small, that can cause us to stop eating, including grief, illness, and anxiety. Even the common cold can make us lose our appetites—and a few pounds. But as soon as we are feeling better again, we go back to our old ways and the weight creeps back up, sometimes even higher than it was before. It seems like a simple equation: Stop eating, lose weight. Start eating, gain it back.

And yet we all know deep down that even the simplest facts can belie a much more complex set of circumstances. While I appreciate that weight loss can be one desired goal in undertaking a cleanse, I hope you will ultimately come away with something more. If you drop your goal-oriented stance of "fasting to lose weight," you will open yourself to a total transformation that has nothing to do with the amount of space at your waistband—and everything to do with the expanding spaciousness revealed within your Self.

There are times that we eat to satisfy hungers or cravings that do not come from our physical bodies. When you stop eating, you literally create a space—space in your stomach, space in your mind, space in your soul. As you go through this juice fast, I will guide you toward true clarity so that you will be fully enabled to choose how you wish to fill this space—or perhaps you will choose not to fill your newly revealed spaciousness but become quite comfortable living with a sense of it. Your way is the perfect way, as you shall see.

When you commit to this seven-day program, I will help you to turn your thinking around so that the point of refraining from solid food becomes not what you will lose but all that you will gain.

Retrain Your Hunger

From a purely physical perspective, fasting—eating sparingly or abstaining from some foods—is one way to allow our bodies a rest from the work of processing. This is *not* an experience of deprivation but just the opposite—an opportunity for enrichment. With this juice cleanse, special care has been taken so that you will not feel deprived. The flavorful broth and nutrient-rich juices that you enjoy each day will nourish your body and your senses, offering a variety of tastes along with nutritional support.

The beauty of this purifying cleanse is that you are not relying on willpower to stop eating. The problem with willpower is that it tends to cancel out intuition. A juice cleanse is not simply an exercise in endurance. You won't need to will yourself through this experience. The Seven-Day Total Cleanse has been created to make you feel pampered and wrapped in comfort and love.

The juices you will enjoy during these seven days are blended with a balance of flavors and a full array of nutrients to be absolutely delicious. I strongly believe that no one should ever drink or eat *anything* that is not delicious and beautiful to behold. I believe that when a food is beautiful to look at, smells fragrant, and tastes delicious, only then will our cells open up to receive it fully. If something tastes like pond scum or looks like mud and you have to gulp it down while holding your nose, every cell in your body is saying, "Oh no!" When the cells say, "Oh yes!" they are open to receive, like a sunflower turned to face the sun. Never ever eat or drink anything, *including the recipes in this book*, if you do not absolutely love the way it tastes.

This is the best reason to learn how to make your own juices, or at least to know how to "tweak" a purchased juice (from a fresh juice bar, please, never from a bottle!) to your taste. This is your opportunity to enhance your intuition and learn to trust yourself. As you become clear about your true desires, you will no longer feel deprived when you abstain from foods you know to be unhealthy.

By the end of these seven days, you will have learned to listen to your Self and your body. In the days after the cleanse, you'll continue to gain clarity. Because you have taken the time to appreciate the juices—savoring the pleasures of tasting familiar foods in unfamiliar combinations—you will have all the tools you need to continue to nourish your physical body in a way that benefits you on the outside *and* on the inside. You will naturally move toward your ideal and natural body weight (and not a weight determined by your degree of willpower or the expectations of others), your skin will glow from deep within, and you will discover the happiness that is your birthright.

Renew Your Body

Fasting and cleansing practices are a reliably effective way to initiate clarity of thought, to cleanse our internal organs and tissues, and to purify the "subtle body" (consisting of the psychological and spiritual aspects of our bodymind). When cleansing is paired with yoga—indeed, as it becomes a regular part of your yoga practice—it is without a doubt the fastest track to your highest and best Self.

If you have never practiced yoga before, a cleanse such as this is the perfect introduction. More than 70 percent of the students who come to me to learn about cleansing have never practiced yoga before. It is a great honor—and a great responsibility—to give students their first yoga experience. It makes me so happy to learn that nearly all of my first-time students have made yoga a part of their lives after the cleanse, in large and small ways.

By combining the documented benefits of juice cleansing with the powerful, dynamic energies of yoga, the Seven-Day Total Cleanse offers you the opportunity to become even more aware of how your mind and your body exert powerful influences on each other. Yoga (from the Sanskrit word *yuj*, meaning *to join* or *union*) is more than just exercise or stretching. It is a lifestyle that allows you to know and observe yourself, find your inner compass, and understand that you are connected to something bigger than yourself—and that you don't have to assume a contorted, gymnastic position to experience it! Yoga is not something you *do*. It is something you *practice*. For each of the seven days of the cleanse, I will give you simple, effective yoga-based exercises, stretches, and breathing techniques specifically designed to enhance and support the powerful mental and physical changes you will be experiencing.

Yoga is about Self experience; that is, experiencing your Self in a conscious way. This is why we sit in postures. We can notice things such as: Am I breathing fully? Can I back off from this edge and find the place where my breath is not blocked or obstructed? Yoga gives you a simple way to feel yourself. It is not meant to create pain but to let you know where you truly are. When you are in a posture and you find it so painful that you realize you are holding your breath, you are not being truthful with yourself. Back off. Be compassionate. Remember always that a yoga pose never puts pain into your body. The pain or discomfort comes from your life experiences—your undigested, unintegrated emotion that has created a particular point of resistance. Yoga poses will never look the same for two different people because no two people share the same life experiences or the same emotions blocking the posture.

Only the breath, and the courage to feel, will shift and cleanse an emotional block. It does not matter if you cannot discover the root of your pain; yoga will resolve it for you on the mat. You do not need to know why yoga works for it to be of benefit, or for cleansing to work its magic. So if you cannot do all the exercises recommended during the seven days of the cleanse, simply do your best. No matter how much you are able to do, you will benefit and learn a great deal about yourself.

Revitalize Your Mind

In this book you will learn not only how to fast from food but also how to break from the relentless stimulation of your busy, overwhelming life. By definition, removing something creates space. After all, a vessel cannot be refilled until it has been emptied. By offering you some simple meditations each day, I will show you how to tune out the "information noise" that clutters your mind and clouds your spirit. The constant interruption of PDAs, the Internet, cell phones, round-the-clock broadcasting—the dis-ease that Yogi Bhajan, the spiritual leader of Kundalini yoga, termed "info-dementia"—has reached epidemic proportions. As a businesswoman with a website, a Facebook page, and a Twitter account, I know only too well how challenging it can be to step out of communication with the rest of the world. However, years of practicing yoga and regular cleansing have shown me how vital truly quiet time is to clarity of mind and purpose.

During your cleanse you will learn how to:

➤ free your body from food choices that weigh you down and compromise your health
➤ retrain your mind to filter out information that burdens your spirit, such as the messages from modern media that often serve only to reinforce our toxic beliefs (that we are not beautiful enough, that we are not achieving enough, that we are not safe from harm in our home or homeland, and so on)
➤ integrate your strongest emotions, deepest needs, and greatest strengths in order to confidently choose what is right for you, right now

Your senses, which have become dulled by the relentless twenty-first-century task of processing, must be sharpened in order for you to exist consciously in today's fast-moving world. Distinguishing which information is serving us and which is not is critical to our vitality on all levels. To be the best, most vibrant specimen of humanity you can be—the best *you*—you must master the art of managing information. During the seven days of this cleanse, you will learn how to tune out the information you do not need, allowing you to discern the information you *do* need in order to benefit from the abundance and goodness that surrounds you.

Begin Today, Benefit Every Day

The daily rituals, exercises, and recipes in this seven-day plan can be done anytime, anywhere, and by anyone. There is no need to close yourself off from the world or retreat from your daily responsibilities. Of course there is an undeniable luxury in allowing yourself a full week for self-pampering and introspection, and the more you can cocoon yourself away while you experience this ritual, the more you will appreciate the "luxury of less." However, there is no reason why you can't experience the full benefits of the Seven-Day Total Cleanse without disrupting your home or work routines. Many of the habits that you will learn are meant to become part of your daily life. So whether you decide to turn your home into a miniresort and linger over each step of this program, or simply choose to incorporate the cleansing rituals into your everyday life, I will show you how to find the time and space you need to overcome the challenges of sensory overload in your environment and to consciously tune into the beautiful, ongoing renewal of your body and mind.

A seven-day cleanse is very complete, but a cleanse can be any amount of time you—in your (hopefully) newfound wisdom—feel will work for you at any given time. Sometimes when you fast you may need a longer time period, and sometimes you may need a shorter one. It will take as long as your life allows—and as long as it takes you to naturally clear the cells of waste and to integrate undigested thoughts and emotions.

In just seven days you can change so much. In just seven days you can attend to each of the seven chakras and begin to understand the connection that is your bodymind. The number seven is a number of great synchronicity: days of the week, colors of the rainbow (that happen to correspond to your chakras)—the full spectrum of light. Just as the juices you will consume will cleanse the physical organs of your body, the color vibrations and the light of the juices will work to cleanse these organs of the emotional energy they are holding. As you cleanse your body, you cleanse your emotions and your mind. In seven days you will realize the truth of one of my most important teachings: what's true in the body is true in the mind.

In just seven days you can change your life, and I am honored to guide you on your journey to clarity.

2

What Makes This Cleanse Different from Others?

A SMALL MIRACLE INEVITABLY occurs whenever we fast: we achieve new clarity concerning our true desires and our life's purpose. A sense of spaciousness is revealed as layer upon layer of nonessential information is cleared away.

Here and elsewhere in this book I frequently use the term *information*. I use this term to refer to anything that is passed through the body, including food, skin-care products, words, and even sights and sounds. Your body is essentially one big filter, and information is what you are filtering. Our amazing, miraculous bodies can discern which information serves our creative purposes and which does not. Our eyes filter and process what we see, our ears use tiny hairs to filter sound, our kidneys and liver filter our blood, our skin filters the sun's rays, our lungs filter the air we breathe, our lymph system filters the water in our bodies, our hearts filter our pain, and our minds filter an unimaginable stream of language, calculations, and more. All of these parts of our bodies are really filtering information.

Indeed, the food we consume through our mouths—and anything put upon our skin, such as soap, lotion, or makeup—is interpreted by our bodies as information, dense with data that must be processed. When food data is introduced into the body, the body must decide what part of this data should be absorbed and how much is needed or desired. The purest components of these nutrients will help the body grow new cells that have enough energy to serve our purpose. With incredible innate intelligence, the body then discerns what will be eliminated. If artificial substances, for example chemical preservatives, are encountered, confusion may occur and the body may "hold on" to these discrete "data" until it can figure out if they are useful. The perfection of our bodies as they work as filters is dazzling. Your body is designed to be well and healthy, its systems working 24/7 to filter out harmful or useless information.

Unfortunately, in the fast-paced times we live in, you are putting information into your body faster than your bodymind can filter it. We don't allow our bodymind the time or space to weigh what is useful and what is to be eliminated. The good news, though, is that your body is creating new cells every moment. We need to give it only a periodic rest from bad information and a period of time for good information input. Simply stopping information overload for a few short days will give your body the time it needs to filter out the inevitable buildup.

The Seven-Day Total Cleanse is different from other cleansing and fasting programs because it addresses the bodymind in full. When you practice a *total* cleanse, you restrict not just food data but also consciously decide what other information you are going to filter through your body. You learn to listen carefully in order to hear what your own bodymind is asking you for and you begin to understand when your body needs time to integrate physical, mental, or emotional experiences.

If you worry that you will be unable to tune into your bodymind successfully, consider this: You were once a baby. You came into this world utterly in tune with your bodymind. And the very cells of your body retain this memory. But as perfectly attuned to our bodymind as we were at birth, we grow into habits that become well-practiced routines and form deep grooves in our lives. These grooves can become deep ruts that easily derail us from the purposeful lives we were meant to live.

Consider that you have likely spent hours upon hours using repetition to teach your Self to ignore and turn away from emotional pain and conflict by numbing your bodymind so that you don't feel it. When a difficult emotion presents itself, do you turn to numbing foods consumed in unconscious portions, or to drugs or alcohol, or to frenetic and constant activity of the body or the mind? Have you fallen into the rut of relying on nonstop stimulation for your body and your mind, keeping them separate and nonintegrated while you exhaust both with what have become habitual activities?

If so, you are not alone. Most of us will do anything to avoid our emotions, and many of us try to rationalize this behavior by convincing ourselves that we are pursuing healthy practices by working out to the point of exhaustion and supplementing a processed diet with more processed supplements. What we cannot, or will not, admit is how we can conveniently avoid feeling simply by relating to our world and our lives exclusively with our minds.

Yogi Bhajan, the master of Kundalini yoga, tells us: "When we relate consciously in partnership with our bodies, our bodies relate consciously to us." This cleanse is designed to give you tools and practices that are easy and fun, approachable by any *body* in any condition, that will allow you to leave your cerebral world and move back into your body. When you fully inhabit your body, you can integrate emotion as you instinctively did as a baby—you cried when frightened, sought comfort when uncomfortable, stopped eating when full.

If you are to return to a natural state of health and your natural weight, and if you want these results to last for the rest of your life, you must gain an awareness of how you push down your emotions and numb yourself, how you cut yourself off from your best Self. Once you honestly admit to the ways in which you numb your bodymind, you have something that you did not have before—a choice. It really is that simple: by becoming aware of our entrenched habits, we become empowered to change them.

You spent many hours as a baby learning what it feels like to be naturally pain free, to be filtering vigorously and freely, and these memories are imprinted into your body. You have that cellular memory within you. Think about how healthfully and quickly the baby grows new cells! When we stop the input of nonessential information and accept only that which supports our bodies' natural affinity for cellular renewal—even if it's only once or twice a year—our cellular rejuvenation speeds up just like a baby's.

Through this cleanse you will become truly integrated and whole, and your new awareness will cause subtle shifts, down to the cellular level, that will never be lost or forgotten. This is what makes this cleanse different from any other you may have already tried or experienced.

The Seven-Day Total Cleanse offers you the perfect opportunity to give your bodymind exactly what it needs. Raw juices are the ideal information for your physical body. They are pure sun energy, alive and complete. They naturally contain the precise enzymes that your body needs in order to clean up depleted, dead, and dying cells and to create fresh, healthy replacements at record speed. Furthermore, the juice recipes in this book show you how to blend juices in such a way that they possess optimal enzymatic action, setting to their task like tiny internal scrub brushes, happily cleaning your physical house while you pamper your bodymind with loving attention and nourishing beauty rituals.

In the next chapter, I'll guide you through exercises that will help you determine the optimal time for *you* to undertake a cleanse. You will learn how to ask yourself important questions like, "What does my body, mind, spirit—my *Self*—need in this moment?" And more important, you will learn how to listen to the answers you receive.

3

When Is the Right Time to Practice a Cleanse?

HOW WILL YOU KNOW when the time is right for you to practice a cleanse? I recommend that you begin the Seven-Day Total Cleanse when you can create enough time and when you feel ready for the positive changes cleansing will bring you. You may feel nervous about committing to seven days of juices. My advice is to simply *begin*, and to then recommit to each day anew.

As I said earlier, many of my students first come to me intending to practice a cleanse as a way to lose weight. Perhaps you are thinking to yourself, "I should cleanse after the holidays, or to get rid of these last five pounds, or to jump-start a diet before bathing-suit season." This is fine. Losing weight is not a trivial reason to cleanse. Any true feeling is a great reason, and in our culture the physical imperative often drives us. Here are the most common reasons people decide to cleanse:

➤ **Seasonal Cleansing.** Many students who have come to practice cleansing with me have followed a seasonal intuition. They feel a need to "spring clean" their bodies or to undertake a cleanse after the frenzy of a holiday season. This is one way we tune into the support of the universal rhythms of nature.

➤ **Cleansing for Beauty.** Weight loss obviously falls into the beauty category, but it also makes sense that if you have recently undergone a procedure like dental work or cosmetic procedures for the purpose of enhancing your beauty, doing something as loving as a cleanse would bring out your deepest and most radiant beauty. A cleanse is a good way to help your body fully clear itself of the (sometimes appropriate) medications required during such procedures. Surgical procedures, even minor ones, put a lot of stress on the body, and though it can rebound, why not give it all the help you can? Help your body help you by cleansing after dosing it with medications. Your liver will love you for it, and your beauty will be enhanced from the inside out.

➤ **Cleansing for Change.** The *real* reason to embark on a cleansing practice is simple: change happens and resistance is futile. There is no better way to facilitate and navigate change than with a cleanse. We are not always in a position to initiate positive change, and often change is not wanted at all: divorce; loss of a loved one, pet, or relationship; loss of a job or a home. Perhaps a devastating illness threatens you or someone you love. We meet all of these events with great resistance, and this causes us great suffering. The Seven-Day Total Cleanse offers you a positive, healthful way to integrate these changes into your Self so that you can continue to learn, grow, and contribute positively to the changing world around you.

On the other hand, rather than dealing with unwanted change, you may be in need of a catalyst for change. The Seven-Day Total Cleanse is a powerful catalyst. If you feel as though you are in a rut in which life has become repetitive, lost meaning, and become dull or purposeless, a cleanse can help move you out of your negative patterns. Even wanting to lose weight is a desire for change.

It doesn't matter whether you are suffering from a change being forced upon you or are desiring new meaning in your life: the Seven-Day Total Cleanse will be the ship to carry you through the breaking waves of change. All you have to do is acknowledge that *change* is the operative word, and the Seven-Day Total Cleanse will help you embrace it.

The Seven-Day Total Cleanse is based on a strong foundation of yogic principles and lifestyle. In yoga, as in cleansing, many of my students come to a practice because they are suffering in some way. Perhaps you feel a sense of struggle or dissatisfaction that is hard to articulate, or which you have trouble justifying to yourself. Accumulated emotional debris—stored emotions that you have ignored or neglected—can manifest in a sense of unease, a feeling that there is something "wrong" about you.

Whatever your reason, the truth is it doesn't matter how you have arrived at your decision to practice this cleanse. What matters is that you have found this book and can now scrub away all those feelings of being "wrong" that you may have been carrying around in your body for years and years. Your authentic and purposeful life—one that you know to be "right"—will emerge in only seven days.

Your body will tell you with absolute clarity when it needs help to change. The cellular "housecleaning" of a juice fast reverses a multitude of physical conditions that are symptoms of living in a world so removed from nature and so toxic to the harmonious balance of the bodymind. There are toxins in our foods and homes and in our air, soil, and water. We unconsciously and unlovingly put toxic substances in and on our bodies every day.

To help you decide if a cleansing practice would be beneficial in changing the purity of what passes through your body, ask yourself the following questions:

➤ Do I eat foods that contain artificial flavors, sweeteners, preservatives, antibiotics, and hormones, or plants grown with pesticides?
➤ Do I crave foods high in sugar or fat?
➤ Do I use alcohol, caffeine, nicotine, or other drugs?
➤ Do I have metal (mercury-filled) dental fillings?
➤ Do I use conventional cleaning products in my home or office?
➤ Is there chlorine or fluoride in my local water supply?
➤ Am I in an urban—or even suburban—area with an increased amount of air pollutants such as sulfur dioxide, carbon monoxide, nitrogen oxides, or hydrocarbons?
➤ Does my home contain lead or asbestos?
➤ Do I use lawn or garden pesticides?
➤ Do I use conventional cosmetics, lotions, shampoos, toothpastes, and other personal products?
➤ Have I recently completed a course of antibiotics, painkillers, or other medications?

➤ Do I routinely take over-the-counter medications such as Advil or Tylenol?

➤ Have I recently had cosmetic or dental surgery that required some form of anesthesia?

If you answered yes to *any* of the questions above, there is no doubt that you would benefit from a cleansing practice. All of the environmental conditions described above can manifest in physical and emotional symptoms. Look at the list below and check off all that apply to you:

☐ I often feel "low energy" or tired.

☐ I have difficulty concentrating or staying focused.

☐ I catch colds easily.

☐ I have bad breath.

☐ I am often congested, or have postnasal drip.

☐ I often suffer from bloating, gas, or indigestion after eating.

☐ I have dark circles under my eyes.

☐ I have skin problems such as eczema, acne, or psoriasis.

☐ I often go for more than one day without having a bowel movement.

☐ I rarely drink water during the day.

Answering yes to three or more of these questions indicates the need for a real change in the way you are treating your body.

Some of you may have tried other "detox" plans that promise to quickly alleviate conditions like those above in a day or two. Many popular "detox diets" tell you that you can simply sweep yourself clean by moving toxic substances out of your body quickly, mainly through the colon. The Seven-Day Total Cleanse is different from these types of "quick detox" approaches, as it is constructed to give your body the time and space it needs to naturally renew itself. This cleanse is not about "stripping" your body clean. No drugs, no supplements, and no harsh colon cleansing are needed, nor are they recommended. Nor is this cleansing practice about forcing your body to behave in a particular way by adding handfuls of supplements to your diet.

Instead, the Seven-Day Total Cleanse emphasizes eliminating the "information overload" your body experiences because of pesticide-treated produce (poison by definition), chemical preservatives (created for the purpose of *preventing* foods from breaking down), added hormones, and highly acidic foods. A *total* cleanse requires both time and mental space to work its magic. It takes time to remove the emotional and physical debris that clogs your bodymind and obscures your clarity. Even when you are practicing a modified version of the Seven-Day Total Cleanse (see pages 177-81), I recommend that you give yourself a number of days before you begin the juice fast to properly prepare your body, allowing the juices to have their maximum effect.

The other important point I want to make—and I cannot stress this enough—is that while pesticides are toxic and negative emotions are toxic, *you*, yourself, are emphatically *not* toxic. Not only are you not toxic, you are a genius healing machine! You only have to give your body time, space, and love, and let the magic happen.

4

What to Expect and How to Cope

WHEN STUDENTS UNDERTAKE THEIR first cleanse, one of the most frequent and urgent questions they have for me is "What will happen over the next seven days?" And even though I have been guiding students through cleansing juice fasts for more than five years, my answer has not changed: no one knows.

This is because the cleansing experience is different for every person. Your personal bodymind is as unique as your fingerprint, and the ways in which you will manifest the results of cleansing will vary with each cleanse you practice. Nevertheless, there are certain outcomes of a cleanse that may cause you some anxiety or stress if they happen.

You should never undertake a cleanse if you have certain medical conditions—diabetes, for instance—without first consulting with your medical care professional. If you experience any unusual symptoms during the Seven-Day Total Cleanse that your inner wisdom cannot guide you through, you should also consult a medical professional. (See the following section, "Why Do I Feel Like This?," for a list of normal symptoms.) However, while it is sometimes appropriate to consult a medical professional, most often you can trust your own inner guidance as you become more practiced at "listening" to how you are feeling. For most of the people practicing a cleanse, the symptoms I describe below can be considered normal "cleansing events" and are not a cause for concern. In fact, such symptoms should be a cause for celebration: they mean your body is doing the work of healing itself.

Why Do I Feel Like This? ....

In the first few days of your cleanse, you may feel worse before you feel better. This is because every cell in your body is dumping the toxic residue that it has absorbed from the air you breathe, the food you eat, and the environment you live in. You may experience mood swings or general crankiness as emotional debris is cleared out along with food debris. If you experience these discomforts, try to think of them as "growing pains"—they are indicators of the growing spaciousness inside you that will result in a remarkable transformation. These "growing pains" will recede as you continue the cleanse. Think of cleaning out a junk drawer in your nice clean kitchen. Before you open it, the kitchen seems shiny and clean. Then you open the drawer, take out the junk, wipe out the dust and crumbs, and begin to replace the useful items. But when you look around the kitchen, now you see a pile of dirty, useless junk. And that too must be swept away. When you are completely through cleaning your junk drawer, you feel much better and your kitchen looks shiny and clutter-free again. And so shall you.

Common "cleansing events" may occur at any given time during your cleanse. Continue to drink lots of pure filtered water and teas to keep flushing them out. Complaints may include:

- acne breakouts
- rashes
- nausea
- headaches
- sleepiness
- general fatigue
- irritability
- light-headedness
- shakiness
- muscle weakness
- constipation
- diarrhea
- runny or congested nose
- ear problems
- body aches

Remember, you may experience one or two of these "events," or you may experience none at all. And no two cleanses will result in the same exact detox events.

Let the word *allow* be your mantra when going through these events. Allow your body to cleanse, clear, and go through the cleanup it needs. Observe what your bodymind is telling you as you move through the seven days of your cleanse. Know that the journey is well worth any rough spots you may encounter along your path.

To keep things in balance, here is a list of all the positive and wonderful sensations you might expect to experience throughout the seven days of your cleanse:

- ➤ exuberance
- ➤ energy
- ➤ deep and restoring sleep
- ➤ a feeling of lightness
- ➤ sharpened senses, particularly those of taste and smell
- ➤ a feeling of comfort "in your own skin"
- ➤ radiant, supersoft skin
- ➤ clear eyes and improved vision
- ➤ lucid dreams
- ➤ mental clarity
- ➤ sexual receptiveness (yes, this does happen!)

How to Cope

Even if you are one of the people who experience some of the less-pleasant cleansing events, there are many things you can do to support and comfort your Self as you move through them. Different sensations are linked to different areas of your body, and as each organ dumps its toxins and begins the renewal process, different symptoms may manifest themselves. Listed below are the major bodily avenues for purification, the physical *and* emotional symptoms you might experience, and specific tools you can use to soothe your bodymind and minimize the discomfort of cleansing events.

Lungs

As your lungs welcome in new breath, they may discharge old toxic emotions and the cellular damage of pollution by triggering excess mucous production. You may also experience a sense of grief, or waves of sadness. To counter these symptoms, take walks in fresh air, enjoy a soothing sauna, fill your lungs with laughter by watching funny movies or reading funny books and comics, practice a breathing meditation, practice heart- and chest-opening yoga exercises (for example, those included in Chapter 9, pages 107–10), and enjoy ginger tea to stimulate circulation and break up mucous.

Kidneys

Overworked kidneys (which can be caused by too much diet soda, stimulating caffeine, and stress, among other things) may signal the release of toxins with more frequent urination, darker or lighter urine than usual, low backache, and a feeling of general anxiety. To counter these symptoms, continue to drink water and tea, promote the free exchange of fluids by taking a sauna, exercise lightly, and use yoga exercises that promote "back body" breathing, such as child pose or forward bends.

Liver

One of the most important filters in our bodies, the liver may signal cleansing events via nausea, bodily chills, episodes of sweating, and emotional releases of anger and blame. To soothe these discomforts, drink extra lemon water, walk in fresh air, have a belly massage, or have an enema. Forgive and release long-held hurts and grudges by journaling them out or burning them off with the "Breath of Fire," *sitali pranayam,* which is particularly effective for releasing anger and promoting forgiveness. (See the directions for Breath of Fire in Chapter 8, pages 93–94, but stick out the tongue and breathe through it as if it were a straw.)

Skin

Our body's largest filtering organ, the skin is the last barrier between internal debris and total release. As you cleanse you may experience body odor; unusual breakouts; rashes; patches of dry, scaly skin; or increased sweating. Immersion in water is critical for both the internal and external body. Dry brushing turns over dead skin cells and reveals radiant new growth. Avoid all deodorants, perfumes, and commercial lotions, as these will only add to your toxic input rather than allow for the toxic release. Instead either allow for the natural odors or use a few drops of tea tree and grapefruit essential oils as deodorant. The body care recipes given later in the book are sufficient to moisturize your skin, as they use pure oils such as almond, sesame, or apricot kernel oil. Olive oil is also a good alternative as a moisturizer.

Colon

As toxins are released from your colon (the organ that stores and processes waste), you may experience physical and emotional sensations that are particularly challenging. Headache, nausea, gas and bloating, and bad breath are some of the physical cleansing events associated with the colon. Emotionally, you may experience fear or anxiety concerning issues related to survival (money, security, attachment to things). To counteract these discomforts, schedule a colon cleanse or an enema on the second day of your cleanse. After a colon cleanse or enema, make sure you get plenty of fresh air, and use yoga poses that comfort and soothe, such as child's pose or knee-to-chest pose. You may also wish to have a massage that concentrates on your belly.

The simple practice of *uddiyana bandha* will also help relieve uncomfortable intestinal detox events. *Uddiyana bandha*, or abdominal lock, is the second of the three interior body "locks" used in asana and pranayama practice to control the flow of energy. It can be practiced alone or in conjunction with *mula bandha*, or root lock (see page 145). To engage this bandha, sit in your "easy for you" position. Exhale your breath, then take a false inhale (draw the abdomen in and up without taking in any breath). Draw the belly up underneath the rib cage. To release, soften the abdomen and inhale. *Uddiyana bandha* tones, massages, and cleans the abdominal organs.

Lymphatic System

Lymph is a fluid that moves through the entire body, cleaning, filtering, and transporting immune cells and other important structures. To imagine how busy the lymphatic system is during your cleansing time, think of it as a busy highway shuttling away all the toxins that your body has accumulated and held onto up until now. As the lymphatic system cleans your body, the entire body responds. You may feel achy or suffer from stiff muscles, and you may develop circles under your eyes. Increasing lymph circulation will speed the cleansing process. Dry skin brushing (see pages 49–50), sauna, fresh air, light exercise, and massage all promote healthy lymphatic circulation.

Mucous Membranes

All of our body passages that communicate with the air are lined with mucous membranes, the moist membranes that cover, protect, secrete, and absorb. As they are cleansed, you may experience a coated tongue, sinus drainage, and increased mucous in your nose or lungs. You can use a tongue scraper or spoon to keep your mouth fresh. Keep your neti pot (see Chapter 10, pages 132–33) in the shower and use it dutifully. Drink plenty of water and detoxifying ginger tea. Fresh air and exercise, as well as breathing exercises (like the Breath of Fire, see Chapter 8, pages 93–94) will also work to revitalize this important line of defense against toxins in your environment.

Mind

Not technically an organ, but an organizer, the mind is deeply affected in the cleansing process. As your mind sheds old beliefs that it can now, in this restful state, discern are no longer serving your higher purpose, emotional and mental debris will be released. You may experience this release as negative thoughts, a judgmental attitude, intolerance, intense food cravings, or unusual dreams. Dreams are the outlet that allows us to resolve unfinished emotional business. As with all other cleansing events, stay present and observe what you are feeling, but do not react to specific feelings. Recognize that these are just other "cleansing events" and that they will pass. Enjoy fresh air and light exercise, choose your favorite yoga poses, turn to your journal, and spark feelings of gratitude. Meditate and laugh, but avoid food talk.

Remember, these cleansing events are not to be feared. They are the *agni* (fire) that is released as you burn off anything that is not serving your highest health and good. Whether you undergo them for a week or only a few days, these cleanses are a map to your personal best, a pathway to your highest purpose. I want you to be fresh and open so you can have space in your life for new joy and new adventures. I want you to be pure and clear so that you can present wonderful things to the world that only you—in your clarity—could bring forth. There are many things I would love to share with you. So here is your map—let's get started!

⪦ PART 2 ⪧

The Seven-Day Cleanse

S YOU REVIEW THE schedule for each of the seven days of your
cleanse, you will notice that there is a specific pattern that should
be followed. Adhere to the schedule as it is given as closely as
possible while still allowing for your own body's rhythms and your
personal daily schedule. Certain steps are repeated in the exact same
way each day. Take the time to read them each day. Do not assume you
know exactly what you should do. You may discover a deeper meaning
in a phrase or word; something that felt one way on one day may feel
entirely different on another. Do not allow yourself to feel bored. Being
bored indicates an internal imbalance. It is not the fault of the external.
Do not fall into the trap of thinking that switching things around or
skipping certain steps will make things more interesting.

Repetition—in yoga, in life, in nature—allows us to go deeper.
The seasons, the cycles of the moon, days and nights: they all repeat
in a loving cycle. This program asks that you offer yourself a loving
cycle of repetition. This is your chance to go deeper into the meaning
of each activity, whether drinking a juice, following a meditation, or
offering your body a beautiful indulgence. If you take this opportunity
to discover the uniqueness that exists even in daily repetitions of the
same actions, you will give yourself the gift of internal transformation
and freedom from "boredom."

How to Begin

Prepare, Precleanse

TAKE THE TIME TO prepare for your cleanse. By consciously attending to some of the details necessary to ensure a calm and ordered environment, both internally and externally, you will remove the potential for becoming stressed or distracted by "to-do" lists *during* your cleanse. Each day has been scheduled for you so you do not have to *think* about what comes next. The intent is to free you from old patterns that tell you to meet certain goals, accomplish particular tasks, or accept particular food, information, or beliefs. Although it is possible to just jump in and begin to follow the Seven-Day Total Cleanse program, I find that most people report a more comfortable and positive experience when they take the time to prepare for the journey.

In preparation for the beautiful gift you are choosing to give your mind and body, I encourage you to gradually eliminate unnecessary stimulants, such as caffeine and sugar, from your diet and to abstain from alcohol and dairy products for five days before beginning. Stopping or even minimizing your intake of these "life killing" unhealthy substances should help you to experience fewer detox symptoms while your body rids itself of the last vestiges of these unnecessary habits and remembers how to use its own natural and powerful energy resources. You may notice that you will feel "cleaner," less bloated, more alert, and more energetic, despite the lack of caffeine or other substances.

If you truly believe that you can't start the morning without that cup of coffee, don't panic. For five days prior to beginning your cleanse, begin to taper off your caffeine intake. For three days substitute increasing portions of water-process decaf coffee in your morning brew until you have completely switched over to decaf for two days prior to the cleanse. From day one, you should replace any afternoon coffee breaks with a cup of detoxifying herbal tea such as dandelion, milk thistle, or a detox blend.

Gradually decrease your intake of sugar, dairy products, and alcohol over three days and completely eliminate these substances from your diet in the two days prior to beginning the cleanse. Be aware of your conscious intention to eliminate these substances. Guided by this book, you will be able to face any discomfort, notice any reactions, and accept the process as your body and mind recalibrate to their natural states.

Through the course of the week preceding your cleanse you need to mentally and physically prepare yourself in order to experience the optimal benefits of the powerful days that follow. Two days prior to beginning your cleanse, you may choose to eat lightly, tapering off your food intake as the day progresses. The day before beginning your cleanse, avoid cooked and prepared foods and enjoy fresh, raw fruits and vegetables instead.

Planning Ahead

Making some simple preparations will allow you to simply relax and experience the optimal benefits of your cleanse. If you have decided that you would like to be able to take solid food during your cleanse, you should purchase and prepare quinoa. Solé, the essential salt and mineral solution used during the cleanse, should also be made ahead of time. If you are interested in naturally assisting your digestive tract in clearing stored waste before you begin the juice phase of your cleanse program, you should schedule a precleanse colonic hydrotherapy treatment or purchase the equipment you will need to perform an at-home enema.

The chapter for each day of the cleanse contains lists of recipe ingredients and other items that you will need for that particular day. If you have minimal storage space in your kitchen, you may want to go shopping for the freshest recipe ingredients each day. However, if it is difficult for you to get to a grocery store or market each day, you should shop for produce in the days just prior to your cleanse.

Quinoa

Some people feel intensely uncomfortable with the idea of foregoing solid food during the juice cleanse. If you have any health restrictions that would prohibit you from consuming only juices, or if you feel very anxious about giving up the "mouth feel" of solid food, I recommend you incorporate a small amount of quinoa into the first few (or even all) days of the cleanse.

Though many people call quinoa a grain, it is actually a seed. Unlike wheat or rice, quinoa contains phosphorus and is high in magnesium and iron, as well as containing a balanced set of essential amino acids. Quinoa is very high in protein (more than ten grams per half cup cooked serving) and is a good source of dietary fiber; it is also gluten free and considered easy to digest. Is it any wonder that the Incas considered it a sacred food and today's nutritionists call it a superfood?

Quinoa is readily available at most supermarkets and health food stores in both bulk and commercial forms. Cooked quinoa has a light, fluffy texture and a mild, slightly nutty flavor. The first step in preparing quinoa is to remove the bitter-tasting outer coating called *saponin*; this process requires soaking the grain in water for a few hours, then changing the water and resoaking the quinoa, or rinsing it in ample running water either in a fine strainer or in cheesecloth. Boxed quinoa typically has been prerinsed, making it an even easier option.

While most people do choose to completely forego cooked foods during the cleanse, others may find that they feel better with a slower withdrawal from solid food. Adding quinoa to your cleansing experience is not "cheating." If consumed consciously, chewing each mouthful until completely liquid, eating quinoa will not deprive you of any of the benefits of this cleanse. This is your first lesson in listening to your body and honoring what it is asking for.

To decide if incorporating quinoa into your personal odyssey is the right choice for you, ask yourself these questions during the five days before your cleanse:

➤ When abstaining from food for a day or more, does your hunger come back with a vengeance, resulting in portion-control challenges or binges that leave you feeling unable to stop eating?

➤ Is your body very toxic at this time? Are you having trouble scaling back coffee, nicotine, and alcohol before your cleanse?

➤ Do you have fear or anxiety about experiencing detox events?

➤ Are you having headaches or an upset stomach during the pre-cleanse days?

➤ Are you at a low weight, or do you sometimes feel light-headed when you go several hours without food?

If you answered *yes* to any of these questions, it may be a good idea to prepare a few servings of quinoa and keep them in your refrigerator so that you can add two or three tablespoons to each serving of broth during your fast. The quinoa will act like the rudder of a sailboat, enabling you to slow down or control the speed of your body's detoxification. It will stabilize your blood sugar, may ease headaches, and should ground you if you feel light-headed. Using quinoa will also offer you a wonderful, conscious chewing practice, allowing you to be more in control of chewing when you return to eating after the cleanse. Here is how to prepare quinoa:

⋛ Quinoa ⋚

- 1½ cups cold water
- 1 cup quinoa

Bring water to a boil and add quinoa. Cover pot tightly and simmer for twenty minutes, or until water is absorbed. Turn off heat and allow quinoa to sit in covered pot for five minutes. Fluff gently with a fork.

YIELDS approximately 3 cups.

The Seven-Day Cleanse

Solé

Replacing essential salts and minerals is an important part of supporting your body during a juice cleanse. Solé is a densely concentrated saline and mineral solution made with Himalayan salt crystals. This solution is so close to the body's natural mineral proportions that the body can fully assimilate it without acting in an imbalanced way (for example, by becoming bloated or hypertensive), which can happen as a result of consuming regular sodium.

Salt acts as a powerful detoxifying agent both internally and externally, pulling toxins from the body. Soaking in saltwater, whether by taking a dip in the ocean or adding crystalline salt (such as Epsom or Himalayan salt) to your bath, draws toxins from your skin. The same thing happens when you add just a few drops of solé to your drinking water. It acts as a magnet, pulling out internal toxins and allowing them to be eliminated naturally while simultaneously supplying minerals in the perfect proportions. Now *that* is information your body understands.

Take your solé each morning shortly after awakening. I keep a small dropper bottle of solé on my bedside table next to a carafe of water so I never forget to take it.

To make solé:

1. Place several Himalayan salt crystals at the bottom of a clean one-quart jar or bottle with a tight-fitting lid.
2. Top with purified (but *not* distilled) water.
3. Leave the container in the sun for several hours or let stand overnight.
4. Check to see if there is salt sediment visible at the bottom of the container. If there is not, add more salt and allow the mixture to stand for several more hours.
5. Continue this process until salt sediment remains at the bottom of the container, indicating that the water is fully saturated.

This solution is extremely concentrated, so use only half a teaspoon per eight-ounce glass of plain or lemon water on the first day and one full teaspoon per eight-ounce glass on each day thereafter. The detoxifying effect of just a few drops of solé is very strong, and taking more than the recommended amounts may make you nauseous. The benefit of solé does not come from consuming it in quantity, but rather through the *regularity* with which you use it. As with everything during your cleanse, less is more!

Daily Juices

The colorful juices you will enjoy each day are full of vibrant, fresh nutrients. For optimal benefits, the juice must be prepared fresh daily. Each recipe (unless otherwise noted) yields twelve to sixteen ounces, or one serving, of juice. If you find that you do not wish to drink all of your juice at the scheduled time, you may save the remainder and finish it at any other time during the day. Most of my students who practice the Total Cleanse agree that the juices are so delicious they can easily finish their daily serving!

≷ Green Elixir for Heart Connection ≷

Green is a color from the sun, the source of all life and energy. Consuming a green elixir along with each daily juice is key to achieving optimal balance and harmony in all the chakras. Only by connecting to our green energy in the fourth chakra can the other six chakras be fully activated and opened.

When taken daily, fresh green juice will facilitate the connection of each of the other six chakras to the green energy of the heart and the sun. You may choose to drink the same green juice for each of the seven days, or you may wish to alternate with any of the green juice recipes found in Chapter 15. On Day 4 you will enjoy an entire day of green juices. In order to minimize work, prepare any green juice you choose in double batches and freeze the extra for the following day.

- 3 green apples
- 2 whole lemons
- 3 stalks celery

- 1 cup torn romaine lettuce
- 2 cups chopped and densely packed dark greens (kale, collards, or parsley)

Push all ingredients through the juicer and gently blend.

THIS recipe will yield a larger batch of juice than you will drink in one sitting. Store the second portion of juice in a vacuum-sealed thermos for the next day or freeze it for use when you are short on time.

Daily Broth

A potassium–rich broth will be consumed daily during your cleanse. The broth may be kept in the refrigerator for up to three days. To keep work to a minimum during your cleanse week, I recommend that you prepare enough broth for the entire week (approximately ten to twelve servings of twelve ounces each) and then freeze it in individual daily portions. Having fewer details to attend to will mean more of your body's energy will be available for cellular cleansing and rejuvenation.

≋ Essential Potassium-Rich Broth ≋

- 2–3 medium potatoes, scrubbed but not peeled
- 3 carrots, scrubbed but not peeled
- 1 large onion (some skin is OK)
- 1 small to medium beet, scrubbed but not peeled
- 2 stalks of celery, halved
- ¼ cup chopped fresh parsley
- 1 bay leaf
- 10 cups of water

Coarsely chop all ingredients.

In a large pot, combine all ingredients and add water. Bring to a boil, then simmer for two or three hours on very low heat.

Using a colander and cheesecloth, strain out all the solids, leaving only liquid.

You can store the broth in the refrigerator for up to two days, or freeze it in daily portions, removing each from the freezer the night before needed.

YIELDS eight to ten servings.

Recommended Teas

You can enjoy as much ginger, milk thistle, dandelion root, or other detoxifying tea as you wish during your cleanse. Other herbs that are supportive and beneficial include peppermint (cleanses and tones), red clover (a blood purifier), fennel or licorice (stimulates the adrenal glands), burdock root (purifies), nettles (rich in minerals), fenugreek (eliminates mucus), flaxseed, and parsley leaf.

You can make your own tea by combining one-half to one ounce of each herb or combination of herbs in a glass jar and shaking well to blend. To prepare tea, pour one to one-and-a-quarter cups of boiling water into a mug or other container and add a heaping teaspoon of tea mixture. Allow the tea to steep for about ten to fifteen minutes, then strain. You may take your tea hot, at room temperature, or cooled.

Do not sweeten your tea during your cleanse. Even if you use stevia—a natural, calorie-free herbal extract—the sweet taste will be out of balance with the other tastes that the body perceives. If there is a strong dominance of any of the five tastes (sweet, sour, bitter, spicy, or salty), cravings will not diminish but will instead grow out of control. Use this time wisely and rest from your sweet tooth. If you really dislike tea without sweetener, it is better to have nothing, or simple water and lemon. You will be surprised at how refreshing hot or cold lemon water can be to your palate. This is the time to heal your body of sugar addiction. Instead of sweetening your tea, look forward to and savor the carefully balanced sweet notes in your juices.

As you will read later in the book, on certain days of your cleanse I recommend specific teas for their restorative properties. However, you may enjoy any of the varieties of tea listed in this chapter on any day of your cleanse.

Gentle Internal Cleansing

As discussed earlier, thoroughly eliminating the toxic waste that remains in your digestive tract is an important aspect of this cleansing program. Having a colonic or enema or using supplements to encourage bowel movements prior to or at the beginning of your fast may minimize detox symptoms over the next few days.

As you remove solid food from your diet, you may notice that your regular bowel movements will stop. This is a normal, healthy reaction to the fact that you are not chewing solid foods (since the very act of chewing stimulates the contractions of the colon that result in elimination) *and* you are not consuming fiber, the "broom" that sweeps the contents of the colon out of the body. Nevertheless, waste remains in your bowels, and eliminating these toxins before they are reabsorbed into your colon is an important element in reducing detox discomfort.

One of the best ways to clean out your system is with pure, simple water by way of a colonic or enema. This is a natural method of cleansing your insides and is safe, simple, and effective. However, if the thought of either a colonic or an enema makes you feel uncomfortable and there are personal reasons why you may not wish to use them, you may also obtain colon and bowel cleansing benefits by taking natural, gentle supplements precleanse. (These are discussed in more detail on pages 46–47.)

Colonics

Think of colon hydrotherapy as a gentle internal bath. A trained hydrotherapist uses professional equipment and plain filtered water to cleanse the entire length of the colon. I recommend the gravity system, which uses only pure water. There are some colon cleansing methods that advocate adding coffee, wheatgrass, or probiotics to your colonic treatment. For the purposes of this program, I recommend you stick with the "less is more" mantra: these colonic additions, though they may be appropriate at other times, are *not* appropriate during this time of rest.

A gravity colonic involves having warm, filtered water slowly released into the colon. The water causes the muscles of the colon to contract (an action called *peristalsis*.) Peristalsis "pushes" feces out through the hose; it is then disposed of in a closed waste system, eliminating any unpleasant smells or sounds. The colon hydrotherapist—who should be by your side throughout the entire session—may apply light massage to your abdominal area to facilitate the process, and you may feel some slight discomfort or fullness. After the session the therapist leaves the room, and you may sit on a toilet to pass any residual water and stools. A typical session lasts forty-five minutes to an hour. You should be sure that the therapist you choose uses a gentle gravity system with a totally disposable speculum and tubing and plain filtered water with no additives. You can find a therapist near you by getting a recommendation from a reputable health professional. Look for a practitioner certified by the International Association for Colonic Hydrotherapy. Undergoing one session prior to or during your cleanse is sufficient. If you suffer from irritable bowel syndrome (IBS) or Crohn's disease, check with your doctor before visiting a colon hydrotherapist.

Enemas

An enema is a practical, efficient, and effective option for cleansing the lower portion of the colon and can be done in the privacy of your own home. A good-quality enema kit can be found in just about any drugstore. Do not use disposable enemas, as they do not hold an adequate amount of water. You will need an enema bag that holds at least one liter of water. Follow the directions that come with the kit. This gentle "inner bath" can be safely administered every day during your cleanse to enhance your internal detoxing experience. The second day of your cleanse is a particularly good time for internal cleansing, as water serves as your guiding imagery for that day.

Supplements

Despite their benefits, many people are squeamish about the idea of colonics or enemas. If the idea of these treatments makes you feel anxious or uncomfortable, you may choose to use one of the following supplements one day prior to or on the first day of your cleanse *only* to stimulate your body's natural elimination. Choose one capsule of Ultimate Cleanse Fiber with one capsule Ultimate Oil *or* one teaspoon of magnesium powder dissolved in an eight-ounce glass of water *or* one teaspoon of salt in an eight-ounce glass of water taken in the morning. If you suffer from irritable bowel syndrome (IBS), Crohn's disease, diarrhea, or loose stools, do not use any of these supplements.

Daily Essentials

There are certain items you will want to have nearby every day during your cleanse. Choose things you find beautiful and inspiring, energizing or soothing; concentrate on colors and textures you find appealing. These little indulgences serve to enhance the pleasure you will feel during this process of self discovery:

➤ A special glass or cup that you will use for drinking your juices. Since each juice recipe should yield about twelve to sixteen ounces of juice, you may decide to enjoy each juice as a single serving from a larger glass, or use a smaller glass and experience the satisfaction of refilling it until all the juice is gone. Choose what feels right for you.
➤ A beautiful journal and a pen
➤ A body brush (a large, natural bristle brush, available at most drugstores)
➤ A yoga mat
➤ A soft, warm blanket or wrap for gently swaddling your body during meditation or beauty treatments

Daily Rituals

On each day of your cleanse you will treat yourself to four important rituals: early morning journaling; dry skin brushing; yoga and breathing exercises; and meditation. Each of these rituals plays an important role in supporting your juice cleanse and in revitalizing and detoxifying your body, mind, and soul. For the seven days of this cleanse, allow yourself the mindful practice of these four simple activities. You will begin to appreciate the powerful force of revitalization that these elemental acts can have on your daily life. Do not be surprised if you find that you want to incorporate these rituals into your daily life when your seven-day cleanse is over.

Morning Journaling

In her book *The Artist's Way*, Julia Cameron links creativity to spirituality and encourages readers to connect with the creative energies of the universe through simple exercises designed to unblock creative energy. One of her best-known exercises is the "Morning Pages," an activity designed to make writing habitual and to overcome internal censorship through the writing of three pages a day about anything at all.

I offer you a version of this exercise to be done each day upon awakening and before you leave your bed. Choose a beautiful blank book that gives you pleasure. Find a pen that feels good in your hand. You will use this journal to set your intention for this unique cleansing experience and will use it each morning of the next seven days (and perhaps far beyond those) to record your first thoughts and impressions upon waking. You may find that you begin having vivid dreams as your mind becomes clearer during the course of this cleanse; use this journal to describe these images from your deepest Self that your mind is processing. Taking fifteen or twenty minutes each morning to transfer the contents of your mind to paper is one of the most interesting and effective ways to become aware of your unconscious (or subconscious) dreams, desires, and even fears. When you write freely and spontaneously, without censoring your thoughts, you not only unleash creativity, you begin the day with a calm, clear mind, with space to accept all that you might learn through your daily experiences. It is quite interesting to go back and review these pages at the end of your cleanse. What you will learn about yourself in this short time is astounding, and you will be amazed at the changes you have wrought.

Dry Skin Brushing

The skin is the largest organ of the body and one of the main channels of elimination and detoxification. Body soaps, creams, antiperspirants, and synthetic fabrics that trap sweat and irritate skin contribute to a variety of skin problems and conditions. But despite everything we do to hinder our skin's natural health and beauty, our bodies still have a natural cycle of renewal. Every thirty-five days we complete a cycle of shedding our skin cells. Think about it: ten times a year we are given the opportunity to literally walk around in a brand-new skin! It is important to detoxify both inside and out to ensure that our renewed skin glows with radiant health.

Dry skin brushing not only removes dull, flaky, toxic skin cells, but also stimulates the lymphatic system. The lymphatic system is an internal network made up of organs, glands, and nodes. A clear fluid called lymph travels through this network, distributing immune cells and other substances throughout the body. It also interacts with the blood circulatory system to drain fluid from cells and tissues. A healthy lymphatic system is essential to a strong immune system and detoxification of our internal organs.

Dry skin brushing helps your lymph system to circulate more vigorously, opens the pores of your skin to encourage discharge of metabolic waste, and improves the surface circulation of your skin. The result? Glowing, healthy skin and a bonus boost of energy.

You will need a natural, nonsynthetic bristle brush that will not scratch the surface of your skin. Look for a brush that feels really great when you brush your back with it, like a delicious back scratch. The rest of your skin will adapt quickly to this and soon find it just as yummy as your back does. You can find one at any drugstore or bath specialty store. I prefer a brush with a long handle that lets me brush hard-to-reach areas of my body. Before showering or bathing, begin to brush your dry skin using long firm strokes. Always brush skin toward the heart. Begin with the soles of your feet and brush up toward your ankles. Continue brushing from ankle to knee; knee to thigh; and thigh to groin, buttocks, and hips. When you reach your abdomen, use circular, counterclockwise brush stokes. Brush lightly around the breast area, avoiding the nipples. Brush from the palms of your hands toward your wrists and continue the pattern, brushing wrists to elbows, elbows to shoulders.

When you have finished, take a warm bath or shower and finish with a cooling rinse to invigorate blood circulation and stimulate surface warmth. To benefit from a cleansing cool rinse without the uncomfortable shock factor, turn the hot shower down just a little bit and get used to the slightly cooler temperature, then turn it down a little more, and allow a moment to adjust. Continue slowly, and just two seconds before you leave the shower, make it cool, but not ice-cold, and then slowly (and carefully) spin once around in a circle before turning off the water and stepping out. You will feel like your aura is ten miles wide! Before toweling dry, massage a pure, natural oil (such as almond oil) into your damp skin.

Because you will be performing dry skin brushing before showering, as well as enjoying detoxifying baths during this ritual, you may choose not to use commercial antiperspirants during your cleanse. As you release toxins your body's pH will become rebalanced and alkaline. As a result, the odor of your sweat may become less noticeable. If you wish, you may apply a mixture of baking soda and a few tablespoons of water under your arms, allowing it to dry before you get dressed. But it is best, if possible, to allow your body to sweat freely during the cleanse in order to aid the efficient removal of toxins.

When you practice dry skin brushing on a daily basis, your skin will become tighter, clearer, and will glow with good health. Your lymphatic system will be renewed and your glands will operate at peak efficiency, resulting in improved digestion, reduced cellulite, and a stronger immune system. What a beautiful thing to do for your body in just a few minutes before your daily shower or bath!

Yoga and/or Breathing Exercises

Whether you already have an established yoga practice or have avoided exploring this ancient art of uniting body and mind, there is no better method for achieving a union of Self. The consensus of physical and mental health experts is growing: yoga is a safe, positive way to improve the way your body and mind feel and function. For each day of the cleanse I will provide you with specific yoga and breathing exercises that will help you to explore your own personal edge of comfort as your body provides vital feedback on what it needs. Don't be surprised if you have strong emotional releases during these exercises. The energy that flows between mind and body can trigger powerful feelings. If you have already established a strong yoga practice or are devoted to your daily gym workouts, you may want to consider modifying your routine during your cleanse. Your body may not have its usual strength and you must honor any need for gentleness.

Those of you familiar with yoga know that the practice invites you to view the world in a different way. The postures turn you sideways and upside down, literally forcing you to change your point of view. So, too, does this cleanse ask you to expand your thinking: while taking away so much, you are not depriving yourself; rather, you are giving yourself a great gift that will last far beyond these few days. No matter what your level of physical activity, bear this philosophy in mind as you move through the exercises each day. Assess the level of activity your body desires and honor it. If you are tired, rest. Relax into each pose; focus on each breath. And remember, even when you are not active, you are still experiencing constant movement in the flow of your breath and the integration of your body's systems as they rid themselves of toxins and are strengthened by pure nutrients.

In our culture of overachievement and excess, the most important lesson you may learn from these seven days is that powering through is not always the answer. When it comes to revitalizing our bodies and clearing our minds, by doing little or nothing we really do so much.

Meditation

Meditation is a mind cleanse. With practice, you can even learn to stop thinking at will. It is refreshing and healing to the entire bodymind. Once considered a largely spiritual pursuit, recent studies have shown that meditation practice provides many health benefits, including stress reduction, increased blood flow, reduction of blood pressure, decreased heart rate, decreased muscle tension, an enhanced immune system, and increased serotonin levels (which influence positive mood and help prevent depression, obesity, insomnia, and headaches). Meditation also leads to improved concentration, focus, and self-confidence. The practice of meditation during your cleanse allows you to release the daily negative influences and energy that can occur whenever you internalize outside beliefs (about behavior, success, appearances, etc.) and feel that you are lacking in some way.

Anyone can meditate at any time. You do not need to go to a special room, learn obscure chants, or seek instructions from a guru. What you do need is twenty minutes of undisturbed private time; a quiet, comfortable space where you can relax and feel safe; loose clothing; some soothing music (classical, new age, or even nature sounds); and a willingness to set aside mental multitasking and self-judgment. Some people are afraid that they will disappear or cease to exist if they allow themselves to reside in emptiness or relax into stillness. What you will discover as you choose to sit quietly with your Self is that not only will you *never* cease to exist, but that you already exist as a far greater being than you have previously imagined. This is the true miracle of both mediation and fasting: when you do *no* thing, you become *every* thing.

To begin a meditation session you may sit, lie down, or prop yourself up with pillows—whatever makes you feel completely comfortable. Many yoga and meditative arts require that you sit with your spine long from your tail to your crown. The common name for this seated upon the floor, cross-legged pose is "easy pose." For many of us who sit at desks or have emotional pain in the body, this pose is easier said than done. In fact, one of my students, who could not sit on the floor comfortably, laughingly renamed "easy pose" as "easy for you to say pose." She had a point—so in the mediation exercises in this book, I encourage you to find your "easy for you" pose. Here are the options:

➤ Sit on an armless chair, near the front edge, and sit tall with your hands resting comfortably on your thighs.
➤ Sit on the floor on a cushion or bolster with your knees lower than your hips and your spine lifted tall.
➤ Sit on the floor with your legs crossed comfortably.

You can choose which variation is most comfortable for you and then put on instrumental music (as recommended for certain meditations) and close your eyes (or focus on a special object such as a flower or a candle). Begin to breathe deeply, inhaling through the nose and exhaling through the mouth. Observe your breath as your inhalations and exhalations become equal in length and power. Allow your breathing to become regular and free your mind to wander. As thoughts pass through your mind, do not attempt to hold on to them. Acknowledge them without the need to dwell on them. If you find yourself mentally making to-do lists or plans for the rest of the day, just notice that you are doing this and smile. Then return your attention to your breath. Allow all tension, stress, and negative thoughts to simply float out of your consciousness. Tension will leave you if you allow it to do so. Notice if you resist this natural release of your tension. As you become practiced at meditation, you will become better at not allowing your thoughts to interrupt your quiet mind.

In this program I offer you a different meditation for each day of your cleanse, each with a particular intention. You may find it helpful to initially focus your mind by pausing on each day's intention. Then allow your mind to wander. If you begin to feel any mental or physical distraction, bring your awareness back to the intention and your breath until your conscious mind quiets again. After twenty minutes, open your eyes if they are closed and savor the internal calm you now possess. Carry this beautiful peace with you throughout the day.

By the end of your cleanse, you will learn to appreciate that you do not have to fill up every corner of your day, your mind, or your stomach. You will come to see that emptiness represents an opportunity for renewal and that spaciousness means limitless possibility.

⋛ DAY 1 ⋚

Red Juice

THE FIRST CHAKRA:
Grounding

....

The best way in life is simply to be. Let the spirit,
let the soul, let the self shine like sunshine.

.... —YOGI BHAJAN ....

DAY 1 OF THE Seven-Day Total Cleanse program focuses on grounding you through the energies of the first, or "root," chakra to prepare the foundation for your experience. Located at the very base of your spine between the anus and the genitals, and associated with the "fight or flight" survival instinct and feelings of security, the first, or base, chakra is the center for our bodily connections, joy, and sensuality. With an emphasis on noting imbalances in physical energy and acknowledging the instinctive forces you are feeling as you embark on this journey of self-evaluation and examination, this first day of cleansing will allow you to get in touch with elements of your most primal being.

Today's Grocery List and Juice Recipe

Today you will enjoy delicious Red Juice along with the Green Elixir for Heart Connection and the Essential Potassium-Rich Broth. The red juice must be freshly prepared in order for you to receive its optimal benefits. The broth may be prepared in advance and kept in the refrigerator for up to three days (see recipe on page 43). You may also prepare extra green juice and freeze portions for the next day (see recipe on page 42). Preparing ahead will mean having fewer details to attend to so that more of your body's energy will be available for cellular cleansing and rejuvenation.

⋛ Red Juice ⋚

Red is the color of the first chakra. Roots, which grow beneath the earth, are embraced securely by the soil and inherently contain the energetic quality of security within them. This wonderful juice provides a powerful beginning for your cleanse, rooted in safety and protection.

- 5 carrots
- 1 medium beet
- 1 medium parsnip
- 1-inch piece of gingerroot, more or less to taste (it is not necessary to peel the gingerroot, though you may wish to, depending on the quality of your juicer)
- Juice of 1 lemon
- Pinch of nutritional sea salt ("nutritional" sea salt refers to high-quality salts containing a naturally high mineral content)

Push carrots, beet, parsnip, and gingerroot through the juicer. Stir in the lemon juice and sea salt.

Today's Recommended Teas

Throughout the day, enjoy as much ginger, milk thistle, dandelion root, or other detoxifying tea as you wish. You may take your tea hot, room temperature, or cooled.

Materials for Today's Creative Inspiration ....

You may already have most of the following items available at home, or you may choose to go out and purchase special new supplies to use during your cleanse. If you are planning to shop, be sure to do so in the days prior to your cleanse. The seven days of the cleanse are *your* time for relaxing, rejuvenating, and resting—not shopping. You will need:

➤ A special glass or cup that you will use for drinking your juices
➤ A beautiful journal and a pen
➤ A small piece of poster board
➤ Colorful pens or markers
➤ Scissors
➤ Two sheets self-sealing laminate

Materials for Today's External Beauty Indulgence ....

Gather the ingredients from this list to prepare for a luxurious and relaxing footbath. The feet are the grounding instruments of the first chakra, conducting the energy of the earth up through your body. Treat them with tenderness and this infusion of black tea, cinnamon, and cloves.

➤ A foot basin or a bowl large enough for both your feet
➤ A clean, white washcloth
➤ A clean, white towel
➤ A pumice stone or coarse file
➤ Pure, fresh oil, such as sesame, apricot kernel, or almond oil. Do not use rancid or old oil, as your body will be absorbing the beneficial fats through your feet!
➤ An eye pillow
➤ A handful of fine pink Himalayan salt
➤ A good size piece of gingerroot
➤ A whole lemon

- ➤ A medium to large stone from the environment nearby
- ➤ A mixture of black tea, cinnamon sticks, and cloves
- ➤ Ylang-ylang essential oil (available in most natural food stores)

What You May Experience Today

You may be feeling many things, including trepidation or fear about how you will react to detox events and a great sense of relief that at last you are *here* and have nothing to do but restore and take care of yourself. It is fasting and cleansing time; in some ways it is like a strange, adventurous vacation. You will be mindfully taking in the pure essence of food in the form of juices rather than the mindlessness of food as we ordinarily consume it. This precious time gives you full permission to stop, rest, reflect, and love yourself with respect and attention.

Schedule for Day 1

Please note that all times are suggested. Stay within a few hours of this schedule if possible, but honor your body's natural rhythms.

7:30 | Awaken, Solé, Morning Journaling

The morning journaling will not work if you use a computer. You must commit to the act of putting pen to paper. As you write, you may very well feel as though your pen is held to the page with a magnetic force as your thoughts pour out into this very sacred notebook. You must agree not to reread these thoughts and you must promise to keep this notebook absolutely safe from anyone else who might happen upon it. That way you will know without a doubt that it will not be read, not even by *you*. So allow your pen to flow. Feel *safe* in writing down all your grievances, undone tasks, unexpressed wishes, and the conflicting beliefs that may not even be your own. Get them all out of your head and onto the page. Allow the pen and the safety you have created for yourself to free your mind. If you begin in safety today, this sense of security will stay with you firmly for the rest of this cleanse. If you do not feel safe, you will never truly be free to let go of the things that obscure your shining essence and your best Self.

If you wish, you can also ask yourself the following questions immediately after finishing your writing and note your answers in your journal. Do not overthink your replies to these questions; simply tap into your intuition and answer honestly and spontaneously.

➤ What is your internal weather report today? That is, if you were the weather, what would you be? Sunny? Storm clouds approaching? Blue skies all the way? Be creative.

➤ What do you fear will be challenging for you today?

➤ What is surprising about how you feel today?

8:00 | First Broth

Enjoy one cup of Essential Potassium-Rich Broth (see recipe on page 43). If you are taking grains, add one to three tablespoons of quinoa to your broth, being careful to chew each mouthful until it is liquid, giving it your total attention, silence, and awareness. Bear in mind that one very important aspect of this cleanse is becoming aware of food and how you consume it. You may also enjoy some detox tea (I like the Yogi Tea brand, available at many health food stores) or ginger tea.

After you enjoy your broth, treat yourself to dry skin brushing before taking a warm shower or bath followed by a cooling rinse. If you like to moisturize after a shower, use only pure, high-quality oils such as almond, apricot kernel, jojoba, or coconut oil. Pure, unmixed oils are immediately absorbed by the skin and do not feel greasy or oily.

9:00–10:00 | Yoga and Meditation

Grounding Yoga Set

Squatting poses work directly and immediately to balance the first chakra. There are several options; choose the pose that is most comfortable for your body.

1. With feet slightly wider than hip distance apart, lower yourself to a squat without allowing your heels to lift off the floor. Keep your hands in prayer pose, over your heart, with your forearms gently pushing your knees comfortably over your toes.

2. Place a block or bolster near a wall and slide your back down the wall until you are squatting to sit on the block or bolster. Keep your knees pointing over your toes in order to release any tightness in your hips. Feel the support of the earth, the wall, and the block. Only when you know you are supported can you truly let go. This is true in this yoga practice and it is true in your life. Do your best!

3. Once you have found a comfortable squatting position, focus your gaze on the floor about three feet in front of you, or to just beyond the tip of your nose. Inhale deeply, then exhale completely. Hold your breath out as you squeeze your rectum and navel inward as tightly as possible. With a little practice, it will feel like you are creating a vacuum as you exhale. Now hold your breath out while pulling energy upward, into and within your body. Once you have mastered this, on your next exhalation keep your breath out longer as you pump your belly gently by pressing your abdominals in and releasing them. Though awkward at first, with a little practice this will feel quite soothing to your intestines and lower belly and will allow your hips to relax.

4. Repeat this sequence seven times and then lower yourself onto your back and rest on the floor with your eyes closed in *savasana*. (Pronounced *sah-vah-sah-nah*, this pose of ultimate relaxation is the final resting pose. It's also sometimes called "corpse pose," which should give you an idea of just how thoroughly you should let go of your muscles.)

Meditation for First Chakra Cleansing: Navigating Change with Grace

Things change; that is the good news and also the bad news. But truly, once we *accept* this fact, in the long run it is always good news. When we resist change that wants or needs to occur, we develop a great imbalance in our first chakra, and the result is always the same:

lower back pain and abdominal and colon problems. We clench our lower abdomens when we are in a state of resentment and resistance to change. Our ability to accept changes that have occurred and to then gracefully move in the present without fear is the gift of a cleansed first chakra. Resistance is the emotion of fear. This meditation will facilitate a sense of safety so that fear can dissolve, the changes of our past can just "be," and you can enjoy the present, allowing your mind a short vacation free from thoughts of resentment regarding changes you may have been resisting.

Be sure to turn your cell phone ringer off and let others know not to disturb you for at least thirty minutes during this meditation. To prepare for this exercise you will need:

> A mug of hot tea or hot water, with lemon if desired
> A warm blanket
> Your journal and pen
> A comfortable (but nonhabitual) place to sit

With the blanket wrapped warmly around you, sit and hold your tea in both hands and enjoy feeling the warmth of the mug. Do not taste your tea yet. Smell the aroma and feel the warmth of the cup permeating your body.

Sip your tea only once, then count three long, slow, deep breaths, observing your body move as it takes in as much breath as it can and empties each breath as fully as it can. After three such conscious breaths, take another sip of your tea. Repeat this for three sips of tea.

Close your eyes and allow them to roll slightly upward as though gazing softly into your forehead. Do not strain; just turn your gaze very slightly in order to give you something to put your attention on besides your thoughts. If negative thoughts appear, focus again on the warmth of the tea and the blanket, perceive your heartbeat, and just feel.

Keeping your eyes closed, "watch" yourself breathe; observe each inhalation and exhalation without trying to control it. Hear the sound *sat (saht)* as you inhale and *nam (nahm)* as you exhale. These primal sounds mean "truth is my name." Allow this mantra to remind your true Self that it is safely grounded in your body and upon this earth. Creating, feeling joyful, and growing happy in your creations here on earth are your birthright. If you narrow the back of your throat slightly, the sound of your breath will become more audible, giving you something to focus on. Continue for about three full minutes, or eighty breaths.

After the final breath, allow your eyes to remain closed and allow yourself to feel that you are becoming a part of everything. Feel yourself a part of the earth; feel your acceptance of things just as they are. The breath and words act together to quiet and cleanse your mind. Sit quietly, enjoy your breath, and accept yourself just as you are. Become aware of the sounds of life: silence, nature, activity outside your door. Return your attention to the warmth and aroma of your cup of tea. Feel the warmth and goodness, the safety and comfort, of this moment and enjoy it fully. Continue for as long as you wish.

Pick up your journal and make a long list of everything you have that is good. Do not confuse this list with a list of that which you desire; keep your list focused on all you already have right now in your life that is good. Smile and finish your tea in peaceful gratitude.

10:00–11:00 | Creative Inspiration: Intention Coaster

Prepare for this project by turning off your phones and computer. Allow yourself an hour free of distraction. You might like to wrap yourself in a comforting blanket, light a candle, and put on your favorite soothing music. Have your journal, your pen, and your art supplies close at hand (see list on page 57).

When we feel the need or the readiness to undertake a cleanse or a fast, it is usually because of a deep yearning for some result. You want something in your life to be different than how it is or has always been. Take some time right now to stop and put a name to what it is you hope to get from this experience. Can you name in three words or less exactly what you are wishing for? Know that whatever it is that you want, since you desire it deeply it is the perfect thing to be wanting. Whether it is as simple and basic as "to lose eight pounds," or something deeper and less concrete, such as "to have more love and affection in my life," what you want is between you and you. Name it now without fear.

In your journal write all the things that you want in your life that you do not have right now. Nothing is too trivial, too vain, or too audacious! Don't leave anything out. It is your right to want whatever it is that you want.

Read over what you have written. Smile, because this is what you are soon to receive. Close your eyes and make your body very comfortable. You may choose to lie on the floor or on your bed. You may want to be wrapped up in your blanket. Settle into a stillness and distill those pages from your journal—that wanting, that yearning—down to only one thing. Can you name it in one word? In three? Relax, smile, and form the word(s) in your mind. On a fresh page in your journal, write the word or words that will represent your intention for this week of cleansing.

Now you are ready to create a visual symbol of your intention. Taking some simple playtime to partake in innocent, childlike art activities like this project is remarkably effective. This is not something most of us normally do. By willingly participating in this activity, you are already accomplishing a very important part of your cleansing journey. You are shifting to a place that is *different* from where you normally are. It is especially nice to do this project with music playing, and perhaps even with earphones on to avoid any outside interruptions. Turn on any music that makes you smile (but not necessarily dance—yet!).

1. Take your glass or cup and place it upside down on the poster board. Trace a circle around the outside rim of the glass.

2. Cut out the circle and write your name on one side.

3. Decorate and embellish the name side of your coaster. This will be a focus tool for every juice you will be drinking, so make it beautiful and special. Give your name a lot of dignity and decorate it with great care and attention. Take your time and enjoy this, using colors that you love, one or many, as pleases you and no one else.

4. When you have completed the name side of your coaster, turn it over to the blank side. On this side write the word or words that you discovered in the beginning of the exercise. Contemplate these words before you commit them to the paper, and refine them if you wish.

5. Now give equal time and effort to embellishing this side of the coaster. Choose colors and designs that add energy to the intention you are writing. This energy will manifest the intention.

6. Press your coaster between two sheets of transparent self-sealing laminate, cutting the edges so the coaster is sealed.

11:00 | First Juice: Red Juice

It is now time to enjoy your first juice of the cleanse, the Red Juice. Enjoy all of your daily juices throughout the cleanse by following this specific ritual:

1. Prepare your juice and pour it into your special glass. Cover it with your coaster with the *intention* side facing down and your name facing up.

2. Imagine your intention infusing the juice and the juice taking in the energy of the intention.

3. Find a comfortable place to sit with a blanket wrapped around you, in the sunshine or wherever you feel very safe and relaxed; you should be neither cold nor hot.

4. Breathe into your belly. Place one hand on your belly and the other on your heart. Notice any feelings that are coming up: anxiety, fear, impatience. Do not dwell on these thoughts, but acknowledge them as you continue to breathe into your belly and allow your heart to open.

5. Assign your hunger level a number between 1 and 5, with 1 being "not at all hungry" and 5 being "extremely hungry."

6. Pick up your covered juice and, with your eyes closed, feel the weight and temperature of the glass.

7. Bring to mind the intention that is face-to-face with the juice under the cover of your coaster.

8. When you are ready, remove the coaster.

9. Engage your senses. Smell the juice. Does your mouth water? Does your hunger level move in either direction? Appreciate the beautiful color of the juice.

10. Take the first sip but do not swallow immediately. Take the time to notice each taste of the juice with every part of your mouth and tongue. Choose when to swallow.

11. Pause and again note your hunger level. Notice if the one swallow of juice shifted that number in one direction or another.

12. Continue to sip your juice consciously, with pleasure. Let your belly be soft and receiving.

13. After half the juice is finished, check in with your hunger. What number level are you now experiencing? You may find that you are no longer hungry, but you may choose to drink the rest of the juice anyway. That is fine. The most important thing is self-observation and self-awareness. It is okay to eat and drink for the pleasure of the taste alone. Enjoy your healthful elixir in luxurious leisure. If you decide you have had enough juice, you may save it for later in the afternoon.

11:30–2:30 | Free Time

Enjoy your day, partaking in activities that give you pleasure and a sense of serenity. The first day of your cleanse might feel unsettling, as it is the first day you are spending out of your habits, routines, and grooves. It may feel like traveling to a strange country where all the signs are in another language and your body feels out of sync with the time zone. Embrace this feeling, because it is just what you want right now: to create safe space while also going to places you have never been before.

At this time you have just had your first delicious juice, so perhaps you are not hungry. Notice that. Or maybe you do feel some hunger pangs; if so, acknowledge them. But also know that your juice has given you everything you need to survive.

Observe and allow yourself to feel whatever you are feeling without reacting to it in your habitual way. There is great power in this practice. You are benefiting greatly as you continue to nourish yourself deeply with the life force energy of the juices. (This life force, the vital energy of all living beings, is called *prana*, Sanskrit for *breath*.) Allow your body to feel radiance, or hunger, or emptiness, or fullness. It is all perfect; you are perfect, and you are simply feeling what you are feeling. What is most important is that you are not reacting to it, but that you are rooted and grounded, firm and steadfast, acting authentically in this moment.

When you react, you repeat. It is insecurity that drives us to move unconsciously, like a robot, doing what we have always done, and therefore getting what we have always received. Notice what you are feeling and allow it all but today, do not "re-act." Instead take a walk, concentrating upon your legs, your feet, and their relation to the firm earth. Run if you feel the urge, skip, or simply walk leisurely. Just allow your legs to move and your feet to carry you at whatever pace your heart wishes to move.

Spend time outdoors, curl up with a book, or take a nap. Indulge your body's desires as much as possible.

Today's External Beauty Indulgence: Luxurious Footbath

There is no part of the body that cannot be healed through the feet.

—GURUNAM (KUNDALINI YOGI, KABBALIST, AND MYSTIC)

The beauty treatment below is a sensuous treat that will help you appreciate the importance of your feet, which literally connect you to the earth. Gather the ingredients to prepare for a luxurious and relaxing footbath (see list on pages 57–58).

We feel the energy of nature and the *prana* of the earth through our feet. Our legs and feet grow and radiate out from our first chakra. Appreciate the beauty of your grounding connection to the earth and honor your intention to begin this journey safely grounded in your true Self.

1. Settle yourself in a comfortable couch or chair. Your feet should easily reach the floor and your head and neck should be supported. Put nine drops of ylang-ylang oil on the stone and place it into the footbath, where its grounding fragrance and energy will be released.

2. Place the foot basin on the floor and fill it three-quarters full with cool water. Add one cup of sea salt, one whole lemon sliced in circles, and two inches of gingerroot cut into slices. Boil water and make a "tea" using one tablespoon of black tea, one stick of cinnamon, and five cloves. Place the teapot within easy reach. You will be adding hot tea to your foot basin as you soak your feet.

3. Grab your iPod or another device for playing your favorite soothing music (see the recommended music at the end of the book for a "Chakra 1" playlist), earphones, cocooning blanket, and eye pillow.

4. Dry brush your feet and legs in long strokes toward your heart. Brush until your feet and legs feel warm. This indicates that the healing lymph in your legs is really moving. Use a file on any coarse skin on your heels and the soles of your feet.

5. Pour half of your hot tea mixture into the room temperature salt water in your foot basin. Slip your feet into the basin and add more hot tea as desired for a deliciously comfortable temperature.

6. Put on your music and eye pillow and rest your head back, comfortably supported by a pillow if needed, until the water has cooled. Add more hot tea and repeat as desired.

7. Put the clean towel on your lap and remove one foot from the water. Firmly squeeze the towel around your foot, massaging the arch in particular. Unfold the towel and use the washcloth to gently begin to clean around the cuticles and under each nail.

8. Interlace the fingers of your opposite hand through your toes and slide your fingers to the base of your toes. Inhale, pause your breath, and then tightly squeeze your fingers against your toes as you exhale. This may be a little uncomfortable or painful, but do your best—it will be worth it! Inhale and pause your breath again, then squeeze your toes tightly against your fingers as you exhale. Inhale a third time, pause your breath, then squeeze both your fingers and your toes together simultaneously, as tightly as you can, for the full length of your exhalation.

9. Imagine this is the foot of your beloved. Massage your arch, your toes, and the ball of your foot with your pure oil mixed with a drop of ylang-ylang essential oil.

10. Offer this same ritual in its entirety to your other foot.

2:30 | Second Juice: Green Elixir for Heart Connection

It is now time for your green juice (see recipe on page 42). Follow the ritual outlined on pages 64–65 to make drinking this elixir as pleasurable as possible and to keep your consumption of the juice as much in the present as you can. Sip your juice slowly and savor the new and delicious tastes you are introducing to your body. If you find that you do not wish to finish all of your juice, you may save it for the 5:00 serving and drink it instead of the potassium broth.

After this second juice, plan to take some free time for yourself. Perhaps a walk sounds inviting. If possible, spend some time in nature. Enjoy the feel of the sun and the freshness of the air. Appreciate all of the ways your body connects to the natural world around you. You may also decide that you would prefer to read, nap, or otherwise spend quiet, restful time alone. If you must take care of personal or family matters during these few hours, try to attend to them consciously, without worry or haste. Maintain the calm and peaceful interior you have established with the centering morning rituals.

5:00 | Second Broth

It is now time for your second portion of Essential Potassium-Rich Broth. Add one or two tablespoons of quinoa, if desired, and drink a smaller portion of Green Elixir or Red Juice, if you have any left over.

Spend the time before the bedtime ritual in quiet activities. Call friends or listen to music, but avoid television and Internet use. Read ahead to the beginning of the next chapter and plan for tomorrow's juices and rituals so you will be prepared for what you will need to do to support your journey.

8:00 | Bedtime Ritual

Take a leisurely warm bath using detoxifying mineral salts (or simply add a handful of Himalayan salt crystals to your bathwater) and then head to bed with a good book. See the recommended reading list at the end of the book for some of my favorite books or, if you have not already done so, read ahead to the beginning of the next chapter of this book so you will be prepared for what you will need to do to support your journey tomorrow. If you find yourself resisting the idea of an early bedtime, allow yourself to relax, and encourage your bodymind to welcome deep rest. You may be pleasantly surprised to find that when your body is free from the stimulating effects of caffeine and sugar and free from the distractions of television or other electronics, you are able to drift off to sleep earlier than you would expect. Sleep luxuriously tonight, in great comfort, knowing you are safe, you are right, and that this process is going to be good.

Today you directed your *drishti* (gaze) into your first chakra and grounded yourself, and now you sit confidently upon this earth, knowing and accepting yourself more. You have brought forth your *intention* for the rest of the week, inscribing it upon your beautiful coaster, and have brought your *attention* back to that original intention each time you offered your juice to your body. Tomorrow this intention will gain even more strength as you climb upward to the second chakra, which controls your creativity and sexuality.

Tomorrow we will explore a bit deeper; your focus shall shift upward from your red earthen roots toward your orange-colored second chakra, the seat of emotion. Tomorrow your practice of observing your body and listening to what it is asking for will only get better. Obtaining clarity in the second chakra dissolves any lingering sense of boredom or restlessness and reconnects you to a sense of excitement and meaning. In the meantime, sleep luxuriously!

7

≋ **DAY 2** ≋

Orange Juice

THE SECOND CHAKRA:
Joyful Self-Expression

Let the drop of water that is you become a hundred mighty seas.
—RUMI, THIRTEENTH-CENTURY MYSTIC AND POET

ON THE SECOND DAY of your cleanse you will explore the creativity, joy, and enthusiasm that emanate from the energetic second chakra. Also called the sacral chakra, the second chakra is located in your abdomen, right below your navel and behind the pubic bone. The second chakra serves as the energy center for the integration of physical and mental creative potential and influences sexual energy and attraction. The element of water is associated with this chakra, and bringing your awareness to the second chakra allows for spontaneous action and honest movement.

Physically, your muscles and organs in the lower abdomen can cling, grip, hold, or contract when there is discord in your second chakra. Because of its powerful influence over emotional connection, imbalances in the second chakra can lead to damage in your relationships. You may be unable to connect purely and intimately with others, or you may become rigid in your outlook on life in general. When this chakra is energetically balanced, you will reap the benefits in the form of increased creativity, sexual energy, and financial abundance.

Today you will learn how to access and appreciate the potential of the second chakra and consider how you wish to fill the wonderful spaciousness you are creating within your Self as you continue your commitment to this cleanse.

Today's Grocery List and Juice Recipe

The color orange is outgoing and busy. It signals cheerfulness and stimulates enthusiasm and creativity. Let this delicious orange juice spice things up and boost your self-esteem and extroversion. There's something about the fragrance and flavor of clementines that makes me feel easygoing and carefree—like I'm on holiday. This is the feeling of creativity.

You will also be enjoying Green Elixir for Heart Connection and Essential Potassium-Rich Broth today (see pages 42 and 43 for recipes). You can choose to drink the same Green Elixir as you did yesterday, or you can pick another beautiful green drink from the juice recipe section in Chapter 15. Restorative, fresh green juice facilitates the connection of each of the other chakras to the green energy of the heart and the sun. As you enjoy today's green elixir, appreciate what it means to open your heart to all of the possibilities and joys of life, love, creation, and expression.

⋛ Orange Juice ⋚

- 3 large carrots
- 3 small mandarin oranges or clementines, peeled
- ¼ small yam, skin on
- 2 stalks celery
- ½ lime, peeled
- 1-inch piece of gingerroot, more or less to taste (it is not necessary to peel the gingerroot, though you may wish to, depending on the quality of your juicer)

Put all ingredients through the juicer.

Today's Recommended Teas

Detoxifying teas remain a good choice today, or enjoy spicy ginger or inspiring orange blossom tea.

Materials for Today's Creative Inspiration

Today's exercise requires props—lots of props! Have fun. No one needs to see you do this. You don't even have to watch yourself.

Gather anything you can find that, in your mind's eye, enhances the image of a sensuous, graceful dancer. Floaty scarves work well. If you're a guy, you might cringe at the thought of dancing with scarves, but you will also benefit! Notice any resistance, and then accept that it's all just part of forcing ourselves to step out of what we think we know to be true, washing away creative blocks. Think of Zorba the Greek or the cool dancers in Bollywood movies. Also good are finger cymbals, jangly coin belts, and whatever else you can find that feels somewhere between ridiculous and fun.

You'll also need some fun belly dancing music or a Bollywood sound-track. Some of my favorites are "Slow Belly Dance Drums" by Drums of the World (from the album *World Drums: African Samba, Taiko, Chinese*); "Hips Don't Lie" by Shakira (from the album *Oral Fixation, vol. 2*); "I Put a Spell on You" by Natacha Atlas (from the album *Ayeshteni*); and "Eye of the Duck" by Natacha Atlas (from the album *Best of Natacha Atlas*).

Materials for Today's External Beauty Indulgence

A luxurious bath is an incredibly sensuous experience. Adding a skin-nourishing massage with evocatively scented rose oil will allow you to connect the power of metal imagery with the physical pleasure of your body. You will need:

➤ A bath or soaking tub (the deeper the better!)
➤ A handful of dried or fresh rose petals

- ➤ Unscented candles
- ➤ A washcloth or silk eye pillow to cover your eyes
- ➤ A clean, thick towel
- ➤ Essential rose massage oil (available at natural and health food stores). You can make your own by mixing rose and sandalwood essential oils into the massage oil base you use each morning following your dry skin brushing. Some good general massage oils for use during this cleanse are sesame, jojoba, apricot kernel, or sweet almond oil. This will be used following the dry skin brushing ritual each day and will also be used as a carrier oil to which to add essential oils for other uses.

What You May Experience Today

You could be experiencing a wide range of emotions today. Anger, restlessness, and resistance, both in the body and in the emotions, are possible. Sudden tears while doing simple yoga poses are common— this is a release of toxic emotions that you have been carrying around for too long. You may feel an uncomfortable edge of hunger that you do not like. If this happens, sip some broth, juice, or lemon water and take time to observe your hunger. Whatever negative feelings you might be experiencing, trust that they will melt away as you progress through this cleanse. You have all the nourishment and all the support you need. Trust yourself and dive deeper.

Schedule for Day 2

Please note that all times are suggested. Stay within a few hours of this schedule if possible, but honor your body's natural rhythms.

7:30 | Awaken, Solé, Morning Journaling

As you journal today, consider letting all your fantasies, thoughts, and fears about sex and sexuality spill out. Remember that this journal is completely sacred and safe and will not be read by anyone, even you. If it creates the sense of safety you need, you are encouraged to burn or shred these pages immediately after writing them. Fill as many pages as you wish (but no less than three), and keep your pen moving even if a word has to be repeated until your thoughts begin to flow again. You may be amazed at how much flexibility you will gain in the hips as you release the words and thoughts you are holding onto your journal pages.

If you wish, you can also ask yourself the following questions immediately after finishing your writing and note your answers in your journal. Do not overthink your replies to these questions; simply tap into your intuition and answer honestly and spontaneously.

➤ What is your internal weather report today? That is, if you were the weather, what would you be? Sunny? Storm clouds approaching? Blue skies all the way? Be creative.

➤ What do you fear will be challenging for you today?

➤ What is surprising about how you feel today?

➤ Did you remember to renew your intention every time you took in nourishment with your juices? How does that feel?

8:00 | First Broth

Begin your day with one cup of Essential Potassium-Rich Broth (see recipe on page 43). If you are taking grains, add one to three tablespoons of quinoa to your broth, being careful to chew each mouthful until it is liquid. Concentrate on the sensation of chewing food, giving it your total attention, silence, and awareness. What do you notice that is different from yesterday?

Even though you will be enjoying a long, soaking bath later in the day, you should still participate in the morning ritual of dry skin brushing followed by a warm shower or bath and finished with a cooling rinse. In fact, because water is the element associated with the second chakra, I encourage you to spend as much time as you are able in or near water today. For those of you with access to the ocean or a lake, you may want to consider packing your juices in a cooler and heading out for the day. However, unless you maintain a chemically free pool, I suggest that you avoid the heavily chlorinated water of most swimming pools during your cleanse. (Our pool at the American Yogini Hohm Retreat is an inground saltwater pool that stays clean without the use of chemicals.)

9:00–10:00 | Yoga and Meditation

Spiraling Yoga Set

Your focus today is on the lower belly. Cleansing spiral exercises will help to rebalance the energy of the second chakra and release any tension and stiffness in your lower back and hips. Don't be afraid to experience the sensuality of these movements; after all, the second chakra influences sexuality and desire. If you have repressed or denied certain emotions, the blockage in this chakra may cause you to fear or deny yourself pleasure, resulting in a resistance to change or an inability to connect with your own feelings. On the other hand, if you have an excessively stimulated second chakra, you may be overly emotional or suffer from sexual addiction or poor boundary-setting. It is therefore important to pay close attention to everything you feel during this session.

Do not force these exercises; rather, allow yourself to flow through the movements just as water swirls and flows through a riverbed.

1. Begin on your hands and knees on your yoga mat. Breathe in as you stretch your back, allowing your belly to drop between your hips and shoulders toward the floor. Let your head fall back as your gaze moves up toward the sky. This is known as cow stretch.

2. Breathe out as you draw your belly up to your spine and arch your back toward the sky. Allow your head to become heavy and drop below your shoulders. You should feel this stretch, known as cat stretch, from the bottom of your spine to the top of your head.

3. Breathe in and relax back into cow stretch, then breathe out smoothly as you move back to cat stretch.

4. Continue to follow your breath as you repeat each stretch three times.

5. Return to a neutral position on your hands and knees.

6. Slowly and rhythmically, begin to move your hips in a large circle to the right. Make seven slow, swirling circles and then return to neutral. Allow your hips and belly to relax and really *flow* in this gentle movement. Next move your hips in a large circle to the left. Repeat seven times, then return to a neutral position on your hands and knees.

7. Cross your ankles and roll back over your feet to sit on the floor with your legs extended out in front of you. (If this is uncomfortable, sit on a pillow or even in a chair with your feet flat on the ground.) Stretch your spine long, reaching the crown of your head upward while releasing your hips to the earth.

8. Bending forward slightly, raise your arms in front of you in a V shape. Moving with your breath, begin to circle your torso over your hips. Make seven long, slow circles to the right, then come to center. Circle seven times to the left.

9. Bending forward, begin to relax totally, surrendering the crown of your head toward your knees, or if you are on a chair, to the space between your knees and toward the earth.

10. Allow your breathing to become long, slow, and deep. Take your attention to the places where the tops of your thighs are touching or facing your belly. As you continue to breathe, allow your belly to remain totally soft as it rises and falls with the breath. Notice how it feels as your belly reaches out to touch your thighs on the inhale and recedes on the exhale, like a wave against the shore. Imagine a sleeping baby, or a dog or cat. Visualize how the rib cage and abdomen move as the infant or animal naps in bliss.

11. Begin to draw breath deeper and lower into the belly so that you feel the lowest part of your belly touching the uppermost part of your thighs with each conscious breath.

12. After seven breaths, performed in complete surrender to gravity and to the movement of the breath in the belly, take your attention to the back of your body.

13. Visualize your lower back, the other side of the belly. Allow your breath to lift and expand your kidneys in the same gentle way you allowed the breath to move your belly. Imagine your kidneys are like little buoys on a gentle sea, rising and falling on the ocean of your breath. Continue for seven deep, slow breaths.

14. Slowly come back to an upright, seated position. Placing your arms behind you, gently lower yourself to the floor to rest in *savasana*.

Meditation for Second Chakra Cleansing: Perpetuity Meditation

The purpose of the mind is to think, to calculate, to differentiate—in short, to separate. The purpose of the heart is to feel, to discover commonality, to unite. The intention of meditation is to quiet and purify the mind. Since the mind typically attempts to create a sense of separateness, this can be challenging. In this meditation I ask you to just feel your way along with your eyes and your heart. Feel what you are seeing and contemplating and allow your mind to rest, as these contemplations purify the second chakra.

For today's meditation, gather the following items:

> ➤ One flower with a visibly open center where the seed pods might be seen, such as an open old-fashioned rose, an orange tiger lily, or a daisy. Even a tiny buttercup will do for this wonderful meditation.
> ➤ Your comfortable meditation seat
> ➤ Music for contemplation. Try "Hold Me, I'm Falling" followed by "Love and Marigolds" and then "Good Indian Girls," all by Mychael Danna from the *Monsoon Wedding* soundtrack. Set these three songs to loop so that you will not be disturbed if they end before your contemplation is complete.

Read through the instructions for this meditation sequence a few times prior to beginning. Then release these directions and just perform this contemplation as best as you can remember.

With your flower, come to your "easy for you" seated pose. You may perhaps even sit comfortably on your couch or, even better, outside in the shade. Listen to your meditation soundtrack music through earphones to help prevent distractions.

Close your eyes and take a few deep, cleansing breaths to slow down your pace for the task of meditating.

Look at your flower; look deep into its center. Just look. Do not analyze; you are simply going to look and notice things about the flower you are holding in your hands. Observe the shape and color of all the parts: the petals, the stem, the stamen, and the undersides of the petals. Contemplate the miracle of reproduction.

Continue to gaze deeply into the flower's center as if into the eyes of your beloved.

Perceive the seeds and contemplate the journey from tiny seed to adult flower.

The flower is attached to the ground. We are not physically attached. Or perhaps this particular flower, like us, is no longer attached to the ground. You are just noticing these things.

If a bee landed upon you, you might fear a sting. If a bee landed upon a flower, the flower would blush and offer its pollen to the bee, then accept any pollen left behind by the bee's delicate feet. Contemplate what the flower feels when it is kissed by a bee. Really look at and into the flower while contemplating these things.

Contemplate the seeds falling to the ground and thirstily soaking up the rain. See the seed breaking apart to reach up and absorb the hot energy of the sun, using this energy to grow higher and bloom again.

Gaze again into the center of this flower. Repeat this sequence of contemplation three times for the three parts of the life cycle: reproduction, birth, and death.

Now close your eyes and imagine your great-great-grandparents. Even if you have no idea what they looked like or who they were, just let yourself imagine them as young people.

Now, separately, imagine them making love on the one occasion that resulted in the birth of your great-grandparents. Imagine your grandparents, maternal and fraternal in turn, full of health, vitality, and youthful radiance. Separately, imagine them finding one another and their tender embrace that one special time when your parents were created. Now visualize your parents as young adults. Imagine them finding one another and the loving union that created you. You may find you feel uncomfortable thinking about your grandparents or parents as loving, sexual beings, but your imaginings do not have to be so graphic that you become uneasy! Instead, contemplate the idea of the generations of love and connection that have brought you here.

Open your eyes and look deep into the center of the flower once again. Do not think; do not get cerebral. Just observe, notice, and feel. When you have completed this contemplative meditation and feel complete, allow yourself some time to sit in peace and simply "be."

10:00–11:00 | Creative Inspiration: Belly Dancing

You can choose to have this experience totally alone or with your very best friends. Go for lots of smiles! Belly dancing is way more fun with the props (see list on page 73). Hopefully you were able to find a sensuously silky scarf—or two, or three! Don't worry about the colors; it's fun with any color. But if you have time to plan ahead, try to find vivid orange and pink scarves in any shades to stimulate the second chakra.

1. Put on your music and dance as if no one is watching—because guess what? *No one is!* Just as with the morning journaling, being alone while you perform this exercise will free your creativity and open up your hips. Float your silk scarves over the air, echoing your body's movements like water echoes the wind. (Remember that water is the element that clears and purifies the second chakra.)

2. Feel and appreciate the sensuality of your body as you let your arms rise above your head and make deep circles with your hips, as if you are looping a gigantic hula hoop.

3. Hold and swish your scarves around like echoes of your hips. Imagine you are cleaning up the space that surrounds you with these graceful, swishing scarves. Move to the music in any way that feels sexy, round, and circular.

4. Keep your first chakra feet—stable and secure from yesterday—firmly on the ground as your hips relax into great circles. There is no wrong way to do this; it is completely improvised through feeling your body move. Let it feel good, let yourself surrender to the rhythm of the music, and completely enjoy your body and the creative impulse that spontaneously erupts from just moving to the music and feeling your body.

11:00 | First Juice: Orange Juice

Just as you did yesterday, enjoy your juice following this specific ritual:

1. Prepare your juice and pour it into your special glass. Cover it with your coaster with the *intention* side facing down and your name facing up.

2. Imagine your intention infusing the juice and the juice taking in the energy of the intention.

3. Find a comfortable place to sit with a blanket wrapped around you, in the sunshine or wherever you feel very safe and relaxed; you should be neither cold nor hot.

4. Breathe into your belly. Place one hand on your belly and the other on your heart. Notice any feelings that are coming up: anxiety, fear, impatience. Do not dwell on these thoughts, but acknowledge them as you continue to breathe into your belly and allow your heart to open.

5. Assign your hunger level a number between 1 and 5, with 1 being "not at all hungry" and 5 being "extremely hungry."

6. Pick up your covered juice and, with your eyes closed, feel the weight and temperature of the glass.

7. Bring to mind the intention that is face-to-face with the juice under the cover of your coaster.

8. When you are ready, remove the coaster.

9. Engage your senses. Smell the juice. Does your mouth water? Does your hunger level move in either direction? Appreciate the beautiful color of the juice.

10. Take the first sip but do not swallow immediately. Take the time to notice each taste of the juice with every part of your mouth and tongue. Choose when to swallow.

11. Pause and again note your hunger level. Notice if the one swallow of juice shifted that number in one direction or another.

12. Continue to sip your juice consciously, with pleasure. Let your belly be soft and receiving.

13. After half the juice is finished, check in with your hunger. What number level are you now experiencing? You may find that you are no longer hungry, but you may choose to drink the rest of the juice anyway. That is fine. The most important thing is self-observation and self-awareness. It is okay to eat and drink for the pleasure of the taste alone. Enjoy your healthful elixir in luxurious leisure. If you decide you have had enough juice, you may save it for later in the afternoon.

11:30–2:30 | Free Time

As I mentioned before, with water as your guiding element, today is the perfect day for a trip to an ocean, lake, or river. If you are able to find a natural source of water, plan to spend some time in or near it. Observe the waves on the sand of a beach or the way water flows around the rocks in a riverbed. The energy of water is always flowing; it is unhindered by what others might perceive as impediments in its path. It moves freely, naturally, gracefully. Visualize your mental and creative energy moving in the same way. Do not allow yourself to become hung up on roadblocks or perceived obstacles to your creative desires. Remember how the creative expression of dance encouraged you to move fluidly and freely, exploring the sensuous possibilities of the body and mind.

Today's External Beauty Indulgence: Rose-Scented Bath

Water, stories, and the body are all mediums that hide and show what's hidden. Study them, and enjoy this being washed with a secret we sometimes know, and then not.

—RUMI, THIRTEENTH-CENTURY MYSTIC AND POET

The beautiful indulgence of a rose-scented bath is an unexpected afternoon treat and a perfect integration after your exuberant dancing and emotional meditation and journaling sessions. Peacefully floating in a tub while surrounded by candlelight allows your mind to drift in unexpected ways.

1. Run a bath with the water just slightly above body temperature. Ideally, you want to be unable to feel a difference between the temperature of the air in the room, the water in the tub, and the heat of your body.

2. Add a handful of Himalayan salt to the bathwater to draw toxins from your skin. Scent the water with a few drops of rose essential oil. For a truly lavish touch, sprinkle fresh rose petals into the bath, or fill the room with fresh, fragrant roses.

3. Ensure that the bathroom will remain quiet or add some soft music to mask the noises of the outside world.

4. Sink into the tub with gratitude and feel your body become weightless as the water slips around you. Close your eyes and allow your other senses to become alive. Appreciate the scent of rose, the silky feel of the water, each note of music, and the rise and fall of your body on the waves of your gentle breathing.

5. When the water has cooled, come out of the tub and pat yourself with a fluffy towel until your skin is just damp. Using essential rose oil (perhaps mixed with another oil of your choice), massage from your feet to your throat, varying the pressure of your massage to offer your skin, your muscles, and your bones the chance to completely relax.

6. As you leave the sanctuary you have created, you may experience an intense feeling of drowsiness or the sense of heaviness in your limbs. Listen to what your body is telling you and rest as needed. You might also experience a burst of creative energy; use this impulse to see where your spirit is telling you to go.

2:30 | Second Juice: Green Elixir for Heart Connection

It is now time for your green juice (see recipe on page 42). Follow the ritual outlined on pages 64–65 to make drinking this elixir as pleasurable as possible and to keep your consumption of the juice as much in the present as you can. Sip your juice slowly and savor the new and delicious tastes you are introducing to your body. If you find that you do not wish to finish all of your juice, you may save it for the 5:00 serving and drink it instead of the potassium broth.

After this second juice, plan to take some free time for yourself. If you must take care of personal or family matters during these few hours, try to attend to them consciously, without worry or haste. Perhaps you can approach these tasks in a new way, challenging your body and mind to take an unfamiliar path, thus stimulating creativity in even the most mundane of activities. Allow spontaneity and do not block new ideas.

5:00 | Second Broth

Now it is time for your second portion of Essential Potassium-Rich Broth. Add one or two tablespoons of quinoa, if desired, and drink a smaller portion of Green Elixir or Orange Juice, if you have any left over.

Spend the time before the bedtime ritual in quiet activities. Call friends or listen to music, but avoid television and Internet use. Read ahead to the beginning of the next chapter and plan for tomorrow's juices and rituals so you will be prepared for what you will need to do to support your journey.

8:00 | Bedtime Ritual

If you like, head back into the bathroom and take a final warm bath using detoxifying mineral salts (or simply add a handful of Himalayan salt crystals to your bathwater). Then head to bed without giving in to any habitual urges to watch television or check e-mails. As you relax and allow your body and mind to settle, use the following waterfall meditation to carry you off into a river of dreams.

Lie comfortably and warmly in your bed with the lights off. Imagine a beautiful waterfall of white light is flowing down on you. It flows down on your head, helping your head to relax. You feel your head relaxing. The light moves down over your neck and shoulders. Your neck and shoulders are relaxing. Now it flows down over your arms. You feel your arms relaxing. It flows down your back. Your back is letting go and relaxing. It flows over your chest and stomach, helping your chest and stomach relax. You feel them relax. It moves down over your legs and feet. You feel your legs and feet letting go and relaxing. The beautiful waterfall of white light is flowing over your whole body. You are very peaceful and relaxed.

You have beautifully completed Day 2 of your cleanse. I hope you are filled with excitement and creative energy and that your feet are firmly grounded beneath you—because tomorrow we will be cleansing the third energy center, located behind your navel. We will dedicate tomorrow to the third chakra, the seat of personal power and confidence. Sleep deeply!

8

≣ DAY 3 ≣

Yellow Juice

THE THIRD CHAKRA:
Confidence and Fearlessness

....

People think I'm disciplined. It is not discipline. It is devotion. There is a great difference.

················ —LUCIANO PAVAROTTI, 1935–2007 ················

THE THIRD CHAKRA LIES in your solar plexus, between your navel and your spine, and, not surprisingly, it controls and reflects emotions concerning power, fear, and anxiety. (Ever wonder why you get a "knot" or a sinking feeling in the "pit" of your stomach when confronting these emotions?) An imbalanced third chakra allows stress to exert an unhealthy influence on your life. Stress manifests itself in physical symptoms such as headaches, insomnia, susceptibility to infections, stomach problems, backache, excessive sweating, and sexual difficulties. When the third chakra is blocked or underdeveloped, you tend to absorb the negative energies of others around you and you may feel powerless or unhappy with your situation in life.

Harmonizing this chakra with a golden juice (as well as your daily green juice of choice) stokes your inner fire and will sustain you as you work toward spiritual growth. As energy flows through this third chakra, you will become confident in allowing your opinions and personal power to serve you.

Today, your joy in movement and inner strength will be ignited through a yoga practice grounded in the powerful "Breath of Fire" breathing technique. The activities you will take part in today will ask you to examine the energy of your inner fire and help you discover how to burn away blockages to reveal your inner strength and become confident and fearless. Today's mantra is *I will.*

Today's Grocery List and Juice Recipe

With a thick armor of skin protecting its juicy, sweet flesh, the pineapple naturally evokes confidence. It's easier to feel confident when we feel protected. Golden pineapple protects you with many important minerals and enzymes, including bromelain, a natural anticoagulant that reduces inflammation and thins mucus.

You will also be enjoying Green Elixir for Heart Connection and Essential Potassium-Rich Broth today (see pages 42 and 43 for recipes). All of the chakras connect through the fourth (heart) chakra. Today the green juice you consume will connect the third chakra to your heart, clearing the path to higher consciousness. Again, you may enjoy the same green juice as you have on previous days, or you may choose one of the others from the juice recipe section in Chapter 15. With today's yellow and green juices, allow the life force of the sun to empower your physical body and light the way for your spiritual growth.

⋛ Yellow Juice ⋚

- ½ of a whole pineapple, scrubbed but with outer peel intact
- 2 stalks celery
- 1 Golden Delicious apple
- ½ cup cilantro
- 1 lemon, peeled
- 1-inch piece of gingerroot, more or less, to taste (it is not necessary to peel the gingerroot, though you may wish to, depending on the quality of your juicer)

Put each ingredient through the juicer, pour into a tall glass, and then gently mix together. Be sure to notice and enjoy the beautiful golden color.

Today's Recommended Teas

Peppermint and ginger teas, which soothe and cleanse the digestive system, would be good choices for today. Harness the power of the sun and brew your own sun tea. Fill a glass jar with purified water and add loose herbs or tea bags. Put a lid on the jar and leave it to steep in the sun, outdoors if possible or on a sunny windowsill. When you drink your tea today, know that you are absorbing the power of the sun, and let it radiate throughout your body and your life.

Materials for Today's Creative Inspiration

You may already have most of the following items available at home, or you may choose to go out and purchase special new supplies to use during your cleanse. If you are planning to shop, be sure to do so in the days prior to your cleanse. The seven days of the cleanse are *your* time for relaxing, rejuvenating, and resting—not shopping. You will need:

➤ Your special juice glass or cup
➤ Beautiful stationery or a card that has meaning for you
➤ A stamped envelope
➤ A pen that feels wonderful in your hand. Look for an unusual color of ink like purple or green, and have fun with your choice.

Materials for Today's External Beauty Indulgence

Today you will smooth and reveal your perfect, glowing skin with a cleansing body paste. You will need:

➤ Three teaspoons of ground almonds
➤ Three teaspoons of oatmeal

- A teaspoon of freshly grated grapefruit peel
- A good pinch of freshly grated nutmeg
- Three drops of bergamot or cedarwood essential oil (which both promote positive balance in the third chakra)
- Two drops of rose essential oil
- Two drops of grapefruit essential oil. You may replace this with neroli oil if you have it.
- Two to four tablespoons of sweet almond oil

Mix these ingredients together to make a paste, adding the oil last to achieve the proper consistency. Store the mixture in a glass jar with a tightly fitting lid until it is time for this afternoon's beauty indulgence.

What You May Experience Today

Day 3 can be thought of as the wild card day of your cleanse. It's impossible to predict how you will feel today, but you will definitely perceive a shift. Your experience may seem more challenging than ever, leaving you feeling ready to abandon ship. Or you may suddenly feel as though you could sail on without solid food forever. Detox symptoms could be more aggravating than ever; you may feel headachy or have body aches and you may notice intense feelings of anger or annoyance. However, you might instead feel ready to run a marathon or skip around the house.

Anything is possible today, for by the end of the third day of your cleanse your body is physiologically altered and you are truly in a fasting state. This means that on a cellular level, your body is in serious cleanup mode. How you will feel today will depend on what your cells have to mop up. There is no way to say what the cellular cleanup crew will have to deal with. But one thing you can be sure of is that it will all be cleaned up soon.

The third chakra is all about commitment, so be strong in your commitment to complete this program; contemplate your fears and release old resentments and anger. Only then will you truly be cleansed and able to achieve perfect bodily balance.

Schedule for Day 3 ....

Please note that all times are suggested. Stay within a few hours of this schedule if possible, but honor your body's natural rhythms.

7:30 | Awaken, Solé, Morning Journaling

Renew your original commitment to completing your journal pages. Today, consider writing out your most pervasive fears. List at least seven things that have made you furiously angry in the past. Keep going if you have more than seven, but do not stop before you have listed at least seven. These seven items could involve something another person did to you or prevented you from doing, or perhaps something you prevented yourself from doing. We are often angry at ourselves for any number of things: for instance, not fulfilling our own potential, not acting in a particular way, or failing to move toward a goal.

Now pick the worst of your items—the one episode that just made you so angry, frustrated, or frightened that you could barely cope. Go ahead and be fearless; name names and say everything you are feeling and all that you felt then. Remember that nobody will read your journal. Take courage in the promise you made to yourself to keep the journal pages safe and private, or to shred or burn them after writing. Notice how you are breathing and feeling as you write out the details of that one chosen episode. Once you have fleshed it out and described it in as much detail as you can remember, imagine someone swooping down from the sky like Superman to create a force field to defend you. List seven things your hero would do and say either to help you or in your defense—avenging, resolving, and correcting that painful episode exactly as you would have had it happen.

Next write out in detail what your life feels like now that you have Superman on your side and this event has been completely resolved.

Realize that there is nothing left to do; you are free from it. All is perfect.

Notice how your body feels. What parts of your body are holding and clinging to each other? Check in with your neck and shoulders, your jaw, and the organs within your "gut." As you perceive each tightly held place, release them one by one. Breathe fully as you release any tension within your body, your belly, or your breath. As you release the physical places of clinging and holding, you also release the anger and fear you have been holding and carrying within you for so long. You can set it all down now and rest. Be fearless in what you write and allow this unedited exploration of your thoughts to lead you to great— and perhaps unexpected—personal growth.

If you wish, you can also ask yourself the following questions immediately after finishing your writing and note your answers in your journal. Do not overthink your replies to these questions; simply tap into your intuition and answer honestly and spontaneously.

➤ What is your internal weather report today? That is, if you were the weather, what would you be? Sunny? Storm clouds approaching? Blue skies all the way? Be creative.

➤ What do you fear will be challenging for you today?

➤ What is surprising about how you feel today?

➤ Did you remember to renew your intention every time you took in nourishment with your juices? How does that feel?

8:00 | First Broth

Begin your day with one cup of Essential Potassium-Rich Broth (see recipe on page 43). If you are taking grains, add one to three tablespoons of quinoa to your broth, being careful to chew each mouthful until it is liquid. Concentrate on the sensation of chewing food, giving it your total attention, silence, and awareness. You may also enjoy peppermint or ginger teas, which are particularly soothing to the stomach.

9:00–10:00 | Yoga and Meditation

Breath of Fire

This powerful yoga breathing exercise energizes and powerfully cleanses your entire body. Concentrate on your solar plexus as you move through this exercise. It may be more challenging than you expect! Be sure to read through the directions prior to performing these exercises so you can flow through them gracefully.

1. Begin by sitting in the "easy for you" pose you established on Day 1 of your cleanse. After you have enjoyed several long, deep, cleansing breaths with your eyes closed, lean forward slightly and stick out your tongue. Place both hands over your navel.

2. Begin breathing over your tongue as if you were a panting dog. Your belly will move rhythmically, with the navel as the control center of this breath, moving in and out like a piston that you can feel in your hands.

3. When you feel ready, lower your hands to your knees, close your mouth, and continue the same rhythm of rapid, even breaths through your nose only. Now you are experiencing Breath of Fire, or *pranayama*. *Prana* means "life force energy" and refers to the breath, the vital life force that moves in and out of our bodies.

4. Practice this Breath of Fire for one to three minutes. You will feel a great, warm sun forming behind your navel—that's how the technique got its name. Feel it grow hotter and hotter as you continue to breath. This rapid, powerful, and rhythmic breath should feel like a bellows stoking a fire deep within your belly as you breathe. You will literally "burn clean."

5. If you get tired or feel you are hyperventilating, slow your breath but keep a definite rhythm. If you are truly dizzy or begin to become unable to maintain an equal balance of inhaling and exhaling, simply stop for a moment, then continue with long, slow, deep breathing. As soon as you can, get right back into practicing the Breath of Fire.

6. Practice this breath for three full minutes; setting a timer is very helpful to keep you going. Eventually, and with not as much practice as you might imagine, this exercise becomes effortless.

7. When you have completed three full minutes of uninterrupted practice, stop and allow your breath to just "be." Lie on your back on the floor and rest for about one minute before continuing on to the next exercise.

If you are new to Breath of Fire, at first this exercise will seem impossible. Just trust, commit, and go. With practice, as you master this breath, your belly will become quite warm, and you may feel as if you have just performed 100 sit-ups. While Breath of Fire is very simple—you are simply sitting and breathing—this technique goes right to your center without delay. Breath of Fire is incredibly toning to the core and is so cleansing that it feels as if you are scrubbing your lungs vigorously with an internal scrub brush. There is no better internal cleansing practice than the breath, and no breath more cleansing than the Breath of Fire.

Knee to Chest Pose

Knee to chest pose will bring an easy balance to your third chakra. As you relax deeply and breathe consciously, your belly will rise to touch your thighs as you hug your knees into your chest. Think of your breath as massaging your belly from the inside out. This pose promotes feelings of safety and comfort—the first steps toward confidence and self-esteem.

1. Begin by lying on your back with your fingers interlinked (a position called the Venus lock) and resting on your solar plexus. If your find that your head is forced to strain back in order to reach the floor, put a rolled towel or a small pillow under your neck.

2. Bring your right knee to your chest and move your interlinked fingers to the top of your knee. Lengthen your left leg to rest straight down upon the floor.

3. Keep your spine flat on the floor and inhale deeply, then exhale all the air in your lungs and belly to form a vacuum. This *uddiyana bandha*, or abdominal lock, is a gentle yet powerful motion of the navel, pulling in and upward, in this case when the abdomen is void of air.

4. Relax as you inhale and lower your leg. Rest.

5. Pull your left knee to your chest and repeat the entire sequence on the other side. Do this two more times for a total of three rounds of twenty-one pulses on each side.

6. Tuck both your knees to your chest and hug them securely with your arms around them. You may bring your chin toward your chest and your head to your knees to tuck yourself into a little ball (like an upside-down version of child pose). Begin Breath of Fire while in this pose, continuing for one full minute. You should set a timer to keep you going. If you do not have a timer or do not want to stop to set one, you can instead count off sixty-four breaths. (Tip: It's easiest to count off eight sets of eight breaths, using the same rhythm as in steps 4 and 5).

7. Inhale deeply, rest your head and feet on the floor, and totally relax for one minute.

8. Repeat step 6 above two more times for a total of three repetitions.

9. Rest in *savasana* with your hands on top of your navel, right hand over left (if you have a male nature, you will instead instinctively rest your left hand over your right). Rest completely and surrender totally.

Meditation for Third Chakra Cleansing

To reach your true potential for growth, you must give up security, embrace adventure, and accept vulnerability. To truly empower yourself, you must be without ego, allowing the forces of the universe to move through and within you. This is difficult because, while the ego is a barrier that stops growth, many of us feel that our ego is our only security. It is only by letting go, by becoming truly open to experience as existence, that we are able to fully surrender to the power within each of us. Out of that surrender comes the power to choose.

In this meditation, allow yourself to experience the vastness of the universe; allow yourself to become an open space, unfettered by ego, expectation, or past experience.

Sit in your "easy for you" seated position (as explained at the beginning of Day 1). You may sit erect in a chair with the soles of your feet completely on the ground. Feel the bottom of your feet in contact with the ground and accept however they present themselves to the floor. You may also choose to sit in a comfortable cross-legged position with a long spine.

In this seated, breathing meditation, you will be inhaling through your nose as you read the first line of the meditation below and exhaling through your mouth as you silently, internally repeat the second line, "So am I." It is important that you keep your eyes open and that you focus and read at the same time as you are inhaling. Think of inhaling and reading as if you are sipping in the words. Imagine each word entering through your eyes and into your heart.

Then close your eyes to "seal" the meaning of what you have read inside your Self.

With your eyes closed, hear the words "So am I" as you exhale. Be mindful of your breath: notice if you are mentally sounding the words while you are holding your breath. If you find that you are, try to exhale out the words, blowing them out of your nostrils as if you were stoking the flames of a fire.

Remember, too, that your energy goes where your eyes go. In yoga, the term *drishti* refers to the place where you place your gaze. I can tell a lot about my students by the way they do or do not use their eyes as they practice. Some feel the need to look all around at others, or at me, or at their own body parts in order to get them to move; others cannot open their eyes. What they do with their gaze reveals much to me about what they need from their practice. By consciously focusing your gaze both inward and outward, you grow effortlessly into "the witness" of your meditation.

In this meditation, focus outward with open eyes as you read the words and then shift your focus inward as your eyes close and you exhale. Begin with a few cleansing breaths as you allow the following image to form in your mind: You are sitting upon the earth, sitting upon the planet as you ride through space, smiling. . . . The core of the earth is miles below you, calm and serene, and you sit upon it, calm and serene.

Open your eyes and inhale as you read: "The earth has a core."
Close your eyes and exhale, affirming silently: "So do I."
Open your eyes and inhale as you read: "The earth is abundant."
Close your eyes and exhale, affirming silently: "So am I."
Open your eyes and inhale as you read: "The earth is magnetic."
Close your eyes and exhale, affirming silently: "So am I."
Open your eyes and inhale as you read: "The earth is fertile."
Close your eyes and exhale, affirming silently: "So am I."
Open your eyes and inhale as you read: "The earth is creative."
Close your eyes and exhale, affirming silently: "So am I."
Open your eyes and inhale as you read: "The earth is resilient."
Close your eyes and exhale, affirming silently: "So am I."
Open your eyes and inhale as you read: "The earth is healing."
Close your eyes and exhale, affirming silently: "So am I."
Open your eyes and inhale as you read: "The earth is beautiful."
Close your eyes and exhale, affirming silently: "So am I."
Open your eyes and inhale as you read: "The earth is powerful."
Close your eyes and exhale, affirming silently: "So am I."
Open your eyes and inhale as you read: "The earth is loving."
Close your eyes and exhale, affirming silently: "So am I."

After the final breath, allow your eyes to remain closed and feel yourself becoming a part of everything. Feel yourself a part of the earth; feel your acceptance of things just as they are. Your breath and these words act together to quiet and cleanse your mind. Sit quietly, enjoy your breath, and accept yourself just as you are.

10:00–11:00 | Creative Inspiration: Letter to Your Self

This project will clear out old demons that block self-esteem and self-consciousness, allowing you to affirm how you choose to see yourself and your potential.

1. On a piece of scrap paper, list seven of the darkest monsters in your life. Write down derogatory phrases that you hear, whether said by others or by your own undermining inner voices. Listen carefully: do you hear parents? Teachers? Siblings? Playmates?

2. Take out your beautiful pen and inspiring card or stationery. Rephrase each negative phrase into a positive affirmation as you render your inner critics powerless. For example, your list may say something like: "You have a terrible singing voice. Don't sing so loud. It's unpleasant to listen to you sing in the shower. Why do you even try?" Respond with honesty and tell yourself what you know to be true: "Dear [me]: You have a strong and distinctive voice full of power. It is joyful when you join in with others who sing. You love music, and it is right and good to participate fully in things you love."

3. Continue with a positive affirmation corresponding to each of the seven judgments from your list.

4. When you have completed your letter or card, seal it in the stamped envelope, address it to yourself, and pop it into the mail. When you receive it a day or two from now, open it and savor the wonderful person that you dare to reveal that you are.

11:00 | First Juice: Yellow Juice

Just as you did yesterday, enjoy your juice following this specific ritual:

1. Prepare your juice and pour it into your special glass. Cover it with your coaster with the *intention* side facing down and your name facing up.

2. Imagine your intention infusing the juice and the juice taking in the energy of the intention.

3. Find a comfortable place to sit with a blanket wrapped around you, in the sunshine or wherever you feel very safe and relaxed; you should be neither cold nor hot.

4. Breathe into your belly. Place one hand on your belly and the other on your heart. Notice any feelings that are coming up: anxiety, fear, impatience. Do not dwell on these thoughts, but acknowledge them as you continue to breathe into your belly and allow your heart to open.

5. Assign your hunger level a number between 1 and 5, with 1 being "not at all hungry" and 5 being "extremely hungry."

6. Pick up your covered juice and, with your eyes closed, feel the weight and temperature of the glass.

7. Bring to mind the intention that is face-to-face with the juice under the cover of your coaster.

8. When you are ready, remove the coaster.

9. Engage your senses. Smell the juice. Does your mouth water? Does your hunger level move in either direction? Appreciate the beautiful color of the juice.

10. Take the first sip but do not swallow immediately. Take the time to notice each taste of the juice with every part of your mouth and tongue. Choose when to swallow.

11. Pause and again note your hunger level. Notice if the one swallow of juice shifted that number in one direction or another.

12. Continue to sip your juice consciously, with pleasure. Let your belly be soft and receiving.

13. After half the juice is finished, check in with your hunger. What number level are you now experiencing? You may find that you are no longer hungry, but you may choose to drink the rest of the juice anyway. That is fine. The most important thing is self-observation and self-awareness. It is okay to eat and drink for the pleasure of the taste alone. Enjoy your healthful elixir in luxurious leisure. If you decide you have had enough juice, you may save it for later in the afternoon.

11:30–2:30 | Free Time

Today is a wonderful day to enjoy a massage. If you can afford the luxury of having a massage therapist visit your home, allow yourself that particularly wonderful indulgence. The stress we experience in our day-to-day lives contributes to the blocking of the third chakra and inhibits our confidence and fearlessness. Managing the stress in your life, including releasing it from your body through massage, can prevent illness, reduce anxiety, relieve sleep disturbances, improve digestion, and help you maintain a healthy weight.

Spend time in the sunlight, soaking up the sun's life-giving rays and absorbing vitamin D, which experts now know works to restore your body at a cellular level.

Today's External Beauty Indulgence: Body-Glow Exfoliation

Laugh, because that is your purpose in life. Love, because that is what you came here for. Shine, because that is important.
—YOGI BHAJAN

After today's bath, get the wonderful body paste you concocted earlier (see pages 89–90). Begin to rub it onto your belly in a circular motion. Start the circular massage at your navel, then rub the paste outward in larger circles until you have covered your entire abdomen. Continue to rub paste all over the rest of your body: legs, arms, chest, hips, and buttocks. This will seem to be a very small amount of paste for your entire body, but it should be rolled onto the body to cover it with a very thin layer, like a second, very thin skin.

When you have covered your body, start rubbing the now-dried paste off your skin, beginning at your navel. You will notice that the paste will brush right off like a powder, leaving your skin incredibly soft and sweet. I have adapted this recipe from *The Complete Book of Essential Oils and Aromatherapy* by Valerie Ann Worwood (New World Library, 1991), modifying the essential oils by using cedarwood oil to create balance in the third chakra's shadow emotions of fear and anger. Pastes such as this are an ancient and still common beauty ritual in both Asia and the Middle East.

2:30 | Second Juice: Green Elixir for Heart Connection

It is now time for your green juice (see recipe on page 42). Follow the ritual outlined on pages 64–65 to make drinking this elixir as pleasurable as possible and to keep your consumption of the juice as much in the present as you can. Sip your juice slowly and savor the new and delicious tastes you are introducing to your body. If you find that you do not wish to finish all of your juice, you may save it for the 5:00 serving and drink it instead of the potassium broth.

After this second juice, plan to take some free time for yourself. If you must take care of personal or family matters during these few hours, try to attend to them consciously, without worry or haste. Be mindful as you approach your tasks. Appreciate what you do well as you meet your own needs or the needs of others. Work without ego and allow yourself the space to *feel* the importance of each thing you do.

5:00 | Second Broth

Now it is time for your second portion of Essential Potassium-Rich Broth. Add one or two tablespoons of quinoa, if desired, and drink a smaller portion of Green Elixir or Yellow Juice, if you have any left over.

Spend the time before the bedtime ritual in quiet activities. Appreciate the power of the kind of laughter that is true "belly laughter." Watch a movie that you know will make you laugh or call a treasured friend and share the joy laughing together can bring.

8:00 | Bedtime Ritual

Take a warm bath using detoxifying mineral salts (or simply add a handful of Himalayan salt crystals to your bathwater) and then head to bed with a good book. See the recommended reading list at the end of the book for some of my favorite books, or read ahead to the beginning of the next chapter so you will be prepared for what you will need to do to support your journey tomorrow.

You have had a very big day today. You have faced a demon or two and emerged victorious; you have also powerfully cleansed your cells with the Breath of Fire, and in doing so you have successfully accessed the confidence and fearlessness so necessary to being the best you can be. Tonight you sleep in fresh, new skin scented with essences that are supporting the growing confidence within you. Sleep in peace.

Dreams cleanse you and deal with unresolved issues. Allow this, and be grateful for dreams. Dreams are your body's natural way of cleansing your nervous system and mind. Welcome this.

Tomorrow is the most wonderful day of the cleanse: Day 4, when your cleanse penetrates the fourth (heart) chakra, revealing your beauty, love, and compassion.

⋛ DAY 4 ⋚

Green Juice

THE FOURTH CHAKRA:
An Open Heart

....

Love and compassion are necessities, not luxuries.
Without them, humanity cannot survive.

················ —TENZIN GYATSO, FOURTEENTH DALAI LAMA ···············

LOCATED AT THE CENTER of your chest on your sternum, the fourth chakra, or heart chakra, is the midpoint of the seven chakras and the gateway to higher consciousness. The heart chakra yokes the lower chakras of the physical to the higher chakras of the mental and spiritual. The heart thus unites body and mind through feeling. When we are connected to our heart, we *feel* things in our body.

Hurtful situations such as divorce or separation, grief regarding a death or abandonment, and emotional abuse may all damage the heart chakra, and this damage can manifest itself in physical ailments such as heart disease, asthma, and upper back or shoulder problems. To heal physically, you must first heal your heart. Today, consuming only green juices will help you unblock the fourth chakra, setting you on the path to unconditional love and compassion. As your heart chakra opens, you often release past traumas and emotional pain.

The space you are creating in this cleanse has the potential to be refilled with an endless supply of universal love. On this challenging day of your cleanse, you will concentrate on opening your heart to give and receive unconditional love and compassion.

Today's Grocery List and Juice Recipe

Today you focus on the fourth (heart) chakra, the gateway to higher consciousness and all-encompassing compassion. Green is the color of the fourth chakra. Just as your heart is centered in the middle of your body, so do green foods, like today's Green Juice, grow in the center of the food world—above the roots and ground, but not so far up into the sky as the fruits and vegetables that grow on vines and trees.

You will also be enjoying Green Elixir for Heart Connection and Essential Potassium-Rich Broth today (see pages 42 and 43 for recipes). You may choose the same green juice each day, or choose one of the others from the juice recipe section in Chapter 15. As you enjoy an all-green-juice day, acknowledge the health and abundance that nature gives to us so freely.

≋ Green Juice ≋

- 1 cup coarsely chopped collard greens
- ½ cup coarsely chopped kale
- ½ cup coarsely chopped dandelion greens
- ½ cup coarsely chopped beet greens
- 3 stalks celery
- 3 green apples
- 1 whole lemon, peeled
- 1-inch piece of gingerroot, more or less to taste (it is not necessary to peel the gingerroot, though you may wish to, depending on the quality of your juicer)

Put the greens through the juicer, followed by the celery, apples, lemon, and gingerroot. Mix gently and enjoy.

Today's Recommended Teas

Enjoy as much detoxifying tea as you like (see page 44). Rosemary or hawthorn teas, both of which strengthen the heart and circulatory systems, are excellent choices for today. To make rosemary or hawthorn tea, combine one teaspoon of herbs with eight ounces of boiling water and steep for three minutes. If you wish, add fresh lemon for flavoring.

Materials for Today's Creative Inspiration

Today's tools can be gathered from your own backyard in season. Otherwise you may wish to visit a grocery or florist to gather the things you will need for today's creative project—a nature mandala. If you are planning to shop, be sure to do so in the days prior to your cleanse.

➤ Your special juice glass or cup
➤ Flowers, leaves, twigs, pinecones, berries, pebbles, etc. Try to gather seasonal things if possible. Celebrate nature's abundance!

Materials for Today's External Beauty Indulgence

Gather the ingredients from this list to prepare for a lovingly shared hand massage:

➤ Sesame oil
➤ Essential oil of your choice (rose, neroli, sweet orange, and frankincense are all choices that resonate with the fourth chakra)
➤ A soft, warm wrap or blanket

What You May Experience Today

Today is the fourth day of your cleanse—bravo! You have made it beyond the three-day adjustment period. You are now in a true fasting state, and are learning to ride the waves of your body's rhythms beautifully. By this point your cleanse may feel very easy for you, but it may also be more challenging. Ultimately, the voyage you are on is yours and yours alone, and you are learning to trust your compass—that is, your intuitive center—to lead you to your purified, clean, and luminous Self.

Schedule for Day 4

Please note that all times are suggested. Stay within a few hours of this schedule if possible, but honor your body's natural rhythms.

7:30 | Awaken, Solé, Morning Journaling

I hope you are keeping up with your journaling ritual. It will free you from psychic weight in ways you cannot imagine. This is such an important cleansing tool. As you write in your journal today, allow your heart to open fully. Write about all the things, activities, and beings (people or pets) that you love, have loved, and will always love. Write about the things that will always make you smile whenever you think of them. Feel these memories all around you. Write about what breaks your heart. Write freely with no concern about spelling, content, or meaning. Just open your heart and let it pour onto the page.

If you wish, you can also ask yourself the following questions immediately after finishing your writing and note your answers in your journal. Do not overthink your replies to these questions; simply tap into your intuition and answer honestly and spontaneously.

➤ What is your internal weather report today? That is, if you were the weather, what would you be? Sunny? Storm clouds approaching? Blue skies all the way? Be creative.

➤ What do you fear will be challenging for you today?

➤ What is surprising about how you feel today?

➤ Did you remember to renew your intention every time you took in nourishment with your juices? How does that feel?

➤ Have you noticed anything that is changed? Are any of your senses sharper or more muted?

➤ How are you sleeping? Have you had any vivid dreams?

8:00 | First Broth

Enjoy one cup of Essential Potassium-Rich Broth (see recipe on page 43). If you are taking grains, add one to three tablespoons of quinoa to your broth, being careful to chew each mouthful until it is liquid, giving it your total attention, silence, and awareness. Bear in mind that one very important aspect of this cleanse is becoming aware of food and how you consume it. You may also enjoy some detox tea (I like the Yogi Tea brand, available at many health food stores) or ginger tea.

After you enjoy your broth, treat yourself to dry skin brushing before taking a warm shower or bath followed by a cooling rinse. If you like to moisturize after a shower, use only pure, high-quality oils such as almond, apricot kernel, jojoba, or coconut oil. Pure, unmixed oils are immediately absorbed by the skin and do not feel greasy or oily.

9:00–10:00 | Yoga and Meditation

Kriya for an Open Heart

Kriya is a Sanskrit word that translates as *action*, *deed*, or *effort*. In Kundalini yoga, a *kriya* is a particular combination of movements that acts to purify the body and nervous system. The series of twists and back bends explained below cleanses your body, energizes your spine, and encourages you to open your heart center to the light.

In all of these exercises, be sure to move carefully and without force. You should not feel uncomfortable in any of these positions, especially the back bends or modified back bends. Appreciate how your body and mind feel during these exercises and modify them to suit your own needs.

1. Begin in a seated position on the floor with your legs extended in front of you. Root the back of your thighbones down into the floor and spread your toes as you flex your feet back toward you. If you are too tight to extend your legs comfortably, bend your knees slightly, sit on a cushion or a folded towel or blanket, or sit in a chair with both feet rooted flat to the earth.

2. Place your hands on your shoulder with your palms facing downward, thumbs in back, fingers in front, elbows level to shoulders.

3. Inhale and twist left. Exhale and twist right. Swing freely from side to side, following your breath. After eight breaths, raise your arms into a V shape and continue the twisting movement for eight more breaths.

4. Pause, inhale, and bring your palms together, arms parallel to your ears and extended above your head. Exhale and bring your hands to your heart center.

5. Repeat this full sequence two more times.

Camel Pose

This is a very intense pose that opens the heart and throat. You may experience some strong emotions, such as anxiety or fear, as you attempt this pose. Move carefully and modify your position as necessary to maintain a feeling of safety.

1. Begin in a kneeling position with your toes pressed into the floor.

2. Bring your arms behind you and press your hands into the small of your back, fingertips facing up or down, whichever is more comfortable for you.

3. Inhale as you lift your heart up and drop your head back. Be sure your hands are supporting your lower back and press the front of your thighs forward as you exhale your heart higher.

4. Using only 30 percent effort, allow the pose to create space as you allow more breath into your heart center. Do not go so deep that your breath becomes forced or you feel panicked or constricted.

5. Continue breathing, allowing each breath to be deeper than the one before. If possible, drop your hands to your heels and allow your head to relax back even more as your chest continues to lift. Strong thighs push forward to support you. Allow the breath to move from your back up through your chest and throat. Feel safe as you allow this to happen. Remember, this pose is beneficial no matter how you practice it. The intention to open your heart as your breath creates space is what matters most.

6. Slowly come upright, reversing the way you went into the pose. Sit on your heels in *vajrasana*, or rock pose. Reach your arms behind your back and interlace your fingers (or grasp a towel if you have tight shoulders). Bring your head forward toward the ground, keeping your butt in contact with your calves. Allow your hands to come up over your head, rinsing out your shoulders. Rest your forehead on the ground and feel your spine lengthen. Return to a sitting position and simply sit with your butt on your heels, hands resting comfortably on top of your thighs—left hand under right for women, vice versa for men. This will happen naturally—watch!

Tabletop, Bridge, and Wheel Poses

Each of these poses is a variation on the back bend, encouraging you to open your heart to the sky. Wheel is an intense back bend. Modifications such as tabletop and bridge are best if you are new to yoga practice or if you have extremely tight back and shoulder muscles or other physical limitations. Begin with tabletop or bridge and move into more challenging postures only if you feel comfortable and safe.

1. From rock pose (described above), sit to one hip and bring your feet in front of you, placing them flat on the floor. Place your hands four to eight inches behind your hips, thumbs facing your hips, fingers pointing away. Straighten your arms, lift your hips, and bring your torso to a tabletop position. If comfortable, allow your head to relax back between your shoulders.

2. Return to a seated position with your knees bent and your feet flat on the floor a few inches from your butt. Lie back and shift each shoulder underneath your torso. Clasp your hands together and check to see that your fingertips can brush your heels. On an inhale, use strong thighs to push your knees together and forward as you lift your hips, butt, and torso from the floor. Feel your shoulders and the backs of your upper arm connecting with the earth. Press the inside edges of your feet into the floor as you lift your hips higher. Protect your neck by keeping your chin toward your chest. Your eyes should be open and soft. Follow your breath for eight breaths and exhale as you return to the floor. Repeat twice.

3. If you are not experiencing any strain in your lower back or neck, you may wish to move into wheel pose. Lie on your back and set your feet about hip-width apart with your heels a few inches from your butt. Bring your hands parallel to your shoulders, palms pressing into the earth, fingers facing toward your toes. Bring your elbows toward each other and as you inhale, press your body up toward the sky. Staying aware of your breath, allow your hips and chest to float up with each inhalation. Stay here for eight breaths if you are able and then, tucking your chin into your chest, roll slowly back to the ground. Repeat twice.

4. Rest in *savasana* with your knees dropping open to the side. For a delicious heart-opening stretch, put a pillow or rolled-up towel just below your shoulders under your back at chest level and let your shoulders fall open across it. Close your eyes and come into awareness of your body resting securely on the earth.

Meditation for Fourth Chakra Cleansing: Open Heart

The heart chakra is also called *anahata* (which means "the unstruck note" in Sanskrit). The heart center can help you to make a stronger connection with your soul. You can do that by calling your soul into your heart center using the healing sound *om* (pronounced to rhyme with *home*). For this meditation, you may wish to begin by chanting *om* three times, feeling the vibration in your heart and throat as you inhale, and then exhale as you vocalize, beginning and sustaining the sound *ahhh-ohhhh-mmmmm*.

Now find a comfortable seated position. You may sit erect in a chair with the soles of your feet completely on the ground. Feel the bottom of your feet in contact with the ground and accept however they present themselves to the floor. You may also choose to sit in a comfortable cross-legged position with a long spine.

You will meditate on the list of phrases below three times each: once in human language (spoken out loud at normal volume), once in the language of lovers (in a whisper), and the third time in the language of universal creative consciousness (silently). If possible, surround yourself with nature sounds or play a recording of nature sounds softly in the background while reciting this beautiful mantra. I recommend some of my favorites at the end of this book.

In this seated, breathing meditation, you will repeat each affirmation three times, inhaling through your nose as you first read the line, exhaling through your mouth as you repeat it in a whisper, and then silently, internally, repeat it once more in the space between the exhalation and your next inhalation. As in all mantras, the sound should be released upon the natural exhalation of your breath. You should begin to feel as if the exhale is indistinguishable from the sound. Remember, to make sound is to breathe. Continue this repetition for each of the affirmations below:

Peace to my left
Peace to my right
Peace behind me
Peace before me
Peace beneath me
Peace above me
Peace in my surroundings
Peace in my heart
Peace unto all
Peace unto me

Light to my left
Light to my right
Light behind me
Light before me

Light beneath me
Light above me
Light in my surroundings
Light in my heart
Light unto all
Light unto me

Love to my left
Love to my right
Love behind me
Love before me
Love beneath me
Love above me
Love in my surroundings
Love in my heart
Love unto all
Love unto me

Your breath and words will act together to quiet and cleanse your mind. When you have finished, sit quietly, enjoy your breath, and accept yourself just as you are.

10:00–11:00 | Creative Inspiration: Nature Mandala

Loosely translated, the Sanskrit word *mandala* means *circle*, but a mandala is much more than a simple shape. The circle represents wholeness, the shape of the world, of cells, and of the very structure of life itself. Contemplating a mandala, we are reminded of our relation to the universe and the world that extends both beyond and within our bodies and minds.

To create today's mandala, you may choose to use only flowers—perhaps even only roses, the symbol of the heart. Or you may choose to celebrate the abundance of nature and use materials that symbolize your connection to the earth and its abundance.

1. Deconstruct the items you collected earlier to create your mandala (see list on page 105). Peel off bark, pull apart petals, break up twigs.

Put each item in a small bowl or cup. This is your artist's palette. Clear a work space on a solid background: a table, the floor, on a towel, outside on your driveway, etc.

2. Begin from the perimeter and outline a circle. Work toward the center, arranging your items in a pattern that pleases you. Leave some white space between the pieces to create your design. Concentrate on the beauty you are creating. Be guided by your heart. Appreciate the textures and colors.

3. When you are finished, admire your beautiful artwork, but understand that it is impermanent—and smile at that. Being open to letting go of things, no matter how beautiful, no matter how much work and time went into them, is essential for a healthy heart. Do not hold things in your heart, for even the things we truly love are only treasured guests in our hearts. As Eckhart Tolle says in his book *A New Earth*: "Everything is destined to dissolve. . . . In the absence . . . everything shines."

11:00 | First Juice: Green Juice

Just as you did yesterday, enjoy your juice following this specific ritual:

1. Prepare your juice and pour it into your special glass. Cover it with your coaster with the *intention* side facing down and your name facing up.

2. Imagine your intention infusing the juice and the juice taking in the energy of the intention.

3. Find a comfortable place to sit with a blanket wrapped around you, in the sunshine or wherever you feel very safe and relaxed; you should be neither cold nor hot.

4. Breathe into your belly. Place one hand on your belly and the other on your heart. Notice any feelings that are coming up: anxiety, fear, impatience. Do not dwell on these thoughts, but acknowledge them as you continue to breathe into your belly and allow your heart to open.

5. Assign your hunger level a number between 1 and 5, with 1 being "not at all hungry" and 5 being "extremely hungry."

6. Pick up your covered juice and, with your eyes closed, feel the weight and temperature of the glass.

7. Bring to mind the intention that is face-to-face with the juice under the cover of your coaster.

8. When you are ready, remove the coaster.

9. Engage your senses. Smell the juice. Does your mouth water? Does your hunger level move in either direction? Appreciate the beautiful color of the juice.

10. Take the first sip but do not swallow immediately. Take the time to notice each taste of the juice with every part of your mouth and tongue. Choose when to swallow.

11. Pause and again note your hunger level. Notice if the one swallow of juice shifted that number in one direction or another.

12. Continue to sip your juice consciously, with pleasure. Let your belly be soft and receiving.

13. After half the juice is finished, check in with your hunger. What number level are you now experiencing? You may find that you are no longer hungry, but you may choose to drink the rest of the juice anyway. That is fine. The most important thing is self-observation and self-awareness. It is okay to eat and drink for the pleasure of the taste alone. Enjoy your healthful elixir in luxurious leisure. If you decide you have had enough juice, you may save it for later in the afternoon.

11:30–2:30 | Free Time

Allowing your Self abundant unscheduled free time is so important. What to do? This is the fun part! Do whatever will make you smile today, right now. The only criteria is that you do it alone: play with your pet, call your best friend, read love poetry by Rumi. Buy yourself flowers and spend time arranging them artfully in a vase, placing them thoughtfully in your bedroom where you will see them as you awake in your bed in the mornings. Think about how you will see them tomorrow when you awake. As you choose the place to set your flowers, imagine placing them in the view of your beloved so that he or she would see a thing of beauty in the moment of awakening. Now do this for yourself. And smile.

Today's External Beauty Indulgence: Shared Hand Massage

I love you without knowing how, or when, or from where,
I love you simply, without problems or pride:
I love you in this way because I don't know any other way of loving.

—PABLO NERUDA, *100 LOVE SONNETS,*
AS TRANSLATED BY STEPHEN MITCHELL

There is nothing more loving than to share innocent, tender touch with another. Enjoy this shared hand massage with someone you care about.

1. Pour a small amount of sesame oil into your palms and add a few drops of essential oil of your choice. Warm the oil by briskly rubbing your palms together.

2. Take your child's, your best friend's, your beloved's hands in yours and examine them lovingly with your eyes. With one hand begin to massage the palm, then each finger from base to tip, and then in between each finger. Be sure to massage the back of the hand as well.

3. Repeat on the other hand.

4. Allow your partner to perform this same ritual on your hands.

5. When you have both had your hands massaged, briskly rub your hands together again to create some heat. Then place your palms over your eyes and hold them gently as you relax your forehead into the darkness. Sit comfortably, swaddled in your blanket, with your palms under the blanket, one hand over the heart and the other hand over the first hand. Keep your eyes closed so you can "see" what is moving

internally with clarity and perceive your heartbeat under your hands. Do nothing more. Just enjoy the stillness, the warmth of the blanket, the comfort of your posture, and the rhythm of your heart.

2:30 | Second Juice: Green Elixir for Heart Connection

It is now time for your green juice (see recipe on page 42). Follow the ritual outlined on pages 64–65 to make drinking this elixir as pleasurable as possible and to keep your consumption of the juice as much in the present as you can. Sip your juice slowly and savor the new and delicious tastes you are introducing to your body. If you find that you do not wish to finish all of your juice, you may save it for the 5:00 serving and drink it instead of the potassium broth.

After this second juice you may plan to take some free time for yourself. If you must take care of personal or family matters during these few hours, attend to them with extra tenderness and compassion. Perhaps for today only, consider not holding any expectation of receiving in return. Practice unconditional giving and loving. Imbue the smallest acts with love and thoughtfulness. Set the table with care or perform some small task that eases the day for your family members. Do these things without asking for recognition. Think of other random acts of kindness you could perform today.

5:00 | Second Broth

Now it is time for your second portion of Essential Potassium-Rich Broth. Add one or two tablespoons of quinoa, if desired, and drink a smaller portion of Green Elixir or Green Juice, if you have any left over.

Spend the time before your bedtime ritual in quiet activities. Perhaps you could connect with someone who loves you. Or listen to music—you can try something from the "Chakra 4" playlist in the recommended music section at the end of this book. Continue to protect your heart today by avoiding television and commercial-laden radio stations. Opt for a CD, DVD, or a downloaded playlist so your heart will receive no interference from conflicting vibrations. Read ahead to the beginning of the next chapter so you will be prepared for what you will need to do to support your journey tomorrow.

8:00 | Bedtime Ritual

Take a warm bath using detoxifying mineral salts (or simply add a handful of Himalayan salt crystals to your bathwater) and several generous drops of lavender and rose essential oils. Then it's off to bed with a good book—if you can keep your eyes open. See the recommend reading list at the end of the book for some of my favorite books or, if you have not already done so, read ahead to the beginning of the next chapter so you will be prepared for what you will need to do to support your journey tomorrow. By now your bodymind's rhythms may have adjusted to an earlier bedtime, and you may notice that you are eager for sleep and that you awaken feeling wonderfully rested.

I hope you enjoyed your day today and that your heart is safe and open. As you sleep, imagine a smile on your heart and continue to enjoy the sensation of your heartbeat deep beneath your sternum. Consider how many other places you can perceive your heartbeat: your belly, your palms, the arches and tops of your feet—even in your throat. Tomorrow we will concentrate on the fifth/throat chakra to sense a great wave of truth within us.

When you awaken, your flower arrangement will be the first thing you see, reminding you to continue to feel your heart chakra open and to release any fear you may be feeling. Bring your attention to your heart beating in your throat tomorrow morning before getting out of bed. As you relax in your bed, gazing at the flowers—no doubt still sleepy—feel the pulse of your heart deep within your throat.

For tonight, sleep luxuriously.

10

≋ DAY 5 ≋

Bright Blue Juice

THE FIFTH CHAKRA:
Truthfulness

....

There is often a big disparity between the way in which
we perceive things and the way things really are.

——TENZIN GYATSO, FOURTEENTH DALAI LAMA

WITH THE TRANSFORMATIVE EXPERIENCES of the past four days providing a solid foundation, you will now create clarity through your higher consciousness chakras. The fifth chakra is associated with the throat area and is centered between the collarbone and the larynx in the neck. It is the locus of communication and truthfulness. After four days of cleansing and self-evaluation, you will have touched your true Self. Today, the fifth day of your cleanse, the time is right to learn to express yourself without fear. On this fifth day you will enjoy gorgeous blue juice (along with your green juice, as always, to facilitate your heart connection with the higher chakras).

When the fifth chakra is imbalanced, you may experience physical manifestations including ear, nose, throat, respiratory, and thyroid problems. Today I'll show you how to cleanse your sinuses with a gentle water irrigation technique using a neti pot and solé to purify your throat. When the energy of the fifth chakra is blocked or turned inward, our voices can become hurtful, our words bitter or destructive.

When this chakra comes into balance, our words become affirming and our communication appreciative of and resonant with one another. Playing with the power of your voice through vocal exercises opens the throat, warming it and inspiring you to consider how you communicate and connect to the rest of the world. Strive to achieve fluency of thought, independent expression, and truthful emotion. Today's mantra is *I am heard*.

Today's Grocery List and Juice Recipe

Blue is calming, relaxing, healing. It is the color of truthfulness, of loyalty. Express yourself freely without fear! Share yourself with the world.

Blueberries are precious and potent—a true "superfood"—containing at least fourteen times more body-cleansing antioxidants than other foods. These precious antioxidants reside in the highly pigmented skin of the berry. By blending the whole fruit into the juice (rather than extracting the blueberry juice and discarding the skins), you offer your body the most out of each ingredient.

You will also be enjoying Green Elixir for Heart Connection and Essential Potassium-Rich Broth today (see pages 42 and 43 for recipes). Whether you choose the same green juice each day of your cleanse or try a different delicious juice from the selection of juice recipes in Chapter 15, you will enjoy the same benefit: harmony between heart and voice.

⧨ Bright Blue Juice ⧨

- 3 stalks celery
- 1 small lemon, peeled
- 1 small grapefruit, peeled
- 1-inch piece of gingerroot, more or less to taste (it is not necessary to peel the gingerroot, though you may wish to, depending on the quality of your juicer)
- 1 pint blueberries

Put the celery, lemon, grapefruit, and ginger through the juicer. Combine the juice mixture with the blueberries in a blender. If you prefer a lighter drink, add purified water to taste.

Today's Recommended Teas

Continue to enjoy as much herbal or detox tea as you wish. Licorice, slippery elm, and fennel are also good choices today because of their soothing properties to the throat. Or just enjoy plain water with lemon.

Materials for Today's Creative Inspiration

For today you will need some very specific items that you may not have on hand. It is worth it to plan ahead and find, order, or download these items prior to beginning your cleanse. You do not want to begin today by having to go out and find these particular things. Plan ahead so that you can enjoy today—it is *your* time for relaxing, rejuvenating, and resting.

➤ Your special juice glass or cup

➤ Your *kirtan* CD or "Chakra 5" soundtrack (see recommended music at the end of the book) downloaded onto your iPod. If you are an experienced yogini and *kirtan* lover, you will already have your favorites. If you are new to this, you are in for a big treat. I recommend Krishna Das's *Pilgrim Heart* album. Download the song "Govinda Hare" followed immediately by "Om Nama Shivaya." Add "Gobinda Gobinda Hari Hari" by Snatam Kaur from her album *Prem* as your third and final call-and-response. Be sure these three songs are downloaded in sequence.

➤ A soft shawl or blanket

➤ Your favorite and most comfortable meditation seat, which could be a pillow, a *zabuton* (a Japanese sitting cushion often used for meditation), or a chair. Or simply use your yoga mat on the floor with a cushion on it.

Materials for Today's External Beauty Indulgence ....

During your cleanse it is beneficial to encourage the cleansing of the mucus membranes that line your nasal cavities, mouth, and throat. They are working harder than ever, and at a very fast pace, to keep up with discharge accelerated by your cleanse. What's needed:

➤ A neti pot (available at most natural food or health stores; you can also sometimes find them in regular drugstores)
➤ Your choice of neti pot salt (either the normal salt that comes with the neti pot or sea salt or solé solution)
➤ Water
➤ Baking soda
➤ Culinary peppermint extract

What You May Experience Today ....

Emotions associated with the throat may come up today. You may feel unaccountably frightened, embarrassed, or just plain silly participating in some of the activities, particularly singing in the shower or making sounds during your meditation. You may feel awkward and doubtful about your ability to perform the nasal cleansing ritual with your new neti pot. Perhaps hunger pangs might be calling you to start eating solid foods again.

Any of these experiences are possible, but they are not necessarily going to happen for everyone. The main point is that, although we are from the same source, we exist here and now in our individual perspectives, and this is a beautiful thing. We are all human, we all have arms, legs, head, and torso, but we are also all different, even as our fingerprints are unique. So expect your cleansing experience to be unique too, not only from person to person, but even from cleanse to cleanse as you move through your life. Be open to all the gifts that open up to you, and you will discover your true purpose and be able to communicate this purpose and your unique beauty clearly to your Self and to others.

Schedule for Day 5

Please note that all times are suggested. Stay within a few hours of this schedule if possible, but honor your body's natural rhythms.

7:30 | Awaken, Solé, Morning Journaling

Before we can ever clearly express ourselves with our voices, we must have clarity within our hearts and minds. It is only when the throat chakra is relating to the heart chakra that we can communicate with truth and understanding. Start your journal in silence today. Let yourself write anything you have not been able to say. Struggle with the words on paper first, and you will feel no struggle as you speak words aloud. Remember that this is just an exercise to clear obstacles and free you for new relationships that will serve your higher purpose. Unleash upon the pages of your journal all that you have left unsaid.

If you wish, you can also ask yourself the following questions immediately after finishing your writing and note your answers in your journal. Do not overthink your replies to these questions; simply tap into your intuition and answer honestly and spontaneously.

➤ What is your internal weather report today? That is, if you were the weather, what would you be? Sunny? Storm clouds approaching? Blue skies all the way? Be creative.

➤ What do you fear will be challenging for you today?

➤ What is surprising about how you feel today?

➤ Did you remember to renew your intention every time you took in nourishment with your juices? How does that feel?

➤ Have you noticed anything that is changed? Are any of your senses sharper or more muted?

➤ How are you sleeping? Have you had any vivid dreams?

8:00 | First Broth

Enjoy one cup of Essential Potassium-Rich Broth (see recipe on page 43). If you are taking grains, add one to three tablespoons of quinoa to your broth, being careful to chew each mouthful until it is liquid, giving it your total attention, silence, and awareness. Be aware of the texture as you swallow. Add a good squeeze of fresh lemon juice to your broth today and appreciate the warmth of the broth as it bathes your throat. After you enjoy your broth, treat yourself to dry skin brushing and then a warm shower or bath followed by a cooling rinse. Lavender, chamomile, rosemary, sage, and thyme (alone or in combination) are all soothing to the throat and are beneficial as steam inhalations. Just before you turn on the water, shake a few drops of essential oil from one of these herbs into a corner of your shower floor where it will not be hit directly by the water. The oil will mix with the steam of your shower, surrounding you for wonderful throat chakra cleansing!

9:00–10:00 | Yoga and Meditation

Jhalandara Bandha (Throat Lock)

This exercise circulates *prana* (breath) within the throat chakra. It offers the opportunity to observe the contrast of the formless (your breath) with the formed (your body). Contrasts exist to point us toward truth. Note the contrasting temperatures—the coolness of your inhalation and the heat of your exhalation. As you inhale your breath and contract your throat, and exhale while expanding your throat, you open the space necessary to reveal your center of truth.

1. To begin, inhale as you drop your chin down toward your chest, then draw your chin back closer to the chest so the back of the neck does not round.

2. Inhale, then exhale, feeling your head hang heavily. Inhale, then exhale as you take your chin to the sky and relax your head back, squeezing and crunching your shoulders toward your ears as you drop your head back to protect your neck and release any tension at the occipital ridge at the base of the skull. Carefully return your head to center upright position.

3. Exhale fully, then inhale as you bring your head to center. Exhale. Inhale and drop your chin to your chest. Do not exhale, but hold your breath inside as long as is comfortable. Bring your chin up and release the breath.

4. Relax and return to neutral, then repeat the steps described above. Feel your throat open both in front and in back as you move in rhythm with your breath.

Lion

While you may feel silly in this pose, it is incredibly beneficial for much of your body. If you have a tight jaw, or if you tend to grind your teeth or clench your jaw, you will feel immediate relief from the stretch in the jaws and tongue. The muscles and tissues of your face are also rejuvenated by the alternating stretching and release. The fixed gaze relieves tense or burning eyes and the stretched fingers benefit tight hands and wrists. This is actually a perfect pose for those of you who spend long days in front of a computer.

1. Move into lion pose by coming to your knees. Place the tops of your feet flat on the floor, and rest your bottom on your heels. Lean slightly forward with your heart center lifted. Place your right hand on your right knee and your left hand on your left knee. Activate your fingers, stretching them into "claws."

2. Open your jaw wide and stretch your tongue as far as possible toward your chin. Roll your eyes gently upward and maintain this posture for about thirty seconds, breathing through your mouth with more emphasis on the exhale. You should hear yourself make an extended *haaaah* sound as you exhale. Allow your inhale to be comfortable and take care of itself, and then allow the elongated exhale to release any tension in your throat, jaw, and face. Don't worry about what you might look like while doing this, this simple move feels really *great*!

Fish

The only way any chakra can fully serve you is by connecting through the heart chakra. As you breathe deeply in fish posture, your heart expands with each of the breaths that pass through your open throat.

1. From your seated position, swing your legs around in front of you and extend them straight out. Placing your hands under the small of your back, make a triangle with your index fingers and thumbs.

2. Keeping your upper arms parallel to your body, bend your elbows and rest your forearms on the floor.

3. Spreading your shoulders wide and pointing your feet strongly, allow your head to sink back toward the floor to expose your throat to the sky. You may rest the crown of your head on the floor if you are able to do so comfortably. If you feel any discomfort in your neck or throat, either lower your chest slightly toward the floor or put a thickly folded blanket under the back of your head.

4. Relax and feel your breath moving gently past your open throat and then filling and expanding your chest. Remain here for eight breaths.

5. Tucking your chin, come out of the pose by reversing the steps you took getting into it. Rest in *savasana* for eight breaths before repeating the pose two more times.

Cobra

The truth is that you are everything! Feel yourself a part of every creature, even the dangerous cobra, as you learn to comfortably inhabit this wonderful pose.

1. Roll over to lie facedown with your chin touching the floor, your legs straight behind you, and the tops of your feet resting on the floor.

2. Place your hands flat on the floor, directly under your shoulders, with your fingers facing forward.

3. Keeping your lower back totally passive and relaxed and keeping your upper arms in contact with or brushing against your sides, gently press your heart and shoulders away from the floor, allowing your heart to open and lift as your head reaches forward and up. Allow the back of your body to curve upward gently. Keep your gaze looking forward. Your torso should be only slightly raised and your pubic bone and hips should remain in contact with the floor. Your arms do not have to be straight, but do make an effort to keep your upper arms in contact with or close to your side ribs. Keeping your upper arms close to your sides as you move in and out of cobra pose not only feels lovely but will ensure that your heart and throat can open freely without the shoulders obstructing them. Bending your elbows allows for a gentle stretch, while moving your hands a bit forward and straightening your arms will create a deeper stretch along the spine. How deep you choose to go is an exercise in knowing your truth and accepting yourself where you are. If you practice with integrity, this memory will follow you off the yoga mat and into your life long after your cleanse.

4. Hold for a few breaths, feeling the gentle stretch along the front of your body from belly to chest to throat. You're mainly aiming to notice how you breathe as you inhabit the cobra. As you inhale, can you allow your breath to open the front of your chest more, as wind might puff out a sail on a boat? On your exhale, can you allow your breath to puff your heart out even more, but passively, as a boat's sail surrenders to the movement of the wind? What is true for you today?

5. Lower yourself to the floor and rest with your cheek turned to one side.

6. Repeat these steps three times, remembering to alternate the side where you rest your cheek when you come out of the pose.

7. Finish by rolling onto your back to rest with your eyes closed in *savasana*. As you rest here, take your attention to your throat. You will perceive a certain energy in your throat. Imagine a small moon is revolving in that space. It may feel tight at first, but by simply noticing the cool temperature of your breath on the inhale and the warmth of your breath on the exhale, and then also noticing your heartbeat just under your sternum, you will feel energy moving quite easily between the heartbeat and that place in your throat.

Meditation for Fifth Chakra Cleansing: Humming Meditation for the Throat Chakra (*Vissudha*)

The Sanskrit word *vissudha* is generally translated to mean "with purity." Each chakra has a "seed sound," or *bija* mantra—a distinct vibration that resonates with the energetic frequency of the chakra. Repeating the *bija* is one of the ways to energize the chakra. The *bija* of the fifth chakra is *ham*.

Sit in your "easy for you" pose. Close your eyes and direct them as if gazing lightly into your forehead.

Now inhale softly, yet deeply, through your nose. As you do, feel the air as it cools the throat. Continue this breath a few times until you truly perceive this cooling of the throat. As you continue this active meditation, keep your attention on the cooling of your throat as you inhale.

On the exhale, create the sound vibration *um,* extending the U sound for the full length of the exhale and ending with the consonant just as you run out of breath.

Cool the throat as you inhale again.

Repeat *uuuuuuuuuuuummmmmmmmmm* until you have exhaled completely.

Cool the throat as you inhale.

Exhale the sound *uuuuuuuuuuuuuuuummmmmmmmmm.*

As you make this sound during your exhale, take your attention to the feeling in the throat during the *uuuuuuuuuu* sound, then transfer your awareness to the feeling in the front of your face, your cheeks, and around the front teeth during the *mmmmmmmmm* part.

Continue to breathe the sound like this for eighteen complete breaths. Then sit quietly and feel the vibration enveloping you.

Exercise the beautiful tuning of your voice throughout the day today. Sing in the shower. Belt out any song you can remember: "Happy Birthday"? "The Star-Spangled Banner"? "Feelin' Groovy"? It's all good.

10:00–11:00 | Creative Inspiration: Your Own Private *Kirtan*

Kirtan, or call-and-response chant, is a give-and-take of breath that puts you into a pattern, quickly abolishing all blockages and resistances that exist in your throat chakra. During a call-and-response *kirtan* session, you share breath and sound with others. In this case, you and your CD *kirtan* leader will trade breaths and share a common vibration. As the singer on the CD (in this case Krishna Das or Snatam Kaur) leads the way with the sound mantra and tune, you relax and enjoy the song, and then "respond" by repeating exactly what the singer has offered. Just as in your yoga exercises, sound should happen only when breath is leaving the body in an exhalation. Do not overthink this, but simply notice the phenomenon as you listen and respond.

Vibration and breath are the most efficient total body cleansing mechanisms there are—better than juices, better than any "superfood," better than one thousand colonics. All of these other means are good, but if you are allowing your breath and your vibrations to freely move through you, your body will maintain a healthy clarity and purity all on its own.

I would like to suggest that the first time you experience a *kirtan*, you should just try to mimic the sounds you hear without reading the sounds written out or trying to understand what they mean. What is so great about doing *kirtan* in private like this is that you feel more free to sound the way you sound, to make funny attempts at replicating new or even strange vocalizations without judgment. You can just immerse yourself in the sound/breath experience and feel the results with no expectations. A child does not learn to speak by first learning to read or by studying the dictionary definitions of words. Get out of your habitual thinking mind, let your mind rest, open your heart, open your throat, drop all worries and judgments, and just give it a try. You will find yourself refreshed with so much breath.

Make yourself comfortable. Allow space for spontaneous natural movement as the breath and sound moves through you. As you hear the sound, inhale, and as you exhale, echo the sound.

Begin to focus on timing your breath to the mantra. Keep your eyes closed. This helps you concentrate on listening to the sounds you are going to repeat; keeps you feeling the sound vibration resonate in your throat, chest, mouth, and head; and of course allows you to feel how the breath gets deeper and deeper to accommodate the sounds.

Kirtan leads us toward a meditative state and helps the mind become quiet. It is in this quiet that we can appreciate the sacred experiences that are always around us. In the silence, you can feel something—a certain vibration. This vibration is the energy of your Self. This vibration is always within you; this vibration *is* you. Experience and enjoy the vibrations of peace, energy, healing, and inspiration that are always surrounding you and within you—just beautiful!

11:00 | First Juice: Bright Blue Juice

Just as you did yesterday, enjoy your juice following this specific ritual:

1. Prepare your juice and pour it into your special glass. Cover it with your coaster with the *intention* side facing down and your name facing up.

2. Imagine your intention infusing the juice and the juice taking in the energy of the intention.

3. Find a comfortable place to sit with a blanket wrapped around you, in the sunshine or wherever you feel very safe and relaxed; you should be neither cold nor hot.

4. Breathe into your belly. Place one hand on your belly and the other on your heart. Notice any feelings that are coming up: anxiety, fear, impatience. Do not dwell on these thoughts, but acknowledge them as you continue to breathe into your belly and allow your heart to open.

5. Assign your hunger level a number between 1 and 5, with 1 being "not at all hungry" and 5 being "extremely hungry."

6. Pick up your covered juice and, with your eyes closed, feel the weight and temperature of the glass.

7. Bring to mind the intention that is face-to-face with the juice under the cover of your coaster.

8. When you are ready, remove the coaster.

9. Engage your senses. Smell the juice. Does your mouth water? Does your hunger level move in either direction? Appreciate the beautiful color of the juice.

10. Take the first sip but do not swallow immediately. Take the time to notice each taste of the juice with every part of your mouth and tongue. Choose when to swallow.

11. Pause and again note your hunger level. Notice if the one swallow of juice shifted that number in one direction or another.

12. Continue to sip your juice consciously, with pleasure. Let your belly be soft and receiving.

13. After half the juice is finished, check in with your hunger. What number level are you now experiencing? You may find that you are no longer hungry, but you may choose to drink the rest of the juice anyway. That is fine. The most important thing is self-observation and self-awareness. It is okay to eat and drink for the pleasure of the taste alone. Enjoy your healthful elixir in luxurious leisure. If you decide you have had enough juice, you may save it for later in the afternoon.

11:30–2:30 | Free Time: Fasting from Words

Be in total silence today during your free time. This is the challenge: no speaking, no listening to words, no reading, no writing. Take two whole hours to fast from words.

Be strong and give this a chance. When your two hours of silence have ended, you may be surprised at how clearly you can communicate what your needs are. It is only two tiny hours of the day. If you wish to listen to a CD, choose instrumental music or nature sounds. The main thing is to avoid words. Allow yourself to be free from understanding and responding to language. This silence is a cleansing rest for the throat, the mind, and the heart.

You do not have to simply sit in a quiet house. Take a walk, knit, paint, draw, nap, or walk alone in nature. But do not speak, listen to someone, respond (even with sign language), read, or listen to the radio. And obviously, absolutely *no* television!

Today's External Beauty Indulgence: Fifth Chakra Cleansing Trio

One of the greatest ways to tap into the truth of who you really are is to begin working with and loving your own human voice.

—GURMUKH, KUNDALINI YOGA TEACHER AND AUTHOR

After performing the following three cleansing actions, you may feel so refreshed that you will want to add them to your daily ritual from now on.

Nose

Begin this cleansing trio during your shower. It is much, much easier to learn and to feel comfortable with neti pot cleansing while already warm, comfortable, and wet and while in a space where you can be free from worries about dripping water around your bathroom or on your body.

1. Fill the neti pot with comfortably warm water. It should probably be a little cooler than the water temperature you shower or bathe in.

2. Stir in a few drops of your solé, or simply use the neti salt packet that comes with most neti pots.

3. Standing in your shower, place the spout of the neti pot into one nostril, on top or closer to the ceiling side, and block off the back of your throat, just as you would if you were at the dentist having your teeth cleaned.

4. Inhale, and hold your breath. Now tip your head sideways, bending slightly at the waist to lean forward. I find it very helpful to lean my forehead against the wall and pivot my head to one side, for more control with less effort.

5. Begin to slowly pour the water from the neti pot into the nose.

6. The solution will naturally pour right out the other nostril, which is closer to the floor. If your nose is very blocked and water does not flow through, you can encourage it by exhaling strongly to expel the water and clear the mucus membranes.

7. Repeat on the other side.

After your shower and neti ritual is complete, massage the inside of your nose with a little of your usual sesame or sweet almond oil. Keep your neti pot right in your shower next to your shampoo and soap, where it will always be ready during your daily shower for a quick nasal cleansing.

Mouth

Make a paste by mixing two tablespoons of baking soda with your solé solution, a little at a time, until a smooth, creamy paste is formed. Stir in one or two drops of culinary peppermint extract. Using your finger, massage your gums and the outside and inside of your teeth. Be sure to reach the molars at the back of the mouth. Rinse, then apply more paste to a soft toothbrush. Brush off any mucus that is clinging to the insides of your cheeks, under the tongue, the roof of the mouth, or the tongue. You will have to rinse the toothbrush with fresh water several times to clear away all the mucus. Now your teeth will sparkle and your mouth will feel clean and fresh.

Throat

In a small cup, mix one part pure solé with three parts water. Gargle loudly. Spit and repeat three times. Be careful not to swallow this solution. Because solé is extremely detoxifying, swallowing too much can make you feel a bit nauseous.

2:30 | Second Juice: Green Elixir for Heart Connection

It is now time for your green juice (see recipe on page 42). Follow the ritual outlined on pages 64–65 to make drinking this elixir as pleasurable as possible and to keep your consumption of the juice as much in the present as you can. Sip your juice slowly and savor the new and delicious tastes you are introducing to your body. If you find that you do not wish to finish all of your juice, you may save it for the 5:00 serving and drink it instead of the potassium broth.

After this second juice you may plan to take some free time for yourself. If you must take care of personal or family matters during these few hours, be conscious of how you use your words and energy to communicate with others. There is no need to change anything about the way you speak and communicate; simply observe, witness, and watch how you communicate. Simply observing creates a shift toward greater clarity in your communications.

5:00 | Second Broth

Now it is time for your second portion of Potassium-Rich Broth. Add one or two tablespoons of quinoa, if desired, and drink a smaller portion of Green Elixir or Bright Blue Juice, if you have any left over.

Spend the time before the bedtime ritual in quiet activities. Continue to resist the urge to turn on the television or use the Internet; you are nearly at the end of your seven-day cleanse, so please hang in there. Call friends, listen to music, or perhaps simply read ahead to the beginning of the next chapter so that you will be prepared for what you will need to do to support your journey tomorrow, when you will purify your sixth chakra and reconnect to your natural intuition.

8:00 | Bedtime Ritual

Take a warm bath using detoxifying mineral salts (or simply add a handful of Himalayan salt crystals to your bathwater) and then head to bed with a good book. See the recommended reading list at the end of the book for some of my favorite books or, if you have not already done so, read ahead to the beginning of the next chapter so you will be prepared for what you will need to do to support your journey tomorrow.

Day 5 is completed—wow! You have regained the ground supporting you, felt your body connect with your heart, strengthened your core power, opened your heart, and voiced your truth. All this awareness and opening will support your work tomorrow, when we turn to your sixth chakra, located just above the brow point on your forehead. It is the seat of your intuition. I will offer you elixirs, tools, and indulgences to assist in the cleansing of this powerful energy center. Sleep well tonight.

11

≋ DAY 6 ≋

Deep Blue Juice

THE SIXTH CHAKRA:
Choosing Clarity

....

*When the winds of change blow, some people
build walls and others build windmills.*

.... —CHINESE PROVERB ....

THE SIXTH CHAKRA IS located in the center of your brow and is also known as the "third eye." When clear and unobstructed, this chakra, the center of intuition and clarity, allows you to differentiate between the wisdom of true knowledge and the noise of distracting information—to see the difference between the wisdom of universal truth and distracting peripheral information that can obscure it.

On this, the sixth day of your cleanse, you may find it a good time to start gently incorporating some solid fruits and vegetables into your juices. Do this by blending them and their skins into your drinks rather than extracting the juices from them and discarding the skins. You will still be totally cleansing. This is a gentle first step toward eating solid foods again and a great way to begin stimulating and toning your digestive system, gently preparing it to once again move solid raw foods through your whole system.

I like starting this process on the day we create clarity in the sixth chakra because creating juices with deep indigo blue color involves berries. Berries of all sorts grow high on bushes, far from the ground and in the air, on the tops of large bushes, winding high upon vines, and up in the trees. These gifts from nature are known to be "superfoods"—that is, they possess the ability to heal the body at a much faster rate than other foods thanks to their enzymatic and antioxidant properties. The skins of these berries contain the highest concentrations of these pigments and are therefore very beneficial to blend directly into your juices, creating beautifully deep-colored and very delicious cleansing elixirs.

Today marks the beginning of the end of your fast. Soon we shall turn our attention to *chewing* solid foods again, but for now, we will begin to break the fast by *drinking* solid foods: easy smoothies that can become your future fast food—a quick, nutritious, and delicious breakfast or meal replacement. Later I'll offer guidance about making wise choices about the food "information" you are putting into your body and suggest the ideal meal to break your juice fast.

Today's meditation will focus on strengthening your awareness of your powerful "third eye" and teach you how to access the love and healing warmth of this chakra. After five days of intense introspection and self-awareness, you will begin to move into a reconnection with the world around you without losing the valuable self-knowledge you have gained.

Today's Grocery List and Juice Recipe

When the body and mind are clear, we can easily see what our next step needs to be. Deep red cherries blend with dark blue blueberries to create a beautiful deep indigo color. The energetic vibration of the color promotes insight.

You will also be enjoying Green Elixir for Heart Connection and Essential Potassium-Rich Broth today (see pages 42 and 43 for recipes). You may choose the same green juice each day of your cleanse, or choose one of the others from the juice recipe section in Chapter 15. In addition, today you will be replacing your second serving of broth with a filling green smoothie. You may choose any of the green smoothie recipes on pages 216–19.

≣ Deep Blue Break-Fast Smoothie ≣

- 2 large apples
- 1 stalk celery
- ½ lemon, peeled
- 1-inch piece of gingerroot, more or less to taste (it is not necessary to peel the gingerroot, though you may wish to, depending on the quality of your juicer)
- 2 cups whole cherries, pitted
- 2 cups blueberries

Put the apple, celery, lemon, and gingerroot through the juicer. In a blender, combine this juice with the cherries and blueberries and blend until smooth.

Today's Recommended Teas

Continue to enjoy as much herbal or detox tea as you wish. Ginger and lemongrass tea are also good choices for today because they uplift your mind and sharpen your senses.

Materials for Today's Creative Inspiration

Today's supplies are simple, and you may already have them at home. Any kind of yarn, string, or even thread will work for the spiderweb exercise. However, if you are planning to shop, be sure to do so in the days prior to beginning your cleanse. Once you begin your cleanse, you do not want to be out running errands. This is *your* time for relaxing, rejuvenating, and resting. You will need:

➤ Your special juice glass or cup
➤ A special journal
➤ A skein of yarn, a ball of string, or a spool of thread

Materials for Today's External Beauty Indulgence

Gather the ingredients from this list to prepare for today's *shirodhara* treatment:

➤ Sweet almond or sesame oil
➤ A cotton towel or washcloth
➤ A small pillow for under your neck (since this could become stained with oil, be sure it is covered with a towel or is otherwise protected)
➤ A larger pillow for under your knees
➤ A warm blanket to place over your body
➤ A small plate or bowl
➤ Music (I recommend *Sapphire Skies* by Dr. Jeffrey Thompson; the entire CD is appropriate, but I especially recommend the track entitled "Prayer")

What You May Experience Today

There is a good reason why we store thoughts deep inside our minds and strive to hide anything that triggers memories of pain or fear: we are trying to protect our fragile Selves. But no matter how high and strong you build your mental walls to avoid feeling emotional pain, the truth is that you can only find peace by confronting these issues with the clarity of knowing what truly matters.

As you move through your day today, you may feel apprehensive about what will happen when you complete this cleanse. You may wonder if you can trust yourself to continue to nourish yourself well or if you will remember to do loving, restorative things for yourself. Your thoughts may race as you think ahead to all you hope to maintain.

Try to remember what Pantanjali, the author of the teachings gathered in the *Yoga Sutras*, tells us again and again: yoga is the cessation of mind. As you enjoy your meditations and beauty indulgence, try to let your thoughts rest and feel a smile upon your forehead. Do not chase down your thoughts, but allow them to flow and witness them without attachment.

Schedule for Day 6 ....

Please note that all times are suggested. Stay within a few hours of this schedule if possible, but honor your body's natural rhythms.

7:30 | Awaken, Solé, Morning Journaling

If you wish, you can ask yourself the following questions immediately after finishing your writing and note your answers in your journal. Do not overthink your replies to these questions; simply tap into your intuition and answer honestly and spontaneously.

➤ What is your internal weather report today? That is, if you were the weather, what would you be? Sunny? Storm clouds approaching? Blue skies all the way? Be creative.

➤ What do you fear will be challenging for you today?

➤ What is surprising about how you feel today?

➤ Did you remember to renew your intention every time you took in nourishment with your juices? How does that feel?

➤ Have you noticed anything that is changed? Are any of your senses sharper or more muted?

➤ How are you sleeping? Have you had any vivid dreams?

8:00 | First Broth

Enjoy one cup of Essential Potassium-Rich Broth (see recipe on page 43). If you are taking grains, add one to three tablespoons of quinoa to your broth, being careful to chew each mouthful until it is liquid, giving it your total attention, silence, and awareness. Bear in mind that one very important aspect of this cleanse is becoming aware of food and how you consume it. In these last two days of your cleanse you will set a foundation for your approach to food and eating that will allow you to sustain the amazing changes you have made in your body and mind over the last five days.

9:00–10:00 | Yoga and Meditation

Balance Poses

These standing poses act to bring your mind into the present. (Have you ever noticed that you always tend to trip or lose your balance when you're zoned out?) When your mind is too busy, it is not in balance. As you practice holding these poses, be sure to focus on your breath. Following your breath is the best way to come into the present. Do not judge yourself as you move into each pose. Thinking too much will inhibit your ability to feel the true balance. You must still your mind in order to still your body. Don't be afraid to modify these poses—bring your foot only to your ankle in tree pose, or touch your toe to the floor in eagle pose. If you remove the fear of falling, you will be able to experience the feeling of being balanced without concern.

Do each of these balance poses at least twice on each side, returning to *tadasana*, or mountain pose, at the end of each.

Tree Pose

As we embody the tree, our roots sink safely into the ground and our crown aspires toward the sun. The physical eyes focus outward to anchor us, and the third eye sees all as it becomes quite clear.

1. Begin in *tadasana*, standing tall with your arms along your sides but not too close; you will want to have some space under your armpits. Your palms and the insides of your elbows should be facing forward, with hands fully open and fingers extended. Take three deep, cleansing breaths, breathing in and out through your nose.

2. Bring your hands to your heart center, palms together. With your left hand, reach down and bring your right foot to your left inner thigh (or left knee or ankle, as is comfortable for you).

3. Bring your hips in line with your thighs and stretch your spine, rooting down into the ground as the crown of your head reaches skyward.

4. Play with your balance: reach your arms overhead as if they were tree limbs reaching for the sky; clasp your hands, extend your pointer fingers, and rest your steepled hands on the top of your head; leave your hands at your heart center and drop your soft gaze to your fingertips.

5. Stay in this pose for eight or ten breaths. If you start to sway, strengthen your thighs, contract your abdominal muscles, and continue to grow upward, as a tree grows toward sunlight.

6. Repeat the pose standing on your right foot, with your left foot pressed against the inside of your right leg.

7. Return to *tadasana*.

Dancer Pose

As always, modify this pose as necessary in order to remain comfortable. If you need to begin by simply holding your foot or ankle and extending an arm, do so. As long as you are conscious of following your breath as you root into the earth and reach out of your spine, you will appreciate your own power as you benefit from this, or any, balance pose.

Don't be afraid to fall out of this pose, or to fall forward. You will find your power in balance only when you find your edge and release the fear of going to that edge (or even possibly beyond it!). It is also beautiful to realize that we are in constant motion, always falling and shifting in and out of center. Balance is a dance—true in these postures and true in life!

1. From *tadasana*, raise your left arm as you reach forward, palm facing inward, thumb facing up.

2. Drop your right hand to your side, palm forward, thumb facing away from your thigh. Rotate your arm clockwise and grasp the inside of your right foot, ankle, or calf.

3. Kick your right shin back toward the wall behind you as you reach forward with your left hand, allowing your torso to follow. Keep your chest and heart lifted, your gaze slightly above and beyond the fingertips of your left hand.

4. Follow your breath as you allow your right knee to continue to point to the floor, extend your left shin back, and reach your left arm forward.

5. Hold this pose for eight or ten breaths before returning upright as you release your right leg to the ground. Windmill your arms, and then repeat this pose with your right arm extended and your left shin kicking back.

6. Return to *tadasana*.

Eagle Pose

This is a wonderful pose for stretching tight shoulder muscles.

1. Once again, begin in *tadasana* with your spine straight; your arms at your sides; your palms facing forward; and your ears, shoulders, and hips in line.

2. In one motion, sweep your arms up and wrap your right arm under your left arm, bending your elbows and twisting your forearms so your palms face each other or touch. It may be that the fingertips of your right hand just reach the palm of your left. This is fine.

3. As your arms begin to move, bring your right leg over your left, crossing at the knee and wrapping your right shin behind your left calf. Let your right toes rest at the inside of your left ankle or on the floor to the inside of your left foot.

4. Bend your left knee deeply as you bring your elbows and knees into line. This may feel a little like twisting as you move your arms slightly right and your knees slightly left to ensure that your hips are even from side to side.

5. Stretch your spine tall and be sure you do not stick your butt out for balance. Tuck your tail, engage your abdominal muscles, and feel the power of your left thigh. Allow the power of your lower body to give freedom to your upper body.

6. Hold this pose for eight calm breaths and then return to *tadasana*.

7. Repeat on the other side, using your right leg for a powerful balance.

8. Return to *tadasana*.

Warrior Pose

In this pose, the front of your body and the inhalation of breath represent your feminine side. The back of your body and the exhalation of breath represent your masculine side. Only when the back of your body is equally as open and strong as the front can you be whole and at your most powerful.

1. From *tadasana*, bring your right foot slightly forward, toes pointing straight ahead, and slowly lift your left leg behind you. Bend your left foot at a forty-five-degree angle and keep your toes pointing straight ahead.

2. Extend your arms upward as you bend your front knee over your right ankle until your right thigh is parallel to the floor. As you exhale, lift your navel toward your spine, pulling up through your pelvic floor muscles (*mula bandha*) and directing both hips equally toward the front of your yoga mat.

3. Allow your shoulders to relax and slide down your spine, away from your ears. Keep your arms fully extended, thumbs to the ceiling, fingers extended toward the sky. Focus your eyes on one point, and continue to lengthen up the front of your body, calmly inhaling and exhaling as you transform into the fearless warrior.

4. Engage the muscles of your right thigh and keep the right toes spread on the floor as you press down on all four corners of the foot.

5. Maintain this pose for eight to ten breaths before returning to *tadasana* and repeating on the other side.

Finish this balance set of poses by standing in *tadasana*. Close your eyes and roll them slightly up toward your forehead to stimulate the pituitary gland. Remain balanced with your eyes closed for eight to ten full, deep breaths, then gently lower yourself to the floor until you are resting in *savasana*.

Meditation for Sixth Chakra Cleansing: Sun Meditation

Find a spot of sunlight, whether indoors or out (if it's cloudy or grey, do this meditation near a bright lamp or a roaring fireplace). Assume your preferred meditation position. You may sit erect in a chair with the soles of your feet completely on the ground. Feel the bottom of your feet in contact with the ground and accept however they present themselves to the floor. You may also choose to sit in a comfortable, cross-legged position with a long spine.

Begin by filling your lungs with air and releasing the breath as you appreciate the spaciousness created by your exhalation.

On your next inhalation, raise your arms and hands up as if to embrace the sun. Exhale as you bring your hands toward your forehead. Cup the sun in your hands as you hold your head in your hands. Feel the warmth and love.

Close your eyes and turn your face to the sun. Stroke your forehead and your eyes, the upper portion of your face, and your ears. Imagine the warmth of the sun heating each part of yourself that you touch.

Lower your hands to your thighs or knees, palms facing upright. Remain conscious of your breathing as you imagine the sun moving to your third eye. The third eye is located in the center of your forehead and is associated with the sixth chakra. It is a metaphysical window into enlightenment. When your third eye is functioning, it allows you to perceive a different dimension. You can "see" things that are invisible to the physical eye but visible to the subtle eye. You may think of this as intuition or psychic ability. As you become more adept at "seeing" with your third eye, your world will subtly transform.

Allow the sun's warmth and love to naturally heal you. Feel the warm point where the sun touches your third eye. Be conscious of a gentle pulsing effect from light to dark to light. Allow the light and warmth to move outward and encompass your entire body, penetrating every cell with light and warmth. Sit quietly and appreciate the fact that learning to get out of your own way and allowing the power of your third eye to awaken is healing and clarifying.

You can practice a variation of this meditation each morning when you awaken by finding a spot in your home where the sun can shine directly upon you. Go to this pool of healing sunlight before beginning your day and allow your third eye to blossom in the bright warmth. Recall this feeling throughout your day when you need to quiet your mind and act with clarity.

10:00–11:00 | Creative Inspiration: Spiderweb

As you go through this exercise, remain calm and present. Stay connected to both your environment and your own physical presence. Observe how your inner instincts are connected to your outer actions.

1. Take your skein of yarn, ball of string, or spool of thread and tie one end to something close to you: the leg of a chair or a table or a spindle on your staircase, for example.

2. Walk to another piece of furniture. If you choose to do this exercise outside, be sure you are around trees, shrubs, and/or on your patio— wherever there are objects that can surround you. If you live in a wide-open loft space, temporarily rearrange your furniture if you have to.

3. As you walk and weave your web, change levels, cross over your path, walk over or under lines of thread as you spin. Trust your intuition. Don't plan your web—let it happen organically.

4. When you are at the end of your thread, pause and notice where you have arrived. Now begin to unravel your web, rolling the ball of yarn back into a whole as you go.

5. If you get to a knot, a tangle, or an impasse, weave your way through the problem until you can progress. Do not cut the yarn. You want to keep your yarn intact. In every part of this exercise, focus your energy.

As the poet William Stafford wrote in his poem "The Way It Is" (1998), "Nothing you do can stop time's unfolding. You don't ever let go of the thread."

11:00 | First "Juice": Deep Blue Break-Fast Smoothie

Today I encourage you to enjoy a "break-fast," a conscious first meal ending any period of fasting. For most of us, *breakfast* (the first meal of the day) has become an unconscious word—one that triggers unconscious eating for no reason other than it is morning and it's what we always do in the morning. Today I invite you to break-fast instead and consciously nourish your body only when it calls for nourishment.

1. Prepare your juice and pour it into your special glass. Cover it with your coaster with the *intention* side facing down and your name facing up.

2. Imagine your intention infusing the juice and the juice taking in the energy of the intention.

3. Find a comfortable place to sit with a blanket wrapped around you, in the sunshine or wherever you feel very safe and relaxed; you should be neither cold nor hot.

4. Breathe into your belly. Place one hand on your belly and the other on your heart. Notice any feelings that are coming up: anxiety, fear, impatience. Do not dwell on these thoughts, but acknowledge them as you continue to breathe into your belly and allow your heart to open.

5. Assign your hunger level a number between 1 and 5, with 1 being "not at all hungry" and 5 being "extremely hungry."

6. Pick up your covered juice and, with your eyes closed, feel the weight and temperature of the glass.

7. Bring to mind the intention that is face-to-face with the juice under the cover of your coaster.

8. When you are ready, remove the coaster.

9. Engage your senses. Smell the juice. Does your mouth water? Does your hunger level move in either direction? Appreciate the beautiful color of the juice.

10. Take the first sip but do not swallow immediately. Take the time to notice each taste of the juice with every part of your mouth and tongue. Choose when to swallow.

11. Pause and again note your hunger level. Notice if the one swallow of juice shifted that number in one direction or another.

12. Continue to sip your juice consciously, with pleasure. Let your belly be soft and receiving.

13. After half the juice is finished, check in with your hunger. What number level are you now experiencing? You may find that you are no longer hungry, but you may choose to drink the rest of the juice anyway. That is fine. The most important thing is self-observation and self-awareness. It is okay to eat and drink for the pleasure of the taste alone. Enjoy your healthful elixir in luxurious leisure. If you decide you have had enough juice, you may save it for later in the afternoon.

11:30–2:30 | Free Time

During your free time today you should walk alone and in silence, outdoors if possible. You might wish to take along a portable music player with your "Chakra 6" soundtrack playing at low volume.

Find a place to rest quietly: a park bench, a beach, a hammock, or a step near a garden. Look around and find something in nature to focus your eyes on. Look at this object carefully: it could be a flower, a blade of grass, a group of sea shells, the edge of the water as it laps up against the shoreline. Examine it well, and try to memorize it. Then close your eyes and see it in your mind.

Now with your eyes still closed, "see" or remember a person or a pet who is beloved to you. Smile. Then open your eyes and look again at the original object, but this time look upon it as if you were looking upon your beloved.

Today's External Beauty Indulgence:
Shirodhara Hair Conditioning Treatment

We are shaped by our thoughts; we become what we think. When the mind is pure, joy follows like a shadow that never leaves.

—SIDDHARTHA, THE FOUNDER OF BUDDHISM, 563–483 B.C.

In Sanskrit, *shira* means *head* and *dhara* means *flow*. This ayurvedic tradition uses the rhythmic flow of a warm oil to calm your central nervous system, rejuvenate your senses, offer important nutritional and restorative benefits to the skin, and promote a state of reflection. *Shirodhara* has proven to be effective for alleviating stress, anxiety, and sleep disorders. It clears the mental debris that can obscure your internal vision and clutter your psyche. When you surrender fully to the meditative state induced by this treatment, you open yourself to peace and joy— the true foundation for inner and outer beauty.

1. Warm sweet almond or sesame oil by putting it in a bottle or bowl and immersing the container in hot water (like you would heat a baby bottle). It can be as warm as you can stand.

2. Take a cotton hand towel or washcloth and fold it into a strip at least four folds deep. Pour the oil into the towel until it is soaked. Lie down and cover yourself with a warm blanket. Make yourself comfortable; perhaps position a pillow under your thighs to elevate your legs and release tension from your lower back.

3. If you desire a small pillow under your neck or head, put another towel over the pillow; oil does stain and you don't need that worry nagging at your mind during this treatment.

4. Turn on the music from your "Chakra 6" playlist (see the recommended music at the end of the book), and place the oil-soaked towel across your forehead, being conscious that you are placing it over your third eye.

5. Relax completely with your arms by your side, palms up, to allow for a clear channel of energy by opening the meridians in your arms and hands to receive what healing and restorative energies the universe has to offer you.

6. Rest for an entire song, about five to ten minutes. The music has a specific biorhythm that will connect with both the right and left sides of your brain and lull you into "quiet mind"—even the busiest mind will quiet and calm with the combined effects of the oil, the pose, and the music. Don't think. Just be. Let the whole nervous system come into balance by doing nothing.

7. If you wish to take more of your mind's energy to the third eye point, allow your eyes to drift upward. As the muscles of your eyes engage to roll up, they stimulate the pituitary and trigger the hypothalamus to signal your body to come into balance.

8. With your eyes still closed, remove the oil-soaked towel and put it on a plate or bowl you've place nearby. Savor the rush of cool air to your forehead. Roll to your right side. (This will help to energize you if you've dozed during this treatment—which would be perfectly understandable.) Rest here for a few minutes. Pull your blanket over your head if you wish and go completely inward, really letting your mask—the face you present to others—drop. Relax your muscles, jaw, nose, and cheeks; let it all drop away. Let your face be what it is without worrying about presenting it to anyone. Enjoy this total freedom.

9. Gently move into a sitting position. If there is extra oil on your forehead, massage it gently into the rest of your face or into your hair. (Leave the oil in your hair until tomorrow, when we will do a special scalp massage and shampoo treatment. You can wear a scarf or bandanna over your hair and put a towel over your bed pillow if you are concerned about creating a mess.)

Appreciate the feeling of *satvic*—pronounced *saht-vik*, this word means *truth* in Sanskrit—touching your true essence and the universal consciousness. For the rest of the day, trust the way you feel. Act the way you feel. Be your truest Self.

2:30 | Second Juice: Green Elixir for Heart Connection

It is now time for your green juice (see recipe on page 42). Follow the ritual outlined on pages 64–65 to make drinking this elixir as pleasurable as possible and to keep your consumption of the juice as much in the present as you can. Sip your juice slowly and savor the new and delicious tastes you are introducing to your body. If you find that you do not wish to finish all of your juice, you may save it for the 5:00 serving and drink it instead of the green smoothie.

After this second juice you may plan to take some free time for yourself. If you must take care of personal or family matters during these few hours, attend to them with extra tenderness and compassion. Do not hold any expectation of receiving in return. Practice giving—and loving—unconditionally. When you give to others without conditions, you are resting your mind; you do not question, judge, or feel conflicted about what you are doing. Be clear and be of service.

5:00 | Green Smoothie

Tonight, instead of the Essential Potassium-Rich Broth, you will enjoy a nourishing and filling green smoothie as you begin your reintroduction to conscious eating. You may choose any of the green smoothie recipes on pages 216–19.

Spend the time before the bedtime ritual in quiet activities. Call only benevolent friends, listen to music from your "Chakra 6" playlist (see the recommended music at the end of the book), and continue to avoid watching television or using the Internet. Read ahead to the beginning of the next chapter so that you will be prepared for what you will need to do to support your journey tomorrow.

7:00 | Bedtime Ritual

Your bath will be a peaceful oasis filled with candlelight tonight; also turn on your "Chakra 6" soundtrack, which was chosen specifically to cleanse your beta thought waves. A good aroma for Day 6 would be a mixture of essential oils including three drops of frankincense, one drop of rosewood, two drops of cedarwood, and three drops of mandarin. These scents assist your mind in seeing intuitively and facilitate a meditative state.

When you head to bed tonight, do not take a book; tonight, just "be." When the body can be still, the mind can be still. Sleep and give intention to your dreams. Intend that your dreams tonight shall resolve all that is unfinished in your life.

Rest deeply and allow any mental walls to dissolve slowly and safely. Imagine you could just put your hand against the wall that you believe keeps you safe from mental pain and fear. Then feel the wall dissolve beneath your hand. Your hand and body weight pass right through this imaginary wall. When the wall dissolves, the monsters you thought were lurking behind it are often found to be more like bunny slippers left under the bed. Nothing is frightening—your memories and feelings become just things to observe with great love and compassion for your Self. Your mind is clear and free. Peace and bliss now feel possible.

≋ DAY 7 ≋

Violet Juice

THE SEVENTH CHAKRA:
Pure Consciousness

....

*No problem can be solved from the same level
of consciousness that created it.*

.... —ALBERT EINSTEIN, 1879–1955 ....

THE SEVENTH, OR CROWN, chakra is located at the top of the head and is the energy center of pure consciousness. When the seventh chakra is fully open, one is able to enter a state of true "beingness"—a transcendental connection with the universal consciousness and a place of inner wisdom. When you operate from this state of beingness, you are free from considerations of personality and ego and are able to experience complete concentration. A blocked crown chakra can be connected to headaches, and may also connect back to the heart chakra, causing high blood pressure.

The past six days have given you the tools you need to change your life. Today, the final day of this program, will teach you how to take these tools and manifest them in your day-to-day life. The internal cleansing you have experienced over the past week will be expressed in a shower meditation that connects you to the rebirth of Self.

Today marks a return to a diet of solid foods, and I will give you exercises designed to remind you how to truly *listen* to your body so that your transition back to eating is as conscious as your decision to embark on this cleanse. Compassionate self-awareness is the focus of the "color wheel" exercise, which provides you with a striking graphic expression of your internal truths and allows you to move toward changing what matters most. On this last day of your cleanse, I hope that you will fully experience the transformative power of honoring your personal journey and carry the luminous results with you into your postcleanse daily routines.

Today's Grocery List and Recipes

Because you will be eating three small meals today, as well as enjoying a clarifying elixir and a final green juice, your shopping list will be more extensive than on previous days. As you return to eating, I want you to particularly savor the taste, smell, and texture of your food, and I encourage you to make a special shopping trip today to ensure that all the food you eat is as fresh as possible. Also, because you will be enjoying break-fast, lunch, and dinner meals today, you may want to drink only half of the usual serving of juice at each "juice break" during the day.

The connection between your heart and your mind—which is facilitated by your daily green juice—is key to following through on the insights you have gained during your cleanse. Whether you choose the same green juice today as you have enjoyed throughout your cleanse or try a different delicious juice from the selection of juice recipes in Chapter 15, you will enjoy the same benefit: focus and a blissful sense of rightness of purpose.

Break-Fast Meal: Fresh Fruit Plate

Pay special attention to color, taste, and texture as you select fresh fruits to enjoy for your first postfasting meal. Some wonderful suggestions include:

Strawberries
Green grapes

Sliced oranges
Deep red cherries (may be used in today's juice as well)
Blueberries (may be used in today's juice as well)
Blackberries
Green or red apples

≩ Voilet Brazil Nut Smoothie ≧

Brazil nut trees are enormous. They can live for as long as a thousand years and grow as high as 150 feet tall. This great height resonates with our seventh and highest chakra, located at the very top of our heads. This is where connection to others can be experienced, particularly when cleansing has made us clear and alert to our senses. The Brazil nut also contains 2,500 times more selenium— which lifts the mood and improves mental performance—than any other nut.

- 3 cups filtered water
- 1 cup shelled raw Brazil nuts
- 1 teaspoon vanilla extract
- 3 medjool dates
- ½ cup whole cherries, pitted
- ½ cup blueberries

Combine all ingredients in a blender and blend at high speed until smooth. Strain through a mesh bag, cheesecloth, or sieve.

Lunch

A salad is a colorful feast for the mouth and eyes. Choose one of the delicious and filling salads described in Chapter 15, and create your shopping list accordingly.

Dinner

A final light meal of vegetable or miso soup will leave you feeling warm and satisfied. Choose either Break-Fast Miso or Break-Fast Vegetable Soup (see recipes on pages 235 and 236).

Today's Recommended Teas

You may continue to enjoy as much tea or water as you wish today. White lotus tea would be an excellent choice because it is beneficial to the crown chakra. You may also want to consider creating a violet-solarized water by putting purified water in a violet or even deep blue bottle. Place the bottle of water in the sunlight for up to twelve hours. The light energy vibration of the colored glass will be transferred to the water, instilling it with the beneficial property of the color. (Blue is calming, violet is spiritually enhancing, and yellow is for mental clarity.)

I hope that by now, drinking pure, fresh water or restorative herbal teas has become a healthful daily habit. Sufficient fluids are vital for radiant skin, accurate perception of hunger signals (since people often mistake feelings of thirst or dehydration for feelings of hunger), and overall energy.

Materials for Today's Creative Inspiration

Today's creative exercise requires items that you probably already have at home. You will need:

➤ Colored pencils, crayons, or markers
➤ White, unlined paper
➤ A small dinner plate or large bowl (small enough to fit on the paper)
➤ A pencil, pen, or thin-line marker

Materials for Today's External Beauty Indulgence

The seventh chakra is sometimes called "The Tenth Gate" or "The Thousand-Petaled Lotus Flower." These names refer to the location of this energy center, at the very top of the head; like a lotus flower, the seventh chakra radiates upward and outward beyond the body. It is the "gate" that forms the connection between our bodies and the energy that supports us, which is beyond the body. Only the highest level of conscious consideration can cleanse and purify your seventh chakra.

An astonishing amount of harmful chemicals and compounds can be found in most commercially made shampoos and conditioners, and they certainly contain no living enzymes. Since you have taken a break from putting preservatives, pesticides, and chemicals into your body, it makes sense to do the same with the products you use on your skin and hair. After all, these products, just like food, enter your circulatory system and circulate throughout your body. These enzyme-rich, alkalinizing treats for your hair will make it shiny, healthy, and more beautiful than it has ever been using any commercial products.

What could be more loving toward yourself than to make these simple, fresh cleansing products to nourish and reveal your beauty on all levels?

Gather the following ingredients to prepare for today's beauty indulgence, which, fittingly, is combined with today's meditation practice, bringing together the connection between all aspects of the bodymind. You will also need clean glass bottles with caps to store your shampoo and hair rinse.

➤ Half an avocado
➤ One quarter of a banana
➤ One egg yolk (but see note below)
➤ One teaspoon of honey (but see note below)

Please note that both the honey and the egg yolk are optional, and the masque is quite effective without them. If you choose to use these animal products, be sure to consider the quality of what you buy. Remember that the wellness of the animals that produced them will become your wellness too; their beauty will become your beauty.

Blend these ingredients in a blender until smooth and store in a covered bowl or glass jar with a tightly fitting lid.

To prepare your special shampoo, gather:

➤ Three tablespoons of castile soap or paraben- and petroleum-free commercial shampoo, which can be found at health food stores.

Dr. Bronner's brand castile soap is now widely available and comes already scented with essential oils such as rose, lavender, or tea tree. Castile soap is made from vegetable oils such as olive, coconut, and jojoba.

➤ One pint Peach Detox Yogi Tea
➤ Five to ten drops of essential oil of your choice

Put all ingredients into a bottle and shake gently to combine. To prepare your special hair rinse, gather:

➤ Three tablespoons apple cider vinegar or lemon juice
➤ One cup Peach Detox Yogi Tea

Combine ingredients in a clean bottle and shake well to mix.

What You May Experience Today

You may feel very eager to start eating solid foods again, or you may be surprised to notice that you feel reluctant to begin to eat again. Either of these feelings is appropriate and normal right now. On one hand, your body is clean and fresh and quite ready to return to eating. On the other hand, you may discover trust issues and fear—fear that you will not nourish yourself properly, that you will not know which foods to choose, that you will not seek out the right foods, or that you will not know how to prepare them. Or you may be very excited to go out and fill your kitchen with exciting and colorful new foods. If you are fearful or reluctant, accept this for what it is. Simply observe it. Do not attempt to change it; just allow it. You have faced many fears and experienced many new things during these past seven days and discovered that you are still OK. Perhaps you believed you could not possibly make it through five or seven days without solid foods, but you did. So now, even as you experience this fear of reentering the world of social eating, deep down you *do* know that somehow you will be OK, you will figure this out.

Schedule for Day 7

Please note that all times are suggested. Stay within a few hours of this schedule if possible, but honor your body's natural rhythms.

7:30 | Awaken, Solé, Morning Journaling

For the past six days you have written every day without looking back. Today is the day to read those things you have put down, if you so choose. To revisit your journal pages, you will need two highlighters: a yellow one and a blue one. Just as you were speed-writing during the daily stream of consciousness writing, you will now speed-read the pages you wrote.

With your yellow highlighter in hand, begin on the first page. As you read, swipe any words that cause you to pause, any phrases that bring a question to your mind, or any sentences that cause you to wonder about something else. Any time a word or phrase that you have written brings to mind another question or makes you wonder about something, swipe it with your yellow marker.

When you have reached the end of your stream of consciousness pages and have swiped all the "questioning" words or passages, go back to the beginning again. This time use your blue highlighter. Now speed-read your journal for the second time. Swipe anything that makes you feel a question has been answered. When you are finished, you may find that you have answered all of your own questions! It is said that we actually know the answers to any question we ask. And that is why we pose them in the first place: because we have fallen into forgetfulness and want to be reminded of that which we already know!

8:00 | Break-Fast

On Day 7, it's bye-bye broth! But remember that the Potassium-Rich Broth you have enjoyed for the past six days is a quick, restorative, and flavorful substitute for commercially prepared soups or broths. It's well worth keeping a supply in your freezer. This morning you will again enjoy a fresh fruit plate and tea or hot water as you break your juice fast.

9:00–10:00 | Yoga and Meditation

The focus today is on creating beneficial blood flow to the brain and energizing the crown chakra. As you practice these exercises and poses, be extremely careful to protect your neck. Do not practice the inversions (headstands, or even modified headstands) if you have high or low blood pressure or problems with your inner ear or dizziness. Do not hold these poses for any length of time if you are menstruating.

If you are at all uncomfortable or nervous about these poses, you will benefit just as much if you lie on your back with your hips elevated on a yoga block or towel and elevate your legs until they are directly over your hips. You may also lie on your back with your legs resting on a wall for even more support.

Gentle Head Rolls

1. Sit comfortably on the floor with your legs crossed. If this is uncomfortable, you can sit in a chair with your feet flat on the floor and your arms hanging loosely at your sides. Begin orbiting your head in a clockwise motion: drop your chin and roll your left ear toward your left shoulder (being careful not to lift your shoulder toward your ear). Relax the back of your neck and allow the heavy back of your skull to drop. Continue this motion, rolling your right ear down toward your right shoulder, and finish with your chin tucked into your neck.

2. Reverse direction, orbiting your head in a counterclockwise direction. The motion should be effortless, with no tension or strain. As you continue to orbit your head, begin to vocalize an *mmmm* sound through your closed lips. The *mmmmmmmm* vibration can easily be felt at the top of the head. It is the final sound of the *om* vibration. *Ahhhhhhhh-oooooooooh* vibrates low (rest your hand on your chest to feel this). Feel the sound of *mmmmmmmm* as it moves up to your crown (move your hand to the top of your head to feel this). The first vibrations actually begin at the base of the spine, but placing your hands on your chest makes it easier to feel them. Enjoy the humming of the *mmmmmmmmm* sound and allow your head to clear with this cleansing vibration.

3. After orbiting your head an equal number of times in each direction, allow your chin to remain pressed into your chest for a *jhalandara*, or throat lock (see pages 124–25 for a reminder on how to practice this important breathing technique).

Easy Headstand

The easiest form of headstand is a straddle with your head on the floor or on a yoga block (or two, or three!).

1. Stand with your hands on your hips. Step your feet widely apart, toes facing slightly inward, heels turned slightly out.

2. Keeping your back flat and your gaze straight ahead of you, hinge forward from the waist.

3. Lower your palms to the floor, about shoulder-width apart, fingertips facing forward, elbows pointing back.

4. Continue to bend forward, rocking your weight into the balls of your feet and keeping your hips over your heels.

5. Place your head down on to the floor between your hands, or if you are not that flexible, on the top of a yoga block or a stack of yoga blocks. It is OK to bend your knees if you feel inflexible. Just be like a child and approach this pose with a fun attitude.

6. Keep your eyes open and your gaze soft. Look out at the world from a new perspective. Continue to follow your breath as you hold this pose for a minute or two.

Tripod Headstand

This more challenging posture offers extra stability for those just beginning headstand postures.

1. Begin with your hands and knees on the mat. You may want to place a folded blanket in front of your hands to cushion your head. Keeping your palms flat on the floor, lower the top of your head to the floor so it's in front of your hands. Keep your elbows directly over your wrists and make sure you can see your hands. Your head and both palms form the points of an equilateral triangle.

2. Once your head and hands feel stable and rooted to the earth, straighten both legs and walk your feet toward your face.

3. Bring your hips in line with your shoulders and press the four points of your hands firmly onto the mat.

4. Engaging your abdominal muscles, rest first one knee and then the other on your triceps. Keep your eyes open and your gaze soft. Follow your breath. Stay here for eight deep breaths. Then slowly lower your feet to the floor.

5. Rest in child's pose (your bottom resting between your heels, your chest resting on your thighs, arms stretched or folded on the floor above your head) or in egg pose (same as child's pose but with your arms wrapped back around, clasping your heels).

Advanced Headstand

This advanced balance pose can grow out of the tripod headstand above by simply extending your legs until they are in a straight line with your hips and shoulders and then pointing your toes. Or work into the pose using a slightly different positioning of your forearms and hands, as directed below:

1. Begin with your hands and knees on the mat. You may want to place a folded blanket in front of your hands to cushion your head.

2. Rest your forearms on the center of the blanket and interlace your fingers. This will be your base of support.

3. Rest the crown of your head on the floor or blanket in between your cupped hands.

4. Raise your knees from the floor and inch your toes toward your face. When you are ready, engage your abdominal muscles and lift your torso with your knees bent.

5. When you feel steady, slowly straighten your legs and point your toes until you are in a beautiful inverted straight line from toe to head. Keep your eyes open and your gaze soft. Follow your breath as you hold this posture for eight breaths.

6. Slowly come out of the pose, reversing the steps you took to get into it: bend your knees, fold your torso, and lower your toes to the floor.

7. Sink back into child's pose or egg pose and rest.

Finish any headstand pose by resting on the floor with your eyes closed in *savasana*, allowing your reenergized blood flow to nourish your entire body. As you become more practiced in headstands, try to do some postures each day. They are wonderfully restorative, increasing healthy blood flow to the brain and stimulating the crown chakra.

Meditation for Seventh Chakra Cleansing: Shower Meditation

The seventh, or crown, chakra is called *sahasara* in Sanskrit, meaning *thousandfold*. It is located at the top of the head and is represented by a thousand lotus petals. This chakra is associated with fulfillment and spiritual energy. Clearing this chakra allows for awareness of the constant creative force in the universe. If you want to be in touch with the energy of this chakra, meditate on your oneness with all humanity and everything in creation.

Today you will combine a powerful meditation with your beauty indulgence to appreciate the connection of bodymind and support the transformative integration that is happening today. Take this time to create the wholesome hair masque, shampoo, and rinse you will use later today before your shower meditation. Keep your hair mask, shampoo, and rinse in tightly covered containers and bottles until later. You can refrigerate the mask if you think you will not use it within one hour. If you have the time now, apply the hair masque and cover your hair with a shower cap or wrap it in a towel.

10:00–11:00 | Creative Inspiration: Lifestyle Mandala

This beautiful exercise, which is inspired by a similar creative inspiration in the book *The Artist's Way* (see the recommended reading list at the end of the book), will give you a colorful and revealing snapshot of where you are right now. Where you go once you have this knowledge is your own choice.

1. Gather your colored markers or pencils and clean, white, unlined paper and find a comfortable, brightly lit (preferably sunlit) spot. Begin by tracing a circle on your paper using a plate or big bowl that is about the same size as your paper.

2. Divide your circle in half, then in quarters, and then draw an X through that to make eight sections.

3. Where the lines join in the center, draw an interior circle that is about one and a half inches around.

4. On the outside edge of the circle, in the white space around it, write "100%," and then at the center circle write "0%."

5. Label each section, beginning from the top and moving clockwise as follows:
Body
Food/eating
Relationship/family
Environment
Community/friends
Right livelihood
Play/adventure
Spiritual attunement

6. If you like, you can now put some music on so that you feel relaxed but focused. There are no right or wrong answers in this exercise. Your answer, whatever it might be, is the right answer at this time. This tells you where you are today, right now, and will empower you to decide where you want to be. So don't analyze or overthink your answers. Pay attention to your inner voice—the one that tells you how you truly feel.

7. Begin with the first section and put a pencil dot somewhere between the center and the edge to indicate where you feel you are in your life right now, with the center part indicating complete dissatisfaction or unhappiness and the edge of the circle indicating 100 percent happy or satisfied. Work your way around the circle, evaluating each area of your life.

8. Once you've worked through all eight sections, choose eight different colored pencils, markers, or crayons. Any color works for any area. Begin at the top and color the section from the center out to where you placed your dot. Use a different color for each section so your wheel is filled with color.

9. Stand back and look at this visual representation of your life. You may be surprised to see that it doesn't much look like a full circle. There may be areas where the color is contracted toward the center and others where it radiates far out to the periphery of the circle. This is good and right because it represents how life really is.

10. Identify the most contracted color, the one closest to the center zone. This center zone is where all colors begin, even those that reach all the way to the outer edge of the circle. This is the zone of compassionate self-awareness. Anything that falls in or near this zone can be expanded through more love, more forgiveness, and more understanding for your Self in that area. In this way you can begin to expand that color.

11. Now, on a separate piece of paper, write down five things you could do to extend that color further toward the periphery. You don't have to commit to these ideas at this point; they just have to be actions that might move you closer to your outer edge.

12. After you've listed the five things you *could* do, list one thing you *will* do, that you *can* do—something small that you can really commit to within the coming week. This one small step doesn't have to be one of the five things already on your list; it can be something utterly practical or simple.

13. Now list five challenges to getting that one thing done. What could come up that might prevent you from doing that one single thing? Write down who, or what, your support system will be to ensure that you have the freedom (and inspiration, if need be) to get that one thing done and to help you get past the potential obstacles you have listed.

Hang this wheel where you can see it. Use it as a meditation tool, an inspiration, a motivator. When you are abstractly looking at the colors (and not obsessing about the issue), envision all the colors extending out from the center and reaching toward the outer periphery until the entire wheel is filled with color.

This is a wonderful exercise to repeat a few times a year. Notice how the colors shift and certain areas of your life move in and out of balance with each other and with the whole. This is your personal supernova—always changing, expanding, contracting, but always a thing of beauty and color. Expansion of satisfaction, like expansion of all things, comes with practice.

11:00 | First "Juice": Voilet Brazil Nut Smoothie

For the last day of your cleanse—as with every other day—enjoy your juice (or, in this case, smoothie) following this specific ritual:

1. Prepare your juice and pour it into your special glass. Cover it with your coaster with the *intention* side facing down and your name facing up.

2. Imagine your intention infusing the juice and the juice taking in the energy of the intention.

3. Find a comfortable place to sit with a blanket wrapped around you, in the sunshine or wherever you feel very safe and relaxed; you should be neither cold nor hot.

4. Breathe into your belly. Place one hand on your belly and the other on your heart. Notice any feelings that are coming up: anxiety, fear, impatience. Do not dwell on these thoughts, but acknowledge them as you continue to breathe into your belly and allow your heart to open.

5. Assign your hunger level a number between 1 and 5, with 1 being "not at all hungry" and 5 being "extremely hungry."

6. Pick up your covered juice and, with your eyes closed, feel the weight and temperature of the glass.

7. Bring to mind the intention that is face-to-face with the juice under the cover of your coaster.

8. When you are ready, remove the coaster.

9. Engage your senses. Smell the juice. Does your mouth water? Does your hunger level move in either direction? Appreciate the beautiful color of the juice.

10. Take the first sip but do not swallow immediately. Take the time to notice each taste of the juice with every part of your mouth and tongue. Choose when to swallow.

11. Pause and again note your hunger level. Notice if the one swallow of juice shifted that number in one direction or another.

12. Continue to sip your juice consciously, with pleasure. Let your belly be soft and receiving.

13. After half the juice is finished, check in with your hunger. What number level are you now experiencing? You may find that you are no longer hungry, but you may choose to drink the rest of the juice anyway. That is fine. The most important thing is self-observation and self-awareness. It is okay to eat and drink for the pleasure of the taste alone. Enjoy your healthful elixir in luxurious leisure. If you decide you have had enough juice, you may save it for later in the afternoon.

12:30 | Lunch: Salad and Tea or Water

Concentrate on color and texture as you create a colorful feast for the mouth and eyes, choosing any of the delicious salads in the salad recipe section in Chapter 15. Keep focusing on your hunger level and allow yourself to feel that edge of hunger. Feeling and simply being with the feeling, rather than immediately acting upon it, is becoming your practice. Allow yourself to *be* on that edge. Notice that you do not fall over dead. You do not become sick. This is a practice of overcoming and examining the fear of being uncomfortable or of being in an unfamiliar place physically. The "edge" is an opportunity to practice self-observation. Notice what emotions, what memories, come up. Notice if these emotions change your breathing and posture in any way. Then see if you can restore your breathing and posture in the face of these emotions by stepping out of your Self and observing calmly. Now have a cup of ginger tea or lemon water. Notice if your hunger diminishes. The point is to learn to note feelings of hunger without immediately reacting to them or giving in to habitual or repetitive behaviors concerning food that are triggered by emotions rather than the biological need to nourish your body.

Today's External Beauty Indulgence: Shower Meditation for Seventh Chakra Cleansing

Beauty—be not caused—It Is . . .
—EMILY DICKINSON, POEM #516, FROM *FURTHER POEMS*

1. If you have not already done so, prepare your fresh hair masque (see pages 159–60 for instructions) and apply to your hair. Cover with a plastic shower cap and sit with your head in the warm sun, outside in your yard or inside near a sunny window. Enjoy your masque and the sun for five to ten minutes as you listen to music from the "Chakra 7" soundtrack recommendations, found at the end of the book.

2. Step into a warm shower but do not wet your hair right away. Right now you have not only the hair masque but also the oil from your beauty ritual yesterday in your hair. Now we will remove both quite easily by massaging shampoo into your dry hair without any water.

There will be no lather, and that is perfect. Don't be disgusted: it is different than what you are used to, and that is the whole point. Get out of your rut and see and feel things in new, delightful ways. If you feel resistance, notice it, know that it is a "detox event," and then drop the drama and just do it—you are going to love the results.

3. Massage a few tablespoons of the shampoo into the roots of your hair. Without water, work the pure shampoo slowly through your hair, adding *small* amounts of water as needed. When the shampoo has been worked through your hair completely, rinse thoroughly. Repeat your shampoo in the normal way. You will enjoy your familiar lather-rich shampoo and all traces of the oil will now be gone. Do not fear: if you use this technique, no oil will linger! Now allow your head and hair to become soaked with the downward flow of water.

4. You will now begin your meditation. Start to massage your entire scalp and head in a swirling motion. Alternate massaging the scalp with tapping the scalp with your fingertips. Massage and tap your brain stem, at the base of your skull, and return to the swirling massage of your entire head.

5. Massage your ears and gently pull them away from your scalp.

6. Begin to visualize the bud of a lotus flower, tightly closed, inside your skull. As you listen to the sound of the water on your head, observe the bud opening up to form twelve petals thirstily receiving the water. The twelve petals grow to twenty-four, then forty-eight. Imagine the gratitude and joy a flower might feel as it receives the water that rains down upon it. Feel the joy and gratitude increase along with the number of petals on the flower until the bud has opened fully to reveal a thousand beautiful petals smiling at the sky and the rain.

7. Now imagine that this unfolding has been happening since the beginning of time, and acknowledge that this is the first time you have noticed it. Smile as a baby smiles at a flower. Realize that you have suspected all along that this unfolding was occurring, and know that now that suspicion is confirmed.

8. Visualize the lotus blossom petals turning from pink to pale violet, then to deep violet, then to pure white, and finally to a luminous glow that pulses with the light of all of these colors.

9. Now shift your attention to the ground and imagine your feet drawing up the water on the floor of the shower. Allow the water to move up through your legs, your thighs, your pelvis, and your belly until it reaches your heart and unfolds in a second lotus flower.

10. Feel both flowers expanding, in your heart and in your head. Follow them as they outgrow the confines of your body to permeate the entire universe and beyond.

11. In a whisper, begin to chant *om*. Draw in a breath and, as you exhale, begin vocalizing *ahhhhh-ohhhh-mmmmm*. Each long, sustained *om* swirls the colors and light through your body and outside of your body, wrapping you in light.

12. For the final ritual before you complete your cleansing shower, begin to turn the water temperature down. Do this very slowly and gradually. Allow your skin to adjust each time you lower the temperature. When it is just cool enough to stand, go for it: turn on the cold water, rinse, and then quickly (and carefully) get out of the shower. You will feel your aura miles wider than your physical body; your aura has also been cleansed, so you will feel incredibly bright. It's a little scary at first. The secret is always to take it slowly and allow time to integrate. Respect this rule with this cold shower ritual and respect it with emotion in your life. By taking time to cleanse, you respect this rule and prosper in your life.

Carry your blissful state with you everywhere you go today. Apply mindfulness and gentleness in all of your activities. Put aside grudges, hang-ups, and beliefs that are not really yours. Let them be reabsorbed into the earth. You are free.

3:30 | Second Juice: Green Elixir for Heart Connection

It is now time for your green juice (see recipe on page 42). Follow the ritual outlined on pages 64–65 to make drinking this elixir as pleasurable as possible and to keep your consumption of the juice as much in the present as you can. Sip your juice slowly and savor the new and delicious tastes you are introducing to your body.

After this second juice, plan some afternoon free time. Savor a nap or take a walk outdoors. Fine-tune your senses by paying attention to all aspects of your environment, whether you choose to remain in familiar surroundings or venture out to explore the sensations of an unexpected place.

After completing your cleanse you may want to make drinking fresh juices a part of your daily routine. Do not hold back because you are still carrying old worries about consuming too many calories. Here is my best advice for you: when you consume consciously, you never have to worry about calories. A calorie is simply a measurement of energy. And calories are wonderful when they are made up of pure *prana* that comes from the sun, as the calories in live, raw juices are.

Processed, high-calorie foods require our body's energy to metabolize them; they do not burn cleanly through our bodies. We are fooled into thinking we need more and more food energy when in fact what we are eating is depleting our energy. When you are nourished by juices, you will naturally crave perfect quantities of the most nourishing and perfect foods available to you. So continue enjoying juices every day as a way to supplement your body and fill it up with *prana*—life force energy. Make juice every day—make extra! Blend your juices with whole fruits and vegetables for a quick, easy, and perfect meal replacement. No fancy powders or supplements are needed—just real food.

It is my sincere hope that you will truly learn to stay conscious of the food you offer to yourself. I believe that simply tuning in to what your body is asking for and being aware of the sources of what you offer your body will bring a powerful and positive shift in your life—for your Self and for all those who are nourished by you in your teachings and your love for them, which is sourced from your love of your Self. As you return to your life postcleanse, you will undoubtedly be faced with times when you must get things done that you don't necessarily prefer doing. With your newfound practice of mindfulness, even these things—or perhaps these things most of all—will be imbued with a sense of great purpose. For in mindfulness you will always have your *drishti*—your focused gaze—upon the desired outcome.

For the rest of today, and for the next few days, I suggest that you keep your intention coaster on the table when you sit down to eat. However, after you complete your cleanse, you should turn it intention side up. As you take a few breaths, assessing your hunger edge and your emotional edge before beginning a meal, consider your intention again. Come back to it again and again.

I will leave you with some conscious eating meditations to practice during break-fast or whenever you need to remember to be present with yourself and therefore present with your food, creating a powerful and complete connection to our natural world.

Mealtime Meditations

Relax your face and muscles. Relax any part of you that is not involved in sitting and chewing. Take the time to taste your food, first with your eyes only, and then with your tongue. Remember what Gandhi said: "Chew your drink and drink your food."

Pause before selecting more food, feeling the warmth of the food you have eaten already as it travels deeply into your body. As you chew, think about the origin of this food: the farmers who planted it, the earth that offered it so lovingly, and the people who harvested the food and brought it here.

As you continue to eat, picture yourself healthy with a feeling of harmony pervading your being. Feel yourself fully alive. Notice if you are breathing fully. Take time to breath. Take five long, slow, deep breaths. Breathing deep into the belly prepares your body to receive fully.

6:30 | Dinner: Miso or Vegetable Soup

After this meal, you may plan to take some free time for yourself. Continue to use the quiet hours before rest to allow your mind and body to slow and relax. Believe that it is fine and healthy to turn off electronic devices and focus on activities that bring pleasure and release stress (instead of generating it). Use this time to really connect with family or friends. Listen with conscious attention, share with truth, and love wholeheartedly.

Over the course of this week you have detoxified your mind and spirit from the dis-ease caused by information overload. If you find yourself slipping back into the patter of checking e-mails "just once more" before bed or keeping your Blackberry on your bedside table at night, practice a "maintenance minicleanse" (see pages 179–80) to remind yourself of the lessons you have learned during the past six days.

7:00 | Bedtime Ritual

By now your quiet and meditative bedtime ritual should be well established. Hopefully you have grown accustomed to taking quiet time, uncluttered by television opinions and noise. Even a half hour of this time can be deeply restorative. Quiet time means pausing for a cup of tea and some beautiful music, relaxing and comfortably chatting with your beloved, or snuggling in bed and reading a story to a child. When you make time for these quiet moments in your life, you will feel healthier and less stressed, and therefore more conscious in your eating practice.

I hope you will take the bedtime ritual you have practiced this week and make it a part of your everyday life. Create a "no negative talk or noise" zone. Resist falling asleep with the TV on. Dare to be more consciously present with yourself, digesting your day during these important hours. Even if I find myself working until the early hours, before I go to sleep I brew some tea and sit on my couch in my room. I take the time to reconnect with myself and, as I said, "digest" my day.

You have spent seven days becoming aware of what your body is asking you for, and now you will simply continue this practice. The ongoing cycle of cleansing does not end here—or ever, in fact. As we eat, absorb, and eliminate in our natural cycle as part of a natural world, we are always cleansing. Your practice will simply extend now to an expanded awareness of all that we take into ourselves. Your good-feeling body will be your natural guide. You will sense with greater and greater ease that your vibrancy and best Self come out of the world around you also being its best.

One thing we know for sure is that we become better and better at those things that we practice. Remember that this increasingly masterful awareness of our bodies, our energy in the form of the food we recirculate through it, and the world this food comes from are all intimately connected. If you have made it this far, you are probably feeling absolutely amazing, and who wouldn't want to continue to feel that way?

Every time you return to your cleansing practice, you become more and more aware of how well you are, how well your body works, and how dependent you are upon the natural world. You will crave natural foods grown in sustainable ways. As your cleansing practice becomes more masterful, you will become more conscious and incapable of fueling your body with unconscious cruelty to animals. After a cleansing fast, it is very common to experience a significant and lasting change in the way you choose to nourish yourself.

Thank you so much for allowing me to guide you this week. Thank you for cleansing your cells and thereby bringing your best Self into our world.

13

Modified Cleanses

I **STRONGLY RECOMMEND THAT** you make the time to do a full seven-day cleanse to gain the complete benefit of a cleanse. However, I do realize that sometimes our busy lives simply cannot accommodate a week off whenever we feel we need it. The two versions of the cleanse that follow are great for maintenance after a cleanse or as quick pick-me-ups any time. Remember, once you have completed the Seven-Day Total Cleanse, you will have the tools you need to continue "clean eating" and to encourage your bodymind to continually renew and revitalize.

Countdown to Cleansing

An important aspect of either of these modified cleanses is the "countdown to cleansing" that precedes them. This countdown is a gentle way to prepare your body for cleansing and allows these modified cleanses to be efficient and most beneficial. If you are already a cleanser, eat a primarily vegan or vegetarian diet, and do not have a daily coffee habit, you can skip straight to the instructions for three days prior to starting a cleanse.

Seven Days (or More) Prior to Starting a Cleanse

These changes are not big or dramatic. They are simple and easy to implement. Notice that even before you begin a cleanse, you are embracing simple *change*.

- ➤ Switch to an organic free trade coffee brand.
- ➤ Choose "free" animal proteins (organic, free-range fish, meat, chicken, eggs, etc.).
- ➤ Reduce the amount of prepackaged, processed food you eat.

Six Days Prior to Starting a Cleanse

For the next three days, follow the menu below to begin to wean yourself from coffee, processed foods, sugar, and "bad" fats.

➤ **Breakfast:** Oatmeal with agave nectar, fresh berries, chopped walnuts, and cinnamon. Morning coffee made with one part organic free trade coffee and one part Teeccino brand grain beverage, brewed in the normal way. Use only half the amount of milk that you would usually add, and choose organic and free range, please. Sweeten with agave nectar if you must—use as little as possible.

➤ **Lunch:** A large green salad with avocado, tomatoes, raw-milk cheese, sweet red peppers, grated carrots, Hohm's House Dressing (see page 240), and pine nuts for garnish. Drink as much Yogi tea, sparkling water with lemon and honey, or filtered water as you wish.

➤ **Mid-day snack:** Fresh juice or a smoothie from our recipe section (see page 215).

➤ **Dinner:** Choose a vegetarian option from our recipe section (see page 222). A small glass of wine with dinner is OK at this point. Taper off any alcohol consumption from day six to day four, decreasing until you cut out wine entirely by day three prior to your cleanse.

Three Days Prior to Starting a Cleanse

Follow the menus for previous days, but omit coffee and substitute Teeccino, herbal tea, or detox tea.

Two Days Prior to Starting a Cleanse

Eliminate any dairy from your diet by this day. Instead, enjoy nut mylks (see page 214) and whole grains of any kind, including oatmeal, brown rice, millet, and quinoa. Decrease the amount of cooked vegetables and fruits you eat and increase your consumption of raw ones. Continue to avoid caffeine.

One Day Prior to Starting a Cleanse

If you feel it is appropriate for your body (and if you have never suffered from IBS, Crohn's disease, or a proclivity toward diarrhea), try going 100 percent raw today, enjoying only salads, fruits, and nut mylks.

Today you may also take one natural fiber supplement—I have been happy with the "Ultimate Fiber" brand—combined with one capsule of "Ultimate Cleansing Herbs" (both made by the Nature's Secret company). These supplements will help your body clear the foods you have been eating prior to the start of your juice fasting days. Alternately, you could have a cup of "Smooth Move" tea, made by the Traditional Medicinals company. Do not take both the supplements and the tea; you want to be very conservative and gentle with your body.

If you are going to undergo a colonic, schedule it for Day 3 of your cleanse. If you are familiar with this procedure, you may want to have more than one, but if you have never done this before and you are going to give it a try, Day 3 would be ideal. With the supplements you take today, the colonic or enema you undergo on Day 3 will be particularly efficient. If you suffer from IBS, having a colonic with only pure filtered water is more than sufficient—do not combine a colonic with fiber supplements. Remember, "Do No Thing" and the magic happens.

Minicleanse

This minicleanse is perfect for the working week or times when you do not want to practice a juice fast exclusively. And it couldn't be easier!

For five days, enjoy any colorful juice for breakfast and a green juice at lunch. For dinner, create a colorful and tasty salad inspired by any of the recipes in Chapter 15 (see page 237).

If you have a job that will make it necessary for you to eat lunch at restaurants or with clients, simply switch your menu around, enjoying a large, raw salad for lunch. Do not use prepared dressings; instead, ask for olive oil and a squeeze of lemon. Then enjoy your green elixir when you arrive home in the evening.

For the last two days of your cleanse (the weekend), follow the daily schedules for any two consecutive days of the Seven-Day Total Cleanse practice. As you become more familiar with cleansing, you will be able to intuit what your body needs and which chakras will benefit from the rebalancing and restorative powers of the juices.

If you wish, reverse the order of the countdown and take another week to transition back to eating three meals (and healthy snacks) each day. Make sure that you take the time to indulge in one or more of the External Beauty Indulgences. This is also a wonderful time to do a week's worth of journaling or create a Lifestyle Mandala (see pages 166–68) to reveal greater clarity about where you are and what you desire at this time.

Weekend Juice Feast

A juice feast is like a juice fast, but you get to consume as much juice as you want. You generally will consume only two or three large glasses of juice a day during a juice fast, but you might crave up to eight glasses a day during a juice feast!

This juice feast could not be easier. Prepare a week ahead of time by following the seven-day countdown described earlier in this chapter. Following the recipe on page 43, make a batch of Essential Potassium-Rich Broth. Then make a batch of juice (any color) and a batch of green juice. Divide each juice into three servings and store them in the refrigerator using glass containers with tight lids.

For two days, begin each day with eight ounces of broth and then alternate between a colored and a green juice, taking an eight-ounce serving every two hours three times during the day. Finish with another eight-ounce serving of broth. Your total intake of broth and juices during the day should add up to about sixty-four ounces. Supplement with water and tea as desired. Treat yourself well during these forty-eight hours. Try one of the External Beauty Indulgences, schedule a massage or a colonic, or just pamper yourself with the luxury of sleep, quiet rest, and meditation.

If you wish, you can reverse the seven-day countdown above to come out of your "juice feast."

≣ PART 3 ≣

Recipes

THE FEATURED RECIPES IN this section are, of course, the vibrantly colored juices that will sustain you during the seven days of your cleanse. But I wanted to include other dishes as well to show you how you can eat healthfully, keeping your body detoxified and energetic, long after your cleanse ends. The most important thing to remember, whether drinking juices or enjoying one of the recipes—which come to us courtesy of some of the most celebrated chefs working with raw and natural foods—is simply this: don't eat anything you don't like.

You might resolve that after you finish your cleanse, you will drink a deep green juice everyday. Of course, I think this is a great idea! But if you are choosing to drink a green juice solely because it is technically supernutritious—because you think it will be "good" for you—with the result that you "take your medicine" by holding your nose and just gulping it down as fast as possible so you will not have to taste it, you are only absorbing a fraction of that juice's benefits. Forcing yourself to drink or eat something you don't like while trying to convince yourself it is "good" for you is, I believe, the root cause of many failures to stick with that initial intention to maintain good food habits after a cleanse. If we do not like our food, we will not want to eat it, no matter how "good" it is supposed to be for us. From there it is a quick trip back to our old ways of thinking and feeling about food and the inevitable return of our body's imbalance—which drove us to feeling a need to cleanse in the first place.

So make sure you are feeding your body with loving attention. If you really don't want something, it won't be good for you. What you eat should have a color that is pleasing to your eyes and a scent that you love—and obviously, it should make your taste buds sing. Choosing foods this way gives a whole new meaning to the word "feedback"; after you have finished the seven days of a cleanse, you will have learned to trust your intuition regarding hunger and become attuned to processing food information on a cellular level. If the past seven days have taught you anything about your relationship to food, I hope it is the value of natural cleansing as part of a natural relationship with the world around us, being nourished by real food rather than a handful of supplements.

14

The Seven-Day Kitchen

NOTHING IS MORE FRUSTRATING, or thwarts good intentions faster, than anticipating a wonderful treat from your kitchen only to find you don't have the right tools or are lacking a crucial ingredient. In order to give your body the good foods it craves, whenever it craves them, there are certain appliances, tools, and ingredients that should be staples in your kitchen.

In this chapter, I'll share essentials from the American Yogini Hohm kitchen and explain why eating local and organic foods is an important part of my cleansing philosophy.

The Right Tools

The amount of money you invest in kitchen appliances is up to you. At a minimum you will need a juicer and a blender. Because the higher quality (professional) appliances make juicing and blending so much easier, I feel that it is worth paying the extra money for them.

I use the Breville brand juicer for everyday home juicing, a Norwalk press to make our home-delivery juices, and the Vitamix brand blender for just about everything else. There are several great models of juicers for home use available. You want to look for a design that is attractive enough to leave out on the counter in plain sight so you will use it daily, and something with as few small parts as possible to make it easy to take apart and clean after you have made your juice. The bottom line is if your juicer requires an hour to take apart, clean, and reassemble, you are probably not going to want to make juice very often.

The Norwalk press juicer that we use for sending juices home with students and delivering juices produces good-quality juice that stays fresh a bit longer, but it is very expensive and is extremely time consuming for small batches of juice. When you are drinking your juices right after you make them, or only storing them for a day or so, a juicer such as the Breville or the Jack LaLanne are the best choices.

The list below suggests a few other kitchen tools that will make recipe preparation easier:

➤ A spiralizer
➤ A vegetable peeler
➤ A sharp knife
➤ A mesh food-filtering bag or sieve—micromesh bags make it easy to create nut mylks or to strain green juices very quickly with little mess or waste. You can also use a traditional sieve or cheesecloth.
➤ A mezzaluna (an old-fashioned, two-handled, half-moon-shaped blade that makes quick work of herb chopping)
➤ Measuring cups and spoons
➤ A coffee grinder for spices and flaxseed grinding
➤ A mortar and pestle for making pesto-type sauces
➤ Mixing bowls
➤ Wooden mixing spoons
➤ Rubber spatulas (use these to get every delicious, precious drop out of your blender and mixing bowls!)

Essential Ingredients

There are certain common ingredients that go into many of the juices and recipes that follow. Some of them may be slightly harder to find in your area than others, although all of them can be found at health or natural food stores or through online sources. If you are not familiar with some of the items on the list below, you may wish to plan ahead and stock your pantry with the following:

➤ **Açaí frozen smoothie packs or açaí powder.** Açaí is a Brazilian berry with anti-inflammatory, antibacterial, antioxidant, and antimutagenic properties. Frozen packets of açaí smoothie, available from the Sambazon company, are more and more common in the frozen section of natural food stores. You can also keep a container of dried açaí powder handy for quick smoothies.

➤ **Agave nectar.** Agave plants grow primarily in Mexico, although they are also found in the southern and western United States and in central and tropical South America. The plants have a large rosette of thick, fleshy leaves that spring from the root of the plant. Agave nectar comes from the heart of the plant and is a natural sweetener.

➤ **Bragg Liquid Aminos.** This is a liquid protein concentrate derived from soybeans that contains sixteen amino acids; use it in place of soy sauce.

➤ **E3Live Supplement.** E3Live® is an all-organic, wild-harvested aqua-botanical that is considered to be one of nature's most beneficial superfoods. It supports the immune, endocrine, nervous, gastrointestinal, and cardiovascular systems, providing sixty-four easily absorbed vitamins, minerals, and enzymes. It is nutrient dense and has more biologically active chlorophyll than any known food. It comes in a frozen liquid form that can be thawed in the refrigerator overnight. You can go to their website at www.E3live.com to learn more about this amazing product.

➤ **Garam masala.** A common blend of spices used in Indian cooking.

➤ **Goji berries (dried) and goji berry juice.** Goji berries are found in the Himalayas and China. These powerful little berries contain an astounding nineteen amino acids, twenty-one trace minerals (including zinc and calcium), are higher in beta-carotene than carrots, have a complete spectrum of antioxidants, and even contain vitamin E (unheard of in most fruits!).

➤ **Grape seed oil**

➤ **Himalayan sea salt**

➤ **Lecithin powder.** Lecithin is a fatlike substance called a phospholipid. It is needed by every cell in the body and is a key building block of cell membranes. Lecithin is an antioxidant and fat emulsifier and benefits both the nervous and circulatory systems.

➤ **Maca powder.** Maca root is a member of the radish family indigenous to Peru. It is a true superfood that contributes to total body well-being and energy. Maca roots are nutritional storehouses of vitamins, minerals, and cellular building blocks that fuel brain function and nourish and balance the body.

➤ **Medjool dates**

➤ **Miso**

➤ **Organic rice**

➤ **Raw almond butter**

➤ **Raw black walnuts**

➤ **Raw Brazil nuts**

➤ **Raw cacao**

➤ **Raw sesame seeds**

➤ **Raw soy sauce.** Nama Shoyu brand is the highest-quality raw soy sauce available in American markets.

➤ **Rice or nut mylk.** Use our recipes to make your own (see page 214); it is also available from most grocery stores.

➤ **Spelt flour.** Flour made from a dietary grain similar to whole wheat but with a nuttier, slightly sweeter taste. Spelt contains more protein than wheat, and the protein is easier to digest. If you are allergic to wheat, you may be able to tolerate spelt.

➤ **Sucanat®.** The name of this sweetener is a contraction of "Sugar Cane Natural" and is made from whole cane sugar. Because it is not refined, it has the deep brown color and distinctive flavor of molasses. Use it just as you would brown sugar for baking or sweetening foods.

➤ **Tocotrienols.** Tocotrienol is part of the vitamin E family and has powerful antioxidant properties that help to promote cardiovascular health. Tocotrienol supplements are available in capsule and tablet form. I use the dark brown powder from the Flora brand.

➤ **Turmeric.** Turmeric contains a unique active compound called *curcumen*, a powerful healer that has been used in India for more than 2,500 years.

➤ **UDO's 3-6-9 Oil.** This high-quality oil, made by the Flora company, is well known as a supplement food for vegans. It contains the "medium chain" fatty acids (once thought to be available only in animal products) that are essential to healthy cells, especially brain cells. This oil is the real key to your ongoing cleansing success! When we start to consume fewer animal products, we think we are hungry and craving meat when in fact we are actually craving *fat*—good fat! Don't be without UDO's in your refrigerator, but get the smallest size bottle you can; it will spoil after only three weeks, even if refrigerated.

➤ **Walnut oil**

➤ **Young coconut flesh and young coconut water.** By the time a coconut falls from a tree, it is older and its flesh is harder and contains less liquid. Besides being highly nutritious, young coconuts also offer benefits for the heart, liver, and kidneys.

Organic and Local Foods

Once you have finished your seven-day cleanse and begin to prepare meals again, you will hopefully understand that clean eating is something that can and should be ongoing. When you are "eating clean," you achieve maximum nutritional impact combined with minimal energy output required by your body for processing. You avoid toxins going in and, by choosing to eat the right kinds of foods, constantly encourage your body in the process of eliminating all kinds of environmental toxins.

The foods that best facilitate the above conditions are foods that adhere to the law of *ahimsa*. *Ahimsa* is a Sanskrit word that means *nonharming*. When the food we choose to consume has not harmed the earth (with toxic chemicals) or the people that produced it (with unfavorable labor conditions), it is at its most potent nutritionally, demands minimal energy from our bodies to process and receive the nutrients, does not add toxins to the body, and allows toxins to exit the body efficiently and quickly.

When you shop consciously following the principal of *ahimsa*, you:

➤ **Protect your health and the health of your family by eliminating pesticides that may cause cancer or other detrimental health effects.**

➤ **Protect our earth by protecting farmland.** Chemical-intensive monocrop farming erodes an estimated three billion tons of topsoil from U.S. croplands each year. Organic crop production practices build long-term soil health and stability. Organic farming practices also eliminate contamination of groundwater, leading to cleaner water supplies.

➤ **Support small farmers and promote a fair economy.**

➤ **Enjoy food with better flavor and absorb more nutrients.** Because organic foods are not treated with fungicides, they must be sent to market as close to harvest as possible, meaning that they are usually far fresher than conventionally produced foods.

Mindful eating extends beyond the act of looking into your fridge or pantry and choosing what you will eat for dinner; true awareness of food asks that you think about and choose the way in which you act as a consumer. When possible, it is best to use locally grown or home-grown foods.

I am fortunate to live in an area with abundant farms; in growing season, our local roadside farm stands overflow with mouthwatering produce. If you have a local farmers' market or a farm offering shares in your area, it is well worth purchasing your produce from these sources.

Organic local produce is best, but if you do not have local organically farmed produce available, you may choose to purchase conventionally farmed local fruits and veggies over organic. It is all part of a balance. Local foods, even if not organically raised, meet the principles of *ahimsa* by using less environment-damaging petro-fuel for shipping. And they are more nutritious because the nutritional components of a living fruit or vegetable degrade by the minute after they are harvested.

Nevertheless, there are certain fruits and veggies that you should only consume if they are organic if it is available, as conventional farming methods consistently use highly toxic chemicals in fertilizing and protecting these crops. Try to choose organic every time when you are buying peaches, apples, pears, grapes, strawberries, raspberries, cherries, cantaloupes, winter squash, green beans, celery, spinach, potatoes, red bell peppers, and tomatoes.

Of course, the ideal is to have your own garden, if your home has space and you live in an area where the weather allows it. Fresh greens, veggies, and fruits picked straight from your yard and immediately juiced or eaten are the best nutritional gift you can give your body!

15

Juices, Smoothies, and Recipes for the Days Following Your Cleanse

YOU'LL NOTICE THAT SEVERAL of the recipes that follow are raw food recipes—that is, dishes where the ingredients are not heated or cooked in any way. Natural ongoing cleansing of our bodies occurs when we are in balance, eating foods that are rich in fiber as well as nutrients and enzymes that are easy to absorb. Raw, vegan foods are ideal for reintroducing your body to consuming solid food in the days following your cleanse. Raw foods are in their most natural form, full of the sun's energizing rays and plump with water drawn from the earth and sky. They instantly connect us to the universe. We share the gravity of the earth that keeps us grounded and safe, the wax and wane of the moon that pulls on the tides around us, governing healthy states of sleep and wakefulness. We absorb so much more than simply vitamins and fiber from raw foods. We draw upon the energy of the sun—and that energy is what illuminates every cell of our bodies and promotes the radiant glow of good health.

The recipes that follow have been taste tested and loved by my students here at American Yogini Hohm, by the satisfied and loyal clientele of The Candle Cafe and Candle 79 restaurants in Manhattan, by the fans of New York–based nutritionist and private chef Shawn Williams, and by clients of New York nutritionist and natural foods chef Laura Rosenberg. I'm grateful to all of these culinary masters, each of whom appreciates the fact that healthy food that tastes heavenly and looks divine feeds both the body and the soul. Enjoy!

Each recipe makes one large (or two small) servings, unless otherwise noted.

Juices

Every juice we create is made with my "five-pointed star of taste" in mind. It's important to realize that our tongues appreciate five different tastes in food and drink: sweet, sour, spicy, salty, and bitter. When we eat things that lean too strongly in only one direction, it results in the body asking for the other tastes. It is "mis-information" to your body's natural intelligence. That is one reason why, when you overdose on sweets or salty snacks, you may still feel hungry and crave more food, while at the same time you don't know exactly what you want. When you consume juices and foods that offer you a balance of all five tastes, cravings are reduced and it is easier to perceive when you have actually had enough.

During your cleanse you may wish to drink all of your juice as a single serving or you may wish to save half of it for later in the day. Use your inner wisdom; it's OK to have less juice more often if that is what you intuit you need. Always notice how you are feeling. You are looking for the edge of sensation, the edge of hunger. Hang out with that edge a bit longer than you normally would, and then take only small sips and simply keep "watching" until you notice you are satisfied.

Please note that it is not necessary to peel gingerroot when it is called for in these juice recipes, though you may wish to do so depending on the quality of your juicer.

Red Juices

Red is the color of passion and vigor. The first chakra is attuned to the color red and governs survival, trust, and security. Let these deep red juices root you to your connection with the earth, the foundation of your energy, and your own sense of personal security.

⋚ Security ⋛

This delicious recipe is particularly strengthening to the bones. Your body feels strong and secure when your skeletal system is supporting you.

- 2 cups cherries, pitted
- 1 small beet (¼ cup diced)
- ¼ of a medium turnip (¼ cup diced)
- 2 red apples
- 3 stalks celery
- 1 lime, peeled
- 1-inch piece of gingerroot, more or less to taste

Put all ingredients through the juicer.

⋚ Safety ⋛

The simplicity of these familiar ingredients will infuse you with a sense of safety. This is a cooling juice, so it is the perfect choice for hot days or when a "detox event" triggers a skin rash or heat flash.

- 3 cups diced watermelon
- 1 lime, peeled
- 1 cucumber
- 1-inch piece of gingerroot, more or less to taste

Put all ingredients through the juicer.

⋚ Grounding ⋛

Because all of its ingredients (except the apples and rhubarb) grow under the soil, this juice is a perfect first chakra strengthener. These roots will help you to harmonize with your own "roots."

- 1 small beet
- 3 medium carrots
- 1 medium parsnip
- 2 red apples

- ¼ cup peeled and diced yam
- 1 stalk rhubarb
- 1-inch piece of gingerroot, more or less to taste

Put all ingredients through the juicer.

≩ Cocoon ≨

This juice is deeply nourishing and warming when it is made with a good amount of gingerroot.

- 1 small turnip
- 3 cups chopped red cabbage
- ½ of a small beet
- 1 Gala apple
- ½ of a lemon, peeled
- 1-inch piece of gingerroot, more or less to taste

Put all ingredients through the juicer.

≩ Stability ≨

Tomatoes and peppers are members of the nightshade family and have very different energetic vibrations than do roots. While the leaves of nightshade plants are often toxic, their fruits contain large quantities of vitamin C. This recipe offers the quality of stability that results when we allow ourselves to grow up from our roots.

- 2 cups chopped tomato
- 3 stalks celery
- ¼ of a red bell pepper
- 4 medium carrots
- ½ cup chopped parsley
- 1 lemon, peeled
- 1 red radish, or more to taste

Put all ingredients through the juicer.

≡ Survival ≡

Our liver is our body's great natural filter; with all the toxins in our modern world, it is constantly working hard to protect our blood from these impurities. The dark reddish-green color of this liver-cleansing juice reminds me of army camouflage—an image of strength and protection.

- 2 cups chopped beet greens
- 1 small beet
- ½ cup chopped Swiss chard (choose red stalks for the best color)
- 3 stalks celery
- 1 lime, peeled
- 1-inch piece of gingerroot, more or less to taste

Put all ingredients through the juicer.

≡ Prosperity ≡

Strawberries grow with great abundance upon a single root, and they are covered with thousands of tiny seeds, just as pomegranates are full of seeds. Seeds offer the promise of unlimited potential and the prosperity and abundance that will be ours.

- 3 cups strawberries
- 1 cup pomegranate seeds
- 1 Gala apple
- ½ of a lemon, peeled
- 1 small jalapeño pepper
- Pinch sea salt

Juice first four ingredients without jalapeño.

With rubber gloves on, seed jalapeño and carefully put through juicer. Use a dropper to add one drop of the resulting juice to the rest of your ingredients and taste; add more, drop by drop, mixing and tasting until you achieve just the right amount of heat for you. Add sea salt before drinking.

Be sure not to skip the jalapeño! Even if you do not like spicy things, a single drop of jalapeño juice will keep you from craving solid foods and feeling hungry, and it helps you cleanse. A single drop will not make the juice too spicy, and you will be surprised by how gorgeous it will make the other ingredients taste! If you do not have a dropper, try dipping a knife into the jalapeño juice and then stirring the rest of the juice with the knife. Repeat until you arrive at the perfect level. You will notice this level changes as your cells get cleaner. What seems spicy or bitter today may taste delicious tomorrow. Be open to what your body tells you.

Orange Juices

Orange is the color of creativity, joy, and enthusiasm. The second chakra governs emotional balance, sexuality, harmony with others, and expression of emotion. The exuberant orange juices described in this section promote courage and optimism. They stimulate your creativity, self-awareness, and authority and balance these traits with kindness and cheer.

⋚ Fulfillment ⋚

Avocado is a very cleansing food and contains a healthy and important fat. Blend only a very small piece into this juice or it can quickly become too thick to drink. Enjoy this if you are feeling unfulfilled. It's very filling—and fulfilling.

- 3 large carrots
- 1 small to medium cucumber
- 1 stalk celery
- ½ of a lemon, peeled
- ½-inch piece of gingerroot, more or less to taste
- 1¼-inch slice of avocado
- Squeeze of lemon, to taste

Put all ingredients except the avocado through the juicer. In a blender, combine the avocado and juice and blend well. Add an extra squeeze of lemon juice just prior to drinking for a "brighter" taste.

≡ Sensation ≡

This juice will stimulate your senses! The grapefruit and ginger make it tangy, while the yam and pear make it smooth.

- 1 large pink grapefruit, peeled
- 1 small sweet potato or yam, peeled and diced
- 1 pear (any variety will do, although Comice, Bartlett, and Anjou are particularly nice)
- 1 stalk celery
- 1-inch piece of gingerroot, more or less to taste

Put all ingredients through the juicer.

≡ Grace ≡

I define "grace" as movement without resistance. In my yoga classes we are in a state of grace when movement occurs only as breath carries us from point A to point B. This is true both on the yoga mat and in our lives.

The meyer lemons that are called for in this recipe are juicier and sweeter than traditional lemons and are particularly effective in stimulating the emotion of desire. If meyer lemons are unavailable, a lime would substitute nicely.

- 4 stalks celery
- 2 navel oranges, peeled
- 3 mandarin oranges, peeled
- 1 meyer lemon, peeled (substitute 1 lime if meyer lemons are unavailable)
- ½ cup mint leaves
- 1-inch piece of gingerroot, more or less to taste

Put all ingredients through the juicer.

≡ Desire ≡

When you are stuck in a rut of boredom and monotony, desire expresses what is truly wanted. When you feel desire, you have begun to know your authentic purpose and path. As your cells are mopped clean by the enzymes in papaya, monotony gives way to creative action.

- 2 cups peeled and diced papaya
- 2 navel oranges, peeled
- 3 clementines, peeled
- 1 meyer lemon, peeled (substitute 1 lime if meyer lemons are unavailable)
- ½-inch piece of gingerroot, more or less to taste

Put all ingredients through the juicer.

⇥ Fluidity ⇤

Water is the element associated with the second chakra, and this recipe contains water-rich cucumber, celery, and apple.

- 4 carrots
- 1 cucumber
- 2 stalks celery
- ½ cup dill
- ½ of a lemon, peeled
- 3 apples
- ½-inch piece of gingerroot, more or less to taste

Put all ingredients through the juicer.

⇥ Sensuality ⇤

The second chakra and the color orange are both connected to our sexual energies and sensual nature. This recipe's intention is to balance, tempering the overly stimulated and firing up the understimulated. Without balanced sexual energy there is no creativity, and without creativity we are powerless to navigate change.

- 2 green apples
- 4 carrots
- ½ of a medium cucumber
- 1 stalk celery
- ½ cup peeled and diced papaya
- 1 small red radish

Put all ingredients through the juicer.

Yellow Juices

Yellow is the color of the sun and of energy, confidence, and happiness. Glow from within by drinking the power of yellow and balancing your third chakra—your personal power center, which helps you overcome inertia and promotes self-esteem and confidence.

⋛ Self-Esteem ⋚

To taste this juice is to soak in pure tropical sunshine. It's also a natural self-esteem boost.

If you can find an organic pineapple, and if your juicer can handle it, pineapples should be juiced with their rinds intact (but well scrubbed). Pineapple rinds contain wonderful and delicious enzymes that will cleanse you more quickly and more deeply.

- ½ of a pineapple (organic if possible)
- 1 meyer lemon or small lime, peeled
- 1 medium cucumber
- 1 stalk celery
- 1 small jalapeño pepper

Juice first four ingredients without jalapeño.

With rubber gloves on, seed jalapeño and carefully put through juicer. Use a dropper to add one drop of the resulting juice to the rest of your ingredients and taste; add more, drop by drop, mixing and tasting until you achieve just the right amount of heat for you.

Be sure not to skip the jalapeño! Even if you do not like spicy things, a single drop of jalapeño juice will keep you from craving solid foods and feeling hungry, and it helps you cleanse. A single drop will not make the juice too spicy, and you will be surprised by how gorgeous it will make the other ingredients taste! If you do not have a dropper, try dipping a knife into the jalapeño juice and then stirring the rest of the juice with the knife. Repeat until you arrive at the perfect level. You will notice this level changes as your cells get cleaner. What seems spicy or bitter today may taste delicious tomorrow. Be open to what your body tells you.

⋚ Commitment ⋛

Grapefruit is a great body cleanser because it contains more than five times the vitamin C of oranges. Grapefruits are rich in bioflavonoids (important antioxidant-enhancing compounds), making this powerhouse cleanser a powerhouse rebuilder as well.

- 2 Bosc pears (hard ones will yield more juice)
- ¼ cup fresh tarragon leaves
- 1 large grapefruit, peeled
- 2 green apples
- 1-inch piece of gingerroot, more or less to taste
- Squeeze of lemon

Cut slits into the flesh of the pears and tuck the tarragon leaves into them before juicing. This will yield more juice from the delicate tarragon leaves.

Put all ingredients except the lemon through the juicer. Add squeeze of lemon juice just prior to drinking. Stir to mix.

⋚ Power ⋛

Turmeric contains a unique active compound called curcumen, a powerful healer that has been used in India for more than 2,500 years. Do not remove the yellow-colored skin of the squashes before juicing. You will be rewarded with the power of magnesium, potassium, and folate to help you cleanse deeply. More power to you!

- 2 yellow summer squash
- 2 stalks celery
- 1 medium cucumber
- 1 apple
- ½-inch piece of gingerroot, more or less to taste
- ¼ teaspoon turmeric, or more to taste (it may taste bitter or astringent to you, so start with the smallest amount)
- Squeeze of lemon

Put all ingredients except the lemon and turmeric through the juicer. Add turmeric and a squeeze of lemon just prior to drinking. Stir to mix.

≣ Spontaneity ≣

When you are sure of your center and shining from your navel power, you will be spontaneous. This recipe is like a great supernova star pouring right into your belly!

- ½ of a pineapple (organic if possible)
- 2 carrots
- 1 stalk celery
- 1 lime, peeled
- ½ cup cilantro
- 1 small jalapeño pepper

Juice first five ingredients without jalapeño. If you can find an organic pineapple, and if your juicer can handle it, pineapples should be juiced with their rinds intact (but well scrubbed). Pineapple rinds contain wonderful and delicious enzymes that will cleanse you more quickly and more deeply.

With rubber gloves on, seed jalapeño and carefully put through juicer. Use a dropper to add one drop of the resulting juice to the rest of your ingredients and taste; add more, drop by drop, mixing and tasting until you achieve just the right amount of heat for you.

Be sure not to skip the jalapeño! Even if you do not like spicy things, a single drop of jalapeño juice will keep you from craving solid foods and feeling hungry, and it helps you cleanse. A single drop will not make the juice too spicy, and you will be surprised by how gorgeous it will make the other ingredients taste! If you do not have a dropper, try dipping a knife into the jalapeño juice and then stirring the rest of the juice with the knife. Repeat until you arrive at the perfect level. You will notice this level changes as your cells get cleaner. What seems spicy or bitter today may taste delicious tomorrow. Be open to what your body tells you.

◌ Energy ◌

This unusual and delicious cleansing juice will completely recharge your prana
(life force energy).

- 2 Golden Delicious apples
- 2 small yellow summer squash
- 2 cups chopped romaine lettuce
- 1 stalk celery
- ½ of a lemon, peeled
- 1-inch piece of gingerroot, more or less to taste

Put all ingredients through the juicer.

◌ Effectiveness ◌

*To increase the benefits of this juice, imagine a golden ball of light deep inside
your belly. Imagine this ball during your yoga or exercises, and then feel it form
as you slowly drink this liquid gold.*

*Golden beets are not too hard to find, but not totally common either.
Anyone who loves vegetables will know what these gentle, sweet cousins to the
common red beet are like.*

- ½ of a pineapple (organic if possible)
- 1 Golden Delicious apple
- 1 golden beet
- 1 meyer lemon, peeled (substitute 1 lime if meyer lemons are unavailable)
- 1-inch piece or gingerroot, more or less to taste
- Tiny pinch Himalayan sea salt

Juice the first five ingredients. If you can find an organic pineapple, and if your
juicer can handle it, pineapples should be juiced with their rinds intact (but well
scrubbed). Pineapple rinds contain wonderful and delicious enzymes that will
cleanse you more quickly and more deeply. Stir in a tiny pinch of Himalayan sea
salt for balance.

Green Juices

Our heart is located right in the center of our body's energy system, linking the three chakras below it and the three chakras above it. It is set into healthy balance by the vibration of the color green. Green foods, just like our hearts, grow in the center of the food world, above the roots and ground, but not so far up into the sky as the fruits and vegetables that grow upon vines and trees. Just as green money is the currency of our economy, leafy and bush-grown greens are the "currency" of our entire bodily energy system.

≡ Joy ≡

Most of these ingredients grow in gardens around my house, and to go and collect a cucumber is like going to a party. They just ramble on like so many smiles.

- 2 cucumbers
- 4 green apples
- Full bunch of mint leaves
- 1 lime, peeled
- 2 stalks celery
- ½-inch piece of gingerroot, more or less to taste

Put all ingredients through the juicer.

≡ Happiness ≡

This juice will bring you the taste of the sunny tropics, the bright energy of collards and green herbs, and the unexpected "pow" of jalapeño. One sip and you will know why we call it "Happiness."

- ¼ of a medium pineapple (organic if possible)
- 1 packed cup of a mixture of equal parts chopped basil, mint, and cilantro
- 3 cups chopped collard greens
- 2 stalks celery
- 1 small jalapeño pepper

Cut deep slits into the pineapple and tuck as much of the chopped herbs as you can inside it. This will make it easier to extract juice from the herbs. If you can find an organic pineapple, and if your juicer can handle it, pineapples should be juiced with their rinds intact (but well scrubbed). Pineapple rinds contain wonderful and delicious enzymes that will cleanse you more quickly and more deeply.

Put all ingredients through the juicer without the jalapeño.

With rubber gloves on, seed jalapeño and carefully put through juicer. Use a dropper to add one drop of the resulting juice to the rest of your ingredients and taste; add more, drop by drop, mixing and tasting until you achieve just the right amount of heat for you.

Be sure not to skip the jalapeño! Even if you do not like spicy things, a single drop of jalapeño juice will keep you from craving solid foods and feeling hungry, and it helps you cleanse. A single drop will not make the juice too spicy, and you will be surprised by how gorgeous it will make the other ingredients taste! If you do not have a dropper, try dipping a knife into the jalapeño juice and then stirring the rest of the juice with the knife. Repeat until you arrive at the perfect level.

Mix well. If you find the taste too bitter, add more pineapple; if you find it too sweet, add more collards and herbs. This is your chance to practice trusting yourself to know what you want, what you like, and what you need.

≩ Innocence ≨

Make this juice for a spring cleanse. Baby vegetables in spring are the epitome of innocence. They look every bit as cute poking their fresh young colors out of the earth as any baby creature taking its first look at the world.

- 3 cups mixed baby lettuces and spinach
- 3 spears of asparagus
- 3 green apples
- 1 medium cucumber
- ¼ cup chopped fennel
- ½ of a lemon, peeled
- 2 red radishes

Put all ingredients through the juicer.

≹ Compassion ≹

There is no greater gift than the gift of compassion for Self. Treat yourself well, and you will radiate a spirit of generosity toward others.

- 1 cup chopped collard greens
- ½ cup chopped kale
- ½ cup chopped dandelion greens
- ½ cup chopped beet greens
- 3 stalks celery
- 3 green apples
- 1 lemon, peeled
- 1-inch piece of gingerroot, more or less to taste

Put all ingredients through the juicer.

≹ Love ≹

Zucchini is so prolific; it never stops flowering and bearing fruit all summer, unconditionally. In drought, in rain, in heat, or in cool nights, we always have all the zucchini (and yummy zucchini flowers) that we need. All love should be so abundant!

- 1 cucumber
- ½ cup chopped mint leaves
- 2 zucchini
- 3 stalks celery
- 1 lime, peeled
- 2 apples
- 3 red radishes

Cut slits into the cucumber and tuck the mint into them before juicing. This will yield more juice.

Put all ingredients through the juicer.

⋚ Playfulness ⋚

"Playful!" is what one guest at my retreat spontaneously exclaimed when he tasted this juice. Everyone laughed and immediately agreed.

- 2 cups chopped romaine lettuce
- ½ cup chopped parsley
- 1 pear
- ½ cup peeled, seeded, and diced papaya
- ½ of a lemon, peeled
- ½-inch piece of gingerroot, more or less to taste

Put all ingredients through the juicer.

⋚ Beloved ⋚

The reddish-green color of this juice comes from the beet greens, the red chard stalks, and of course the surprising pomegranate. It's very appropriate for a heart chakra cleanse, as pomegranates are well known as a tonic for the heart and as a cholesterol reducer.

- 1 cup chopped beet greens
- 2 cups chopped chard
- 3 Gala apples
- ½ of a pear
- ½ cup pomegranate seeds
- 1 lemon, peeled
- 1-inch piece of gingerroot, more or less to taste

Put all ingredients through the juicer.

Bright Blue Juices

Blue is deep; blue is pure. Blue is peaceful waters, tranquil skies, true-blue friends. . . . Blue is the color of serenity and contemplation. When the fifth chakra is balanced, we can use this calm and steadfast energy to communicate our deepest truths to ourselves and those around us. These bright blue juices communicate with your body to clear the way for you to trust your intuition and act upon your creative and spiritual desires.

⋛ Truth ⋚

Blueberry skins contain the greatest gifts these fruits have to offer; rather than putting them through the juicer, blend them whole into your cleansing elixir.

Throat Coat tea, which is called for in this recipe, is made by Traditional Medicinals and can be found in health food stores nationwide. If you cannot find it, simmer a cinnamon stick in about four cups of water with a fourth of a fennel bulb and the peel of one orange. Boil, steep for thirty minutes, and then strain.

- ¼ cup mint leaves
- 2 apples
- 1 lime, peeled
- ½-inch piece of gingerroot, more or less to taste
- 1 pint fresh blueberries
- 3 drops solé solution
- ½ cup room temperature Throat Coat tea

Put mint, apples, lime, and ginger through the juicer. Combine juice, blueberries, solé, and tea in blender and blend thoroughly.

⋛ Communication ⋚

Anyone can communicate in harmony if he or she wishes. Here the sunny, tropical pineapple gets into friendly communication with the deep blue northern blueberry. Drink, appreciate, and communicate!

- ½ of a pineapple (organic if possible)
- 1 stalk celery
- 1 lemon, peeled
- ½-inch piece of gingerroot, more or less to taste
- 1 pint blueberries

Put pineapple, celery, lemon, and gingerroot through the juicer. If you can find an organic pineapple, and if your juicer can handle it, pineapples should be juiced with their rinds intact (but well scrubbed). Pineapple rinds contain wonderful and delicious enzymes that will cleanse you more quickly and more deeply. In a blender, combine juice and blueberries and blend well.

⅀ Good Vibrations ⋹

Make a double batch of this juice and feel twice the good vibrations!

- 1 handful of blueberries
- 8 ounces of rice or almond mylk (see page 214 for nut mylk recipes)

In a blender, combine all ingredients and blend at high speed until they are a nice blue-violet color.

Deep Blue Juices

Deep blue, or indigo, is a color full of dignity and integrity. It is energetically attuned to the sixth chakra, promoting true inner vision and mental clarity. Let these deep blue juices work their magic on your ego, banishing fears and lack of discipline and bringing balance and true clarity.

⅀ Intuition ⋹

Cleansing is the time that our intuition returns. This blackberry recipe is rich but good. Blackberries grow in a wild, rambling way, obscuring a path we are certain is there. Our minds can also obscure a path we know to be true. Drink this juice slowly and seek clarity.

- 3 cups blackberries
- 1 cup blueberries
- 1 cup black cherries, pitted
- 1 apple
- ½ of a lemon, peeled
- ½-inch piece of gingerroot, more or less to taste

Put all ingredients through the juicer.

This recipe contains nearly every berry in my local area (the northeast United States). Berries are superfoods; that means they have an unusually high level of antioxidants. Supercleansing superfoods like fresh, raw berries lead you to your deeper knowledge.

- 1 cup blackberries
- 1 cup raspberries
- 1 cup blueberries
- 1 cup black cherries, pitted
- 2 stalks celery
- 1 lemon, peeled
- ½-inch piece of gingerroot, more or less to taste

Put all ingredients through the juicer.

Violet Juices and Aura Enhancers

Purple is the perfect balance of red and blue, strength and dignity. The seventh chakra is the doorway to universal connection. We strive to be powerful and one with the universe, to balance intellect and spirit, to live with meaning, passion, and excitement. Beyond the seventh chakra is our aura (the "eighth chakra") where all the colors come together in a pure white energy. The juices and other drinks that follow fortify the seventh chakra and beyond, with the white elixirs vibrating with the energy of innocence, purity, and truth—what we carry forward when we are empty, open to all wonder and possibility, and committed to the truth of our journey.

≣ Seventh Gate ≋

Grapes grow on vines that climb toward the sky. Grape seeds are beneficial and add the right level of bitterness. Add a little water to this recipe, as the berries and fruits are extremely dense and sweet; water also helps to bring clarity and lightness. If you cannot find fresh sour cherries, use sweet cherries and add a squeeze of lemon to your juice before drinking.

- 1 cup black grapes with seeds
- 2 cups blackberries
- ½ cup sour cherries, pitted
- ½-inch piece of gingerroot, more or less to taste
- Filtered water
- Pinch Himalayan sea salt

Put all ingredients except water and sea salt through the juicer. Pour juice into a glass and add water to reach desired consistency. Add salt and mix well.

⇉ Connection ⇇

Cherries and apples grow high upon trees, just as your seventh chakra resides high up the body at the top of your head. Blackberries ramble in the wild, as the mind will also ramble. In this juice, the gingerroot will help keep you grounded as your mind opens peacefully.

- 3 cups cherries, pitted
- 1 cup blackberries
- 2 Granny Smith apples
- ½-inch piece of gingerroot, more or less to taste
- Filtered water
- 1 ounce bottled goji berry juice
- Squeeze of fresh lemon juice

Put all ingredients except water, goji berry juice, and lemon juice through the juicer. Pour juice into a glass and add water to reach desired consistency. Add goji juice and a squeeze of fresh lemon.

⇉ Wisdom ⇇

Black walnut trees are nearly as tall as the mighty Brazil nut tree, stretching their branches to the sky, just as your eighth chakra reaches out beyond your

*physical body. Walnuts contain significant amounts of omega-3 fatty acids—
rare in the vegetable world. What are omega-3s good for? Brain health, of
course! Nourish your brain and welcome the wisdom of the universe.*

- 3 cups filtered water
- 1½ cups black walnuts
- ½ cup frozen banana slices
- 1 teaspoon vanilla extract
- 1 teaspoon walnut extract

In a blender, combine water and walnuts and blend on high speed until frothy.
Pour into a mesh bag to filter, thoroughly squeezing all milk from the pulp.

Pour fresh-squeezed walnut milk back into blender. Add banana slices and the
vanilla and walnut extracts and blend well.

≡ Understanding ≡

*Sesame seeds are formed in pods that grow upon tall grasses. They are higher
in absorbable calcium than dairy milk. As sesame cares for the bones and
Brazil nuts care for the mind, this recipe cares for both the finite density of our
bones and the infinite complexity of our mind.*

- 3 cups filtered water
- ½ cup sesame seeds
- ½ cup Brazil nuts
- ½ of a vanilla bean, split and scraped
- ¼ cup raw honey (optional)

In a blender, combine water, sesame seeds, and Brazil nuts and blend until liquefied. Strain liquid through a mesh filter or cheesecloth bag.

Return strained liquid to blender and add vanilla bean and honey (if using);
blend well.

Beyond the Spectrum

These recipes are great for supporting you both during and after a cleanse. The updated version of the Master Cleanser and the dairy-free rice and nut mylks should be standards in your repertoire.

≩ Radiance ≧

This is our version of the well-known "Master Cleanser." This version uses agave nectar in place of the traditional maple syrup. The lemon juice must be fresh squeezed—if the juice is not alive, this drink is just low-cal lemonade!

- Juice of 2 lemons
- 1 quart filtered water
- ¼ cup agave nectar
- ½ teaspoon Himalayan sea salt
- Pinch of cayenne pepper

In a blender, combine all ingredients and blend well. Keep a quart of this in your refrigerator during your cleanse. Enjoy between juices or as a simple replacement for some of the juices whenever extra energy or relief from detox events is needed, or when making fresh juice is just not possible.

Fresh Mylks

Enjoy these just as you would cow's milk: with your breakfast oats, on their own, or as a treat with one of our indulgent dessert recipes. You can use a little in your tea or simply drink it warm as part of a comforting and relaxing bedtime ritual.

≩ Almond Mylk ≧

Although almonds are called for here, you can experiment with cashews, walnuts, or Brazil nuts to make flavorful, enzyme-rich mylks that nourish and comfort.

- 1 cup almonds
- 3 cups filtered water
- 1 tablespoon raw honey
- 1 teaspoon vanilla extract
- Fresh nutmeg

In a blender, combine almonds and water and blend on high until mostly liquefied. Pour liquid through a mesh bag or cheesecloth to filter, squeezing out excess liquid.

Return liquid to blender. Add honey, vanilla extract, and nutmeg and blend well.

≩ Rice Mylk ≨

This is a wonderful choice for those who are allergic to nuts but still want some comfort. Warm this mylk as you would a baby bottle, placing a glass or a glass jar of it in a bowl of hot water for a few minutes.

- 1 cup organic rice (uncooked)
- 3 cups filtered water
- 1 cinnamon stick
- ¼ cup agave nectar

Soak the rice, water, and cinnamon stick overnight at room temperature. In a blender, combine all ingredients and blend on high speed until smooth. Pour through mesh filter or cheesecloth to strain.

Smoothies

Smoothies are filling and nutritious and take less time to whip up than you think. With the benefits of fruits, veggies, and the addition of E3Live® Cubes, they're as good as a meal!

≡ Trinity Ice Cubes ≡

At American Yogini we premix and store small batches of this simple recipe.

- 8 green apples
- 1 lemon, peeled
- 1 lime, peeled
- 2-inch piece of gingerroot, more or less to taste

Put all ingredients through the juicer. Freeze juice in ice cube trays. When frozen, remove from trays and store in an airtight, freezer-safe container. Use these cubes in juices to create instant smoothies or to chill or thicken any cleansing juice recipe.

≡ E3Live® Cubes ≡

E3Live® is an all-organic, wild-harvested aqua-botanical that is considered to be one of nature's most beneficial superfoods. It supports the immune, endocrine, nervous, gastrointestinal, and cardiovascular systems, providing sixty-four easily absorbed vitamins, minerals, and enzymes. It is nutrient dense and has more biologically active chlorophyll than any known food. It comes in a frozen liquid form that can be thawed in the refrigerator overnight. Visit our website at www.americanyogini.com for a link to this, our favorite superfood product.

Thaw E3Live® in your refrigerator. Pour carefully into ice cube trays and refreeze. Remove cubes from the tray as soon as possible and place them in a freezer-safe, airtight container to use when needed in the recipes below.

≡ Green Glow ≡

The color is gorgeous! And the taste is just . . . wow!

- 1 lime, peeled
- 4 green apples
- 1-inch piece of gingerroot, more or less to taste

- ½ cup fresh mint leaves
- ½ cup fresh chopped parsley
- ⅛ of an avocado

Put lime, apples, gingerroot, mint, and parsley through the juicer. In a blender, combine juice with avocado and blend on high until smooth.

≩ Pure Love ≨

I have a Pure Love smoothie every single day. I make it in large batches, as it easily becomes the base for any number of smoothies.

- 3 green apples
- 1-inch piece of gingerroot, more or less to taste
- 1 whole lemon, peeled and seeded
- 4 romaine lettuce leaves
- 1 kale leaf, torn, stem removed
- ¼ cup chopped cilantro and parsley leaves, measured together
- 1 cup fresh pineapple chunks (do not substitute canned!)
- 1 teaspoon seeded and chopped fresh chili pepper
- ½ cup water

Put apples, ginger, and lemon through the juicer. In a blender, combine juice with romaine, kale, cilantro and parsley, pineapple, and chili pepper. Blend on high until liquefied. Add water if you would like a thinner consistency.

≩ Frosty Joy ≨

Grab a Frosty Joy instead of coffee when you need a morning energy kick or midafternoon pick-me-up!

- 7 Trinity Ice Cubes (see recipe on page 216)
- 2 E3Live® Cubes (see recipe on page 216)
- 3 cups chopped romaine lettuce
- 1 small or ½ a large cucumber, peeled and seeded
- 7 frozen banana slices
- Filtered water

In a blender, combine Trinity Ice Cubes, E3Live® Cubes, romaine, cucumber, and frozen banana and blend on high, adding small amounts of water to reach your preferred consistency.

Yields 2 large servings. Share with someone you love and care about, or save one for later.

≩ Wild Abandon ≨

Could wild foods, aka "weeds," be our true superfoods? Victoria Boutenko, a pioneer raw food educator (www.rawfamily.com) thinks so, and I agree. Purslane grows everywhere in the continental United States and is absolutely delicious. It is sold at some farmers' markets—check your local CSA (community-sponsored agriculture) organization. It also contains more antioxidants than you can shake a stick at!

- 2 apples
- 2 pears, 1 peeled, cored, and sliced
- ½ of a lemon, peeled
- 1 cup chopped purslane
- ¼ cup arugula
- ¼ cup cold filtered water

Juice apples, the whole pear, and lemon. In a blender, combine juice with purslane, arugula, and the sliced pear. Blend well. Slowly add ¼ cup of water to reach your preferred consistency.

≩ Super Human ≨

With this many immune system–boosting antioxidants, this smoothie will make you feel like a superhero!

- 3 E3Live® Cubes (see recipe on page 216)
- 7 Trinity Ice Cubes (see recipe on page 216)
- 1 pint broccoli sprouts
- 1 stalk celery, chopped

- 1 cup peeled, seeded, and cubed cucumber
- Filtered water, as needed

In a blender, combine E3Live® Cubes, Trinity Ice Cubes, broccoli sprouts, celery, and cucumber and blend until smooth, adding filtered water a tablespoon at a time to reach your preferred consistency.

⋛ Pink Spring ⋚

Here on the East Coast, strawberries and rhubarb come into season at the same time. After the winter, we watch the miracle of their perennial offering and anticipate this delicious seasonal smoothie. Because they grow and ripen at the same time, they are like good friends together in this breakfast smoothie. It's a favorite post-yoga meal in the earliest days of summer.

Raw oats, which are called for in this recipe, are not easy to find, and you will probably have to go online to buy them. You can also substitute organic rolled oats—they are not really raw, but they are still a great, convenient option for protein.

- 1 stalk rhubarb
- 2 stalks celery
- 1-inch piece of gingerroot, more or less to taste
- 2–3 cups fresh or frozen strawberries
- ¼ cup raw oats

Put rhubarb, celery, and gingerroot through the juicer. In blender, combine juice, strawberries, and oats and blend on high until smooth.

Good Mylk Shakes

Can you really treat yourself to milk shakes? You certainly can when you indulge in delicious nut mylk! Almonds, cashews, hazelnuts, Brazil nuts, macadamia nuts, walnuts—they all make delicious, rich, nondairy mylk.

⋛ Bollywood Festival ⋚ ═══════════════════

Exotic and fresh, this mylk makes us feel like belly dancing! Make sure you specifically look for "young" coconut flesh and water. By the time a coconut falls from a tree, it is older, its flesh is harder, and it contains less water. Besides being highly nutritious, young coconuts also offer benefits for the heart, liver, and kidneys.

- ¼ cup young coconut flesh
- ¼ cup young coconut water
- 1½ cups basic almond mylk (see recipe on page 214)
- 7 frozen banana slices
- 1 cup frozen strawberries
- 1 teaspoon vanilla extract
- 1 cup frozen mango slices
- 2 tablespoons agave nectar, more to taste if the fruit is less sweet
- 2 teaspoons garam masala
- 1 teaspoon mild curry powder

In a blender, combine young coconut flesh, young coconut water, nut mylk, frozen banana slices, frozen strawberries, and vanilla extract and blend on high until smooth. Pour into a pitcher.

In a blender (no need to rinse blender after first use, as any leftover liquid will help these ingredients to blend better), combine frozen mango slices, agave nectar, garam masala, and curry powder. Blend on high until smooth.

To serve, fill a tall glass half full of the white mylk and top with some of the mango-spiced blend. Serve with Indian Bollywood music and garnish with cocktail umbrellas, fancy straws, and happy intentions.

MAKES 4 servings.

⋛ Chocolate Malted ⋚ ═══════════════════

This recipe takes me back to my childhood: a cold chocolate malted on a hot summer day. This shake provides you with emotional and nutritional fulfillment. After your cleanse, you will realize that each is just as important as the other. Enjoying treats like this is necessary for true health!

- 3 cups basic almond mylk (see recipe on page 214)
- 2 tablespoons raw almond butter
- 14 frozen banana slices
- ¼ cup raw cacao
- 2 tablespoons maca powder
- 2 teaspoons vanilla extract

In a blender, combine all ingredients and blend on high until creamy. Serve in a nostalgic ice cream soda glass with a paper soda fountain straw.

≡ Creamsicle ≣

A purely fun drink, this is cool, creamy, and refreshing.

Please note that it is important not to use more than a single drop of essential oil in any recipe. It is also important that you use only pharmaceutical-quality essential oils when using them to flavor foods. If you cannot find this precious oil, substitute with 1 teaspoon of orange extract.

- ¼ cup young coconut flesh, frozen if possible
- ¼ cup young coconut water
- 1 cup basic almond mylk (see recipe on page 214)
- 3 mandarin oranges, peeled and seeded
- 7 frozen banana slices
- 1 teaspoon vanilla extract
- 1 drop mandarin orange essential oil

In a blender, combine all ingredients and blend until creamy and smooth.

≡ Macanana ≣

The tastes of maca and banana are very friendly in this smoothie, which is reminiscent of a vanilla malted shake. Again, do not use more than a single drop of essential oil and be sure to use only pharmaceutical-quality essential oil; you may substitute with 1 teaspoon of orange extract if necessary.

- 2 heaping tablespoons maca powder
- 1 fresh banana (or 10 frozen banana slices for a colder, creamier shake)
- 2 cups basic almond mylk (see recipe on page 214)

- 3 medjool dates
- 1 teaspoon vanilla extract
- 1 teaspoon banana extract
- 1 drop vanilla essential oil

In a blender, combine maca powder, banana, almond mylk, and dates and blend until creamy. Add vanilla extract, banana extract, and a drop of vanilla essential oil. Blend well.

Raw, Semiraw, and Cooked Recipes for Before or After Your Cleanse

Humankind cannot live by juice alone, no matter how delicious and nutritious. So here are some tasty, healthy, cleansing recipes to enjoy any time you are not cleansing.

Breakfast

As they say, breakfast is the most important meal of the day. These power-packed, clean breakfasts will get you off to a great start, providing you with beautiful sun energy to illuminate your day.

⅀ Raw Porridge ⅀

As Goldilocks would say, this is "just right."

- 1 cup peeled, seeded, and cubed papaya
- 1 cup strawberries (reserve a few for topping)
- 1 teaspoon vanilla extract
- ¼ cup almonds, soaked overnight
- 4 sour green apples
- 1 sweet red apple
- Sprinkle of cinnamon

In a blender or food processor, blend the papaya, strawberries, and vanilla extract until smooth. Add almonds and pulse to chop. Add apples and continue to pulse until you have achieved a nice, chunky texture.

Serve this refreshing raw porridge in a bowl and top with fresh strawberries and a sprinkle of cinnamon.

MAKES 2 servings.

⋚ Superfood Breakfast Smoothie ⋚

This is so good. You'll be good to go the entire day without even getting hungry at lunchtime!

Any juice will do for this smoothie, so if you are planning on making it, try to remember to set aside a portion of any juice you make the day before.

- 1½ cups of juice
- ½ cup rolled oats
- 1 tablespoon tocotrenols
- 1 tablespoon lecithin
- 2 bananas
- 1 frozen packet of açai or 2 tablespoons açai powder
- 1 tablespoon of agave nectar
- 1 cup filtered water

In a blender, combine juice, rolled oats, tocotrenols, lecithin, bananas, açai, and agave nectar and blend until smooth. Slowly add small amounts of water to reach your preferred consistency.

Lunch or Dinner Plates

Any of these dishes are perfect for a hearty lunch, a delicious dinner, or to serve to guests. We serve them all the time to our guests at American Yogini Hohm.

⋛ Spaghetti Squash Several Ways ⋛ ═══════════

Natural food chef Shawn Williams offers this dish, which works well as either a side or a main course. It's perfect in any season.

- 1 medium-size spaghetti squash
- Salt and pepper to taste

Preheat oven to 350°F.

Cut squash in half. Place cut side down on a baking sheet and bake for thirty to forty-five minutes, until soft enough to pierce with a fork (skin will be slightly brown).

Use a fork to scrape the squash flesh out; it will look something like strands of spaghetti.

Toss the squash flesh with one of the toppings below—or, if you want to get crazy, divide the squash and have it a couple of different ways for variety.

MAKES a full meal for 1 person or a side dish for 2 to 4 people.

Suggested Toppings

➤ Drizzle with 1 or 2 tablespoons of extra-virgin olive oil or UDO's oil combined with 1 tablespoon of your favorite fresh herbs (sage, thyme, basil, and parsley all work well).

➤ Dice four or five tomatoes and cook in extra-virgin olive oil with garlic and a small amount of water to make a homemade marinara sauce; add fresh herbs if you wish.

➤ Top with ¼ to ½ cup of the Roasted Cherry Tomato and Zucchini Sauce recipe that follows.

⋛ Roasted Cherry Tomato and Zucchini Sauce ⋛ ═══════

This is a delicious summer dish and a wonderful way to celebrate an abundant offering of zucchini and tomatoes from the garden.

- 1 box of cherry tomatoes
- 1 zucchini
- 1 clove of garlic, chopped
- Olive oil

- Salt and pepper, to taste
- Fresh or dried herbs, capers, and/or olives (optional)

Preheat oven to 350°F.

Toss tomatoes, zucchini, and garlic with a little olive oil and salt and pepper and bake for about twenty minutes, or until the tomatoes are slightly blistered. Toss with herbs, capers, and/or olives if desired.

MAKES about 1½ cups.

≩ Raw "Tuna" Salad ≧

This recipe is one of my favorite fast snacks, and it also makes a complete and comforting meal when served with Carrot Lemon Soup (see recipe on page 233). It's the emotional equivalent of a tuna salad sandwich with cream of tomato soup, just like my mom made for me when I was a child.

- 2 stalks of celery
- 1 cup soaked almonds
- 1½ teaspoons Bragg's Liquid Aminos or Nama Shoyu soy sauce
- 1 tablespoon white miso
- 1 clove garlic

In a blender or food processor, combine all ingredients and blend until smooth. Serve on sliced circles of zucchini or stuffed inside celery sticks.

≩ Heirloom Tomato and Avocado Tartar ≧

My dear friends at New York's Candle Cafe offer this delicious and seasonal treat. Eat it as an appetizer or make a meal of it!

- ¼ pound oyster mushrooms
- 2–3 tablespoons extra-virgin olive oil (or enough to coat the mushrooms)
- Juice of 2½ lemons
- Salt and pepper, to taste
- 2 avocados
- 1 pound heirloom tomatoes, seeded and diced
- 2 cucumbers, peeled and diced

- 1 shallot, finely sliced
- ½ bunch scallions, finely sliced

Clean mushrooms by pulling them apart and gently wiping them with a damp cloth. Chop mushrooms into a medium-sized dice.

In a small bowl, combine mushrooms, olive oil, two tablespoons of the lemon juice, and salt and pepper. Set aside to marinate while preparing the remaining ingredients.

Cut the avocados in half. Carefully press the tip of a sharp knife into the avocado pit, twist, and pull gently to remove. Score the avocado flesh every ¼ inch, horizontally and vertically, cutting it into a medium-sized dice. Scoop flesh out of the peel with a large spoon and place into a bowl with the tomatoes, cucumbers, shallots, and scallions.

Add the mushrooms to the large bowl of prepared vegetables along with the remaining lemon juice. Add salt and pepper to taste.

Gently mix all ingredients with a large spoon, making sure not to mash the avocado. Enjoy!

MAKES 4 small appetizers or 2 meals.

⋛ Chickpea and Sweet Potato Curry ⋛

Laura Rosenberg (MS, RD, CDN) is a nutrition professional and a trained chef. She graciously offers some recipes she makes for herself after cleansing.

- 1 (15-ounce) can chickpeas or 1 cup dried chickpeas, soaked
- 5 cups peeled and diced sweet potato (about 1½ pounds)
- 1 tablespoon olive oil
- 1 tablespoon peeled and minced fresh gingerroot
- 3 cloves garlic, minced
- 2 carrots, diced
- 2 scallions, chopped
- 2 large tomatoes, diced (about 2 cups)
- 2 tablespoons curry powder
- 4 ounces coconut milk
- ⅓ cup chopped fresh cilantro
- Sea salt and pepper, to taste

If using dried, soaked chickpeas, they will need to be pressure-cooked, following manufacturer's instructions.

Steam sweet potatoes for ten minutes. Cover to keep warm and set aside.

Heat oil in a large skillet, and then add gingerroot, garlic, and carrots. Sauté for three minutes, and then add scallion, tomatoes, and curry powder. Cover and cook for three to five minutes on low heat.

Stir in chickpeas (if using canned, add the extra liquid in the can as well) and simmer uncovered for five minutes.

Add coconut milk and sweet potatoes. Cook on low heat, stirring gently, for two minutes. Add cilantro. Season with sea salt and pepper.

Serve over Coconut Quinoa (see recipe below).

MAKES 4 servings.

≣ Coconut Quinoa ≣

- 1 cup quinoa, well rinsed
- 6 ounces fresh young coconut milk
- 1 cup water
- 1 teaspoon sea salt

Toast quinoa in medium saucepan until dry and fragrant. Add coconut milk, water, and salt and bring to boil.

Simmer until done, about twenty to thirty minutes. Fluff with fork before serving.

MAKES 2 cups.

≣ Moroccan-Spiced Chickpea Cake ≣

I think the chefs at The Candle Cafe and Candle 79 are geniuses. It's just "love on a plate" as far as I'm concerned. If ever you are in New York, don't miss the chance to eat at either of these two restaurants. You'll probably see me there!

Continuing with meals inspired by exotic ingredients, this gluten-free dish from The Candle Cafe will transport you to your own Arabian nights.

- 3 cups cooked chickpeas (about 1½ cups uncooked)
- ½ cup chopped onions

- 8 tablespoons extra-virgin olive oil
- ½ cup chopped celery
- 1 tablespoon sea salt
- 1 tablespoon Old Bay spice
- 1 teaspoon cumin
- 1 teaspoon paprika
- 2 tablespoons chopped fresh parsley

To cook chickpeas, soak overnight and then boil in water for thirty to forty-five minutes.

Sauté onions in 4 tablespoons extra-virgin olive oil and let cool. Repeat with celery and the rest of the olive oil.

Blend chickpeas in food processor for five minutes, or until ground. Using a bowl, blend ground chickpeas with all other ingredients. Form mixture into cakes (about palm size). To serve, top chickpea cakes with vegetables, curry sauce, and toasted almonds and spoon apricot chutney alongside on plates (recipes follow).

MAKES 4 servings.

≣ Mixed Vegetables ≣

- 1 cup chopped white onion
- 1 cup diced Yukon gold potatoes
- 1 cup fresh corn
- 1 cup diced zucchini
- 1 cup extra-virgin olive oil, divided
- 1 teaspoon salt
- 1 tablespoon chopped fresh parsley

Sauté all ingredients separately, using 4 tablespoons of oil for each. Mix all ingredients.

MAKES about 4 servings.

≩ Red Pepper–Coconut Curry ≨

- 1 medium-sized white onion, chopped
- 4 tablespoons grapeseed oil
- 3 roasted red peppers, peeled and seeded
- 1 cup coconut milk (young coconut milk if possible)
- 1 teaspoon curry powder
- 1 teaspoon cumin
- 1 teaspoon sea salt
- 4 tablespoons chopped fresh cilantro
- 3 tablespoons tomato paste

Sauté chopped onion in grapeseed oil until soft. Let cool.

Mix all ingredients in a blender. Blend until smooth. Put into saucepan and reduce for ten to fifteen minutes on medium heat.

MAKES about 2 cups.

≩ Toasted Almonds ≨

- ½ cup sliced almonds

Toast almonds in a 350°F oven for ten minutes.

≩ Apricot Chutney ≨

- 1 cup chopped white onions
- 3 tablespoons grapeseed oil
- 3 cups diced apricots
- ¼ teaspoon salt
- 2 tablespoons agave nectar
- 2 tablespoons peeled and chopped fresh gingerroot
- ½ cup water

Sauté onions in grapeseed oil until soft. Add all other ingredients and reduce for twenty-five to thirty minutes on medium heat.

MAKES about 3 cups.

≡ Raw Zucchini "Pasta" ≡

A taste of Italy from right here at Hohm. . . . Serve with Favorite Sauce (recipe follows). The sauce is also great on zucchini disks or manna bread. Drizzle some extra UDO's oil or flaxseed oil over your pasta sauce before eating. Delicious!

- 1 or 2 fresh whole zucchinis, raw

Use a spiralizer to shave the zucchini into a basic pasta shape. Alternatively, make lots of long strips with a vegetable peeler, or shred on the French fry setting on a mandolin.

MAKES 2 servings.

≡ Favorite Sauce ≡

- 6 sundried tomatoes in oil, or dried, soaked for half an hour
- 1 pint cherry tomatoes
- ½ of a sweet red pepper, seeded
- ½ cup pine nuts, soaked in water for about three hours
- 1 or 2 cloves garlic, to taste
- 2 tablespoons Nama Shoyu soy sauce
- ½ cup fresh basil leaves
- ½ of a lemon, peeled and seeded
- Cayenne pepper and sea salt, to taste

In a blender, combine sundried and cherry tomatoes, sweet red pepper, pine nuts, garlic, soy sauce, basil, and lemon. Process until well blended. Adjust seasoning with cayenne and sea salt as desired.

MAKES 2 servings.

Soups

Whether hot or cold, soups are one of those foods that nourish us both inside and out. These recipes are just as tasty on hot summer days as they are on winter nights. With an abundant salad, any soup becomes a full meal. Remember to eat a raw salad at least as big, if not bigger, than your serving of cooked soup at mealtimes to round out the enzymes (although soup can be enjoyed alone as a satisfying snack as well).

≣ Live Cucumber and Avocado Soup ≣

My beautiful Candle Cafe friends offer this to us. I love this soup because I almost always have these ingredients on hand. Mint grows in my garden and avocados have gotten to be a kitchen staple. It's just so easy and so good.

- 8 cucumbers, roughly chopped
- 4 avocados, peels and pits removed
- 1 jalapeño pepper, seeds removed
- ½ bunch cilantro
- 1 sprig mint, stems removed
- Juice of 1 lime
- 2 tablespoons salt

FOR GARNISH
- 1 small radish, julienned
- 1 ear of sweet corn, kernels cut from ear
- ½ of a red bell pepper, seeded and julienned

In a high-speed blender, combine all ingredients and blend on high until well pureed (about one to two minutes).

Place a chinois-style strainer over a one- or two-quart container. Pass the puree through the strainer, pressing it through with a spatula if necessary. Taste and re-season as desired.

Garnish with radish, red pepper, and corn kernels. Enjoy!

MAKES 4 servings.

⋚ Butternut Squash Chestnut Soup ⋛

Another great recipe from our friends at The Candle Cafe—a spicy new take on a traditional holiday starter.

- 4 tablespoons olive oil
- 1 large leek, trimmed and chopped
- 1 cinnamon stick
- 1 whole nutmeg, halved
- 1 stalk lemongrass, chopped
- 2 cardamom pods or ½ teaspoon dried
- 1-inch slice of fresh gingerroot, peeled and chopped
- 1 dried chipotle pepper
- 2 large butternut squashes, peeled and diced
- 2 cups peeled chestnuts, fresh or frozen
- 2 tablespoons fresh sage or 1½ teaspoons dried
- 5 quarts filtered water
- 1 tablespoon pure maple syrup
- 1 teaspoon salt

In a large stockpot, heat olive oil. Add leek and sauté until soft, about ten minutes. While leek is sautéing, place cinnamon stick, nutmeg, lemongrass, cardamom pods, gingerroot, and chipotle pepper in a twelve-inch square of cheesecloth. Knot securely or tie with string to make a pouch and set aside.

Add butternut squash, chestnuts, sage, and the spice pouch to the pot. Add the water, making sure there is enough to cover the mixture by one to two inches. Bring to a simmer and reduce heat to low for thirty to forty-five minutes or until squash is tender and falls apart. Set aside to cool.

Discard pouch. Add maple syrup and salt. In a blender, puree soup until creamy. If consistency is too thick, add a small amount of water.

Garnish with Caramelized Pears (recipe follows) and maple syrup.

MAKES 6 servings.

⋚ Caramelized Pears ⋛

- 1 tablespoon grapeseed oil (or canola or safflower oil)
- 3 pears, peeled and diced

- 3 tablespoons pure maple syrup
- 1 teaspoon cinnamon powder
- 3 tablespoons balsamic vinegar

In a pan, quickly heat grapeseed oil on high. Add pears and sauté for five minutes. Reduce to medium heat and add maple syrup, cinnamon powder, and balsamic vinegar. Cook for ten to fifteen minutes until pears are soft and vinegar has become syrupy, coating pears. Set aside to cool.

MAKES 6 garnishes.

≣ Carrot Lemon Soup ≣

Don't be intimidated by the idea of "decorating" the top of your soup—it's just fun, like painting with your condiments. This is the way we serve all the raw soups here: with an explosion of tastes placed on top just before serving. It makes every spoonful like a party in your mouth!

- 6–10 carrots
- 1 lemon, peeled
- 1 avocado, peeled and cubed
- ¼ cup chopped dill

FOR GARNISH
- 3 tablespoons chopped dill
- Cayenne pepper, to taste
- Roasted pumpkin seed oil
- UDO's 3-6-9 oil
- Nama Shoyu soy sauce
- Nasturtium blossoms (optional)

Put carrots and lemon through the juicer.

Reserve half of avocado and place the other half in the blender along with the chopped dill and the carrot-lemon juice and blend well.

To serve, ladle soup into soup bowls, place reserved avocado cubes in center of soup, and garnish with chopped dill and a careful sprinkle of deep red cayenne pepper. Finish with decorative drizzles of the dark amber pumpkin seed oil, the lighter golden UDO's oil, and a few more drops of dark brown Nama Shoyu. Set nasturtium blossoms alongside of bowl. Beautiful!

MAKES 4 appetizers or 2 meals.

⋛ Cauliflower Soup with Truffle Oil ⋛

I love it that chef and friend Laura Rosenberg lives and works nearby because she always has great things to do with the abundance of cauliflower we harvest in the fall. And she's so practical: many of her recipes can be made ahead using high-quality packaged goods.

- 2 tablespoons extra-virgin olive oil
- 1 leek, white part only, finely chopped
- 1 pound cauliflower florets (about 5 cups)
- 2 (14.5-ounce) cartons of vegetable broth
- Salt and pepper, to taste
- 1 teaspoon white truffle oil or extra-virgin olive oil
- 1 tablespoon thinly sliced chives

Heat olive oil in a heavy, large pot over medium heat. Add leek and sauté until tender, about eight minutes.

Add cauliflower and sauté two minutes. Add broth. Cover and simmer until cauliflower is tender, about twenty-five minutes.

Working in batches, transfer soup to blender and puree until smooth. Return soup to pot.

Season to taste with salt and pepper. Ladle soup into bowls. Drizzle with truffle oil and garnish with chives.

Soup can be prepared one day ahead, cooled slightly, and then covered and refrigerated. To serve, bring soup to simmer.

MAKES 6 servings.

⋛ Vegetable Soup with Quinoa ⋛

Cooked soups are comforting in cold or rainy weather. Here is another one from Rosenberg, my go-to girl for cold-weather seasonal cooked foods.

- 1 large onion, diced
- 2 carrots, diced
- 2 ribs celery, diced
- 4 cloves garlic, minced
- 1 small sweet potato, diced
- 1 small rutabaga or parsnip, diced
- 3 tablespoons extra-virgin olive oil
- 8 cups vegetable stock (or substitute Essential Potassium-Rich Broth; see recipe on page 43)
- ½ cup quinoa, well rinsed
- 1 cup string beans, cut in 2-inch pieces
- ½ cup chopped spinach, kale, or chard
- Sea salt and fresh pepper, to taste

In a large stockpot, sauté onion, carrots, celery, garlic, sweet potatoes, and ruta-baga or parsnip in olive oil for eight to ten minutes over medium heat. Add stock and reduce heat to simmer.

Add rinsed quinoa and cook for about fifteen minutes.

Add beans and spinach, kale, or chard and cook until vegetables are just soft-ened, about three to five minutes.

Season with sea salt and fresh pepper.

MAKES 6 servings.

≡ Break-Fast Miso ≡

Not a breakfast soup, this is a light meal for the day you break your fast. Warm, nourishing, and easy to digest, this is one of my favorite pick-me-ups whether I have been fasting before I make it or not.

Instant, dehydrated sea veggies, which are called for in this recipe, can be found in most natural food stores; if you cannot find mixed dried sea vegeta-bles, try arame (seaweed), which is more readily found.

- ¼ cup chickpea miso
- 1 teaspoon tahini
- 1 teaspoon mixed dried sea vegetables

- 1 scallion, thinly sliced (white part and part of green)
- 1 medium to large baby bella mushroom, sliced
- Squeeze of lemon juice

Put miso and tahini into a large soup bowl. Mix in a small amount of warm water until paste dissolves. Add the sea vegetables, scallion, and mushroom, and then stir in hot water until bowl is full. Allow to "rest" for about three to five minutes—the perfect amount of time to take some long, deep breaths into your belly—and add lemon just before eating.

MAKES 1 serving.

≡ Break-Fast Vegetable Soup ≡

This is a favorite—a soul-nourishing, half-raw, half-cooked soup. The root vegetables are quickly cooked and served with an abundant amount of raw herbs.

- 1 red onion
- 1 stalk celery
- 1 carrot
- 1 parsnip
- 1 small yam
- Extra-virgin olive oil (enough to sauté vegetables)
- 1 quart filtered water
- Handful finely chopped fresh herbs (try parsley, cilantro, thyme, or oregano)
- Sea salt and pepper, to taste
- Squeeze of lemon juice

Chop onion, celery, carrot, and parsnip into a small, uniform dice. Chop the yam into one-inch cubes. Sauté all the vegetables in olive oil until onions are transparent, three to five minutes.

Add the water and bring to a boil, then immediately turn heat down to low, cover tightly, and simmer about ten minutes more.

Ladle into bowls and top with the fresh herbs, salt and pepper to taste, a squeeze of lemon juice, and a drizzle of extra-virgin olive oil.

MAKES 4 servings.

Salads and Dressings ....

Salad has become my favorite and most desired staple meal. This is partly so because I am often too busy to prepare an elaborate meal, and salads are the easiest way to create a completely nutritious raw meal. Truly, it's the most delicious and fun to eat meal I could wish for. When I feel really hungry and have that "need food right now" feeling, being able to make a quick salad is how I ensure I'm always just a few minutes away from a satisfying meal.

The key to being able to create interesting and varied salads on demand is to prepare components, keep them handy in the refrigerator, and then simply assemble the flavors you are yearning for. When I do my produce shopping, I take the time to prewash, pre-chop, pre-dice, and pre-shred anything that I pick up that day. Then I store each veggie in separate airtight containers or, more often, use serving bowls with dinner or dessert plates turned upside down as a cover. In this way I can avoid using plastic or foil, placing less stress on our natural environment. If we acknowledge our natural world—if only during our cleanse time—our natural world will take care of us.

When you dress your salads with interesting, fresh dressings made with cold-processed oils and fresh, raw, living ingredients, you get the bonus of a nutrient-dense antioxidant infusion that balances your body, staves off cravings, and keeps your body in a perfect state of naturally cleansing itself.

The sky's the limit when creating delicious healthy salads. Let your imagination and your cravings guide you as you consider any of the following combinations:

➤ Butterhead lettuce with broccoli and alfalfa sprouts

➤ Mesclun mix with sliced avocados, sliced tomatoes, and chopped soaked almonds

➤ Mesclun mix with basil, mint, and cilantro leaves, shredded carrots, and julienned sweet pepper (this combination is particularly good with Thai Half-Cup Dressing; recipe on page 241)

➤ Mono-mixes of plain romaine lettuce, spinach, and butterhead lettuce let you really taste the flavors of the dressings

➤ Go traditional: mesclun mix with cherry tomatoes and cucumber

➤ Toss julienned cucumber, jicama, and carrots over butterhead lettuce

➤ Tri colored: arugula, endive, and red leaf lettuce

➤ My favorite is the "Big Meal" salad with everything but the kitchen sink: mesclun mix, shredded carrots, shredded beets, chopped tomatoes, chopped cucumber, sliced avocado, sweet onion, mixed chopped mushrooms, sprouts, and—why not?—pignoli nuts or chopped presoaked almonds

⊰ Mexican Salad with Fiesta Dressing ⊱

My daughter, Harriet Halloway, is not only a comic but also a professionally trained chef. She knows I love salads so she's always coming up with new tastes like this one.

- 4 cups chopped romaine lettuce
- 1 cucumber, roughly chopped
- ½ cup fresh corn kernels
- 1 tomato, roughly chopped
- ½ of an avocado, diced
- ½ cup finely chopped fresh cilantro
- 2 tablespoons UDO's oil

In a large bowl, toss all salad ingredients with UDO's and Fiesta Dressing (recipe follows).

FIESTA DRESSING
- Juice of 2 limes
- ½ cup extra-virgin olive oil
- 1 clove garlic
- 1 teaspoon sea salt
- ¼ cup filtered water
- 2 tablespoons chopped red onion
- 1 teaspoon chopped chili pepper

In a blender, combine all dressing ingredients and blend on low speed until well combined.

MAKES 2 main course salads.

⇛ Mesclun Salad with Roasted Beets, Caramelized Onion, Spiced Pecans, and Champagne Vinaigrette ⇚

Laura Rosenberg again! I have been cleansing so long that I now prefer the taste of raw beets. I tried this recipe with thinly sliced raw beets in place of the roasted ones and found it to be fantastic. If you want more enzymes, you can use raw beets too; just slice them paper-thin with a mandolin.

- 4 medium beets
- 6 tablespoons olive oil
- Sea salt to taste
- 2 large onions, sliced thin
- ½ cup whole pecans
- 2 tablespoons pure maple syrup
- 1 tablespoon canola oil
- 1 teaspoon tamari
- ⅛ teaspoon cinnamon
- Pinch cayenne pepper
- 1 pound mesclun, baby spinach, or arugula

Preheat oven to 400°F.

Trim and wash beets. Toss with 3 tablespoons olive oil and salt. Place on a parchment-paper-lined baking sheet and bake for thirty to forty-five minutes, until soft.

Slowly caramelize onions in the remaining olive oil in a large sauté pan until golden brown.

Remove beets from oven. Put in a bowl and cover with plastic wrap. Let cool. Peel and cut beets into one-inch dice, slices, or wedges as preferred.

Toss pecans with maple syrup, canola oil, tamari, cinnamon, and cayenne. Bake in 350°F oven on a parchment-paper-lined baking sheet for ten minutes. Check often to prevent burning. Rough chop when cool.

In a large bowl, toss mesclun with vinaigrette (see recipe below). Top with diced beets, onions, and pecans.

CHAMPAGNE VINAIGRETTE
- ¼ cup champagne vinegar
- 1 shallot, finely diced
- 1 tablespoon pure maple syrup
- 1 teaspoon sea salt
- 1 tablespoon Dijon mustard
- ¾ cup extra-virgin olive oil

Put vinegar and shallot in a bowl and let sit for ten minutes. Add maple syrup, salt, and mustard and whisk. Stream in olive oil slowly, whisking to combine.

MAKES 4 servings.

Dressings

Dressings are just as important as the salad when eating raw foods. Choosing quality ingredients and living, high-nutrient oils turns salad dressing into the equivalent of a vitamin supplement. Store these dressings in clean glass jars so you can quickly see what you want and shake it together in seconds. You can even use these same jars to make these recipes, rather than a blender.

⧽ Hohm's House Dressing ⧼

This is the dressing we offer for our pre-fast welcome salad. Here's the recipe, from our "Hohm" to yours.

- ¼ cup UDO's 3-6-9 oil
- ½ cup extra-virgin olive oil
- ⅔ cup fresh-squeezed lemon juice
- ⅔ cup fresh-squeezed orange juice
- 1 teaspoon minced gingerroot
- ¼ cup chickpea miso
- 1 tablespoon Nama Shoyu soy sauce

In a blender or glass jar, combine all ingredients and blend (or gently shake) until well combined.

Makes about 2½ cups.

⋛ Harriet's Basil Lime Dressing ⋛

My daughter Harriet, an excellent chef, makes this dressing when she visits me. We always have lots of fresh basil in the garden. Spoon this over fresh tomatoes from the garden or enjoy it on plain mixed lettuces or healthy sandwiches in place of mayonnaise.

- 1 cup fresh basil leaves
- 1 clove garlic
- 1 tablespoon peeled and grated fresh gingerroot (about a 1-inch piece)
- 1 cup lime juice
- 1½ cups extra-virgin olive oil
- Sea salt and black pepper

In a blender, combine basil, garlic, gingerroot, and lime juice and blend until liquid. On low speed, add olive oil until emulsified. Season to taste with salt and pepper.

Makes about 3 cups.

⋛ Thai Half-Cup Dressing ⋛

Half a cup of everything for a taste that is halfway to heaven.

- ½ cup fresh basil
- ½ cup fresh mint
- ½ cup fresh cilantro
- ½ cup sesame oil
- ½ cup pineapple juice
- ½ cup lime juice
- Fresh jalapeño pepper, to taste
- Nama Shoyu soy sauce, to taste

In a blender, combine all ingredients and blend until liquid. Add water if you prefer a thinner consistency.

MAKES about 3 cups.

⋛ Mary's Basil Lime Dressing ⋚ ━━━━━━━━━━━━━━━

Harriet's not the only one in our family that appreciates our abundant summer crop of basil! My recipe using fragrant basil and tart lime is a household favorite.

- 1 cup fresh basil leaves
- 1 clove garlic
- ¼ cup Nama Shoyu soy sauce
- Juice of 2 Granny Smith apples
- Juice of 2 limes
- 1½ cups extra-virgin olive oil
- Drizzle of UDO's 3-6-9 oil

In a blender, combine basil, garlic, and soy sauce with apple and lime juices and blend until completely liquefied. Put the blended mixture into a glass jar with a tightly fitting lid, add the olive oil and UDO's, and shake gently until well mixed.

MAKES about 2½ cups.

⋛ Healthier Italian Dressing ⋚ ━━━━━━━━━━━━━━━

Sweet and savory with healthy garlic and herbs. Mangia!

- 1 or 2 medjool dates, pitted
- ½ cup balsamic vinegar
- 1 cup extra-virgin olive oil
- 1 clove garlic, minced
- ¼ cup chopped fresh oregano or 1 tablespoon dried
- ½ cup finely chopped parsley

In a blender, combine dates with vinegar and blend until smooth. Pour into a glass jar and add olive oil, garlic, oregano, and parsley. Shake until fully combined.

MAKES about 2 cups.

⋚ Lemon-Orange Miso Dressing ⋚ ══════════════

A dressing to tempt your taste buds, based on my five-pointed star of tastes.

- Juice of 1 lemon
- Juice of 1 orange
- 1-inch piece of gingerroot, juiced
- ¼ cup chickpea miso
- 3 tablespoons Nama Shoyu soy sauce
- ½ cup olive oil

In a blender, combine lemon, orange, and gingerroot juices with miso and soy sauce and blend well. Slowly add oil at medium speed until dressing is creamy.

MAKES about 1½ cups.

⋚ Tarragon Lemon Shallot Dressing ⋚ ══════════════

A quick, easy, and elegant recipe that is a subtly flavorful way to dress almost any salad.

- 1 cup extra-virgin olive oil
- Juice of 1 lemon
- 1 teaspoon apple cider vinegar
- 1 tablespoon Nama Shoyu soy sauce
- 1 tablespoon agave nectar
- 1 tablespoon chopped tarragon
- 3 tablespoons minced shallot

In a blender, combine olive oil, lemon juice, apple cider vinegar, soy sauce, and agave nectar and blend slowly. Pour mixture into a glass jar and add chopped tarragon and shallot. Shake until well mixed.

MAKES about 1½ cups.

Desserts

When desserts are made with conscious care and adhere to the principles of *ahimsa*, they really serve you well. Every ingredient is nourishing; there are no excessive sugars that are void of nutritional currency in these desserts. Every bite offers valuable sun energy, so you will be nourished, satisfied, and not likely to overindulge. Cleansers always love dessert!

⋛ Chocolate Mousse Pie ⋚

This rich-tasting, luxurious Chocolate Mousse Pie from The Candle Cafe is great for any occasion. For an excellent variation, make it with a combination of chocolate and peanut butter chips.

There are a few ingredients in this recipe that you may not be familiar with, including kuzu, an organic root starch used as a thickener. What a delicious way to give it a try!

PIECRUST
- 1 cup spelt flour
- ¼ cup cocoa powder
- ¼ cup sucanat
- 1 teaspoon baking powder
- 1 teaspoon baking soda
- ½ cup soy milk
- ½ cup maple syrup
- ¼ cup safflower oil
- ½ cup water
- ½ teaspoon vanilla extract
- ¼ teaspoon almond extract
- 2 tablespoons chocolate chips

CHOCOLATE MOUSSE
- 2¼ cups chocolate chips
- 1 cup plus 2 tablespoons vanilla soy milk
- ½ teaspoon cocoa powder
- ½ teaspoon kuzu

- 1¼ blocks (20 ounces) silken tofu
- ¼ cup pure maple syrup
- 2 teaspoons vanilla extract
- 1 teaspoon almond extract

Preheat the oven to 325°F.

To prepare the crust: Mix the flour, cocoa powder, sucanat, baking powder, and baking soda together in a large mixing bowl. In another bowl combine the soy milk, maple syrup, oil, water, and vanilla and almond extracts. Add the wet ingredients to the flour mixture and stir well to combine. Pour the mixture into a baking pan and bake for thirty-five minutes. Let baked dough cool in the refrigerator for about an hour.

Crumble the baked dough and press the crust crumbs into a nine-inch pie plate. Sprinkle with chocolate chips.

To prepare the mousse filling: Place chocolate chips, 1 cup of soy milk, and cocoa powder in a bowl. Dissolve kuzu in the remaining 2 tablespoons of soy milk and add to mixture. Place the mixture in a double boiler and heat over simmering water on medium heat, stirring occasionally, until melted. Transfer to a mixing bowl and let cool slightly.

Place the tofu in a blender and blend until smooth. Add the maple syrup and vanilla and almond extracts and blend again. Fold into the chocolate mixture until well blended.

Pour the chocolate mixture into the piecrust and chill two hours or overnight before serving.

MAKES 1 nine-inch pie.

⧭ Chocolate Truffles ⧭

Chocolate? Truffles? What's not to love? These special treats make an elegant presentation after a meal. Or savor their sophisticated flavor with a special beverage when you are feeling indulgent.

- 1 (16-ounce) jar of raw sunflower seed butter
- 1 cup organic raw chocolate powder
- 1 cup raw agave nectar
- 1 teaspoon maca powder

- 2 teaspoons vanilla extract
- 1 drop vanilla essential oil
- ¼ teaspoon cayenne pepper
- 1 pinch of Himalayan sea salt

GARNISH POSSIBILITIES
- Strawberry slices
- Coconut flakes
- Macadamia nuts
- Grated orange rind
- Fresh thyme sprigs

In a food processor, blend all ingredients until smooth.

Press into a decorative mold—I use a tiny heart-shaped one—then turn out of mold right away onto a parchment-paper-covered cookie sheet. Continue until all the dough has been used. Garnish—use your imagination!—and enjoy.

MAKES about 3 dozen truffles, depending on the size of the mold.

⅀ Chocolate Fudgesicles ⅀

This recipe takes me back to my childhood. Cold, chocolatey, and completely delicious, not to mention full of heart-healthy fats and antioxidants!

- 1 avocado, peel and pit removed
- ½ cup raw cacao powder (use a little more for a really intense fudge taste)
- ½ cup agave nectar
- 1 teaspoon vanilla extract

In a blender, combine all ingredients and blend until smooth. Pour into popsicle molds and freeze. They're ready when you are and they are the best fudgesicles you have ever tasted!

MAKES 4 fudgesicles.

Recommended Books, Music, and Other Resources

Books ....

The following list represents books that would be perfect bedtime reading during your cleanse, and others that would best be read following your cleanse for continued education and inspiration. Please save cookbooks and books about food for after your cleanse has ended, as books about food will drain energy from you that should be used for cleansing your bodymind. Enjoy books from the first list during the cleanse and books from the second list in the days following your cleanse so you can truly feel what it is like to energize yourself with sheer positivity rather than thoughts about food.

Books for the Days of Your Cleanse

A New Earth: Awakening to Your Life's Purpose by Eckhart Tolle
Lifting the Veil: Practical Kabbalah with Kundalini Yoga by Gurunam (Joseph Michael Levy)
Bringing Yoga to Life: The Everyday Practice of Enlightened Living by Donna Farhi
Nonviolent Communication: A Language of Life by Marshall B. Rosenberg
The poems of Rumi (There are many collections available, and all of the poetry is beautiful and meaningful.)

The Artist's Way: A Spiritual Path to Higher Creativity by Julia Cameron

The Hidden Messages in Water by Masaru Emoto and David A. Thayne

The Eight Human Talents: Restore the Balance and Serenity Within You with Kundalini Yoga by Gurmukh

The Book of Understanding: Creating Your Own Path to Freedom by Osho

Meditations from the Mat: Daily Reflections on the Path of Yoga by Rolf Gates and Katrina Kenison

Books for After Your Cleanse

Animal, Vegetable, Miracle: A Year of Food Life by Barbara Kingsolver, Camille Kingsolver, and Steven L. Hopp

Skinny Bitch: A No-Nonsense, Tough-Love Guide for Savvy Girls Who Want to Stop Eating Crap and Start Looking Fabulous by Rory Freedman and Kim Barnouin

The Omnivore's Dilemma: A Natural History of Four Meals by Michael Pollan

In Defense of Food: An Eater's Manifesto by Michael Pollan

Raw Food Life Force Energy: Enter a Totally New Stratosphere of Weight Loss, Beauty, and Health by Natalia Rose

Eating for Beauty by David Wolfe

Conscious Eating by Gabriel Cousens

Depression-Free for Life: A Physician's All-Natural, 5-Step Plan by Gabriel Cousens

Cookbooks

Fresh: The Ultimate Live-Food Cookbook by Sergei Boutenko and Valya Boutenko

The Candle Cafe Cookbook: More than 150 Enlightened Recipes from New York's Renowned Vegan Restaurant by Joy Pierson, Bart Potenza, and Barbara Scott-Goodman

I Am Grateful: Recipes and Lifestyle of Café Gratitude by Terces Engelhart

Everyday Raw by Matthew Kenney

The Raw 50: 10 Amazing Breakfasts, Lunches, Dinners, Snacks, and Drinks for Your Raw Food Lifestyle by Carol Alt

Rainbow Green Live-Food Cuisine by Gabriel Cousens and the Tree of Life Café Chefs

Websites

www.juicecleanse.com. This is the official website of the American Yogini Hohm Juice Cleanse. It features recipes, resources, advice, and support for your cleanse. I have included every option I could think of to make undertaking and completing a juice cleanse as easy as possible. For example, you can join an online community of cleansers or order fresh juices to be delivered to your door.

www.rawchef.com. This is the website of my first raw chef teacher, and one of the greatest raw food chefs in the world, Chad Sarno.

www.sacrednourishment.com. This is the website of Alison Shore Gaines, who has been my guide through countless cleansing juice fasts for years. She has also created a wonderful CD with brilliant guided meditations for conscious eating.

www.treeoflife.nu. The official website of the Tree of Life Rejuvenation Center run by Dr. Gabriel Cousens, a pioneer in raw food and spiritual nutrition.

www.matthewkenney.com. The website of Dr. Matthew G. Kenney, a world-famous chef and entrepreneur who is always opening new restaurants and launching new raw food products. Visit his inspiring website to keep up with what's new and where to go to find great raw food.

www.rawfamily.com. The official website of the Boutenko family, also known as the Raw Family. I love their homey newsletters, which always offer super simple recipes.

www.greennapkinchefs.com. The official website of Laura Rosenberg (MS, RD, CDN), who is a nutrition professional and a trained chef. Some of her delicious, healthful recipes have been re-created in this book.

CDs and Daily Playlists

I have consciously included only instrumental music or music not in a Western language for these daily playlists. This is so that your mind can benefit from positive and cleansing vibrations without having to process any information. Because these sounds are foreign and different, they will put you into a "beginner's mind" and prime your cells for opening up to change in a safe and loving way.

Chakra 1: Earth

Wake Up/Early Morning

"A Path to Solitude" from *Forest Piano* by Dan Gibson
"Hymn to the Old Growth" from *Forest Piano* by Dan Gibson

Yoga and Personal Time

"Om Nama Shivaya" from *Pilgrim Heart* by Krishna Das
"Thunder" from *Didgeridoo Trance Dance* (Vol. 1) by Andy Graham
"Tempo" from *Percussions d'Afrique: African Drums* by Madou Djembé
"Hand Drums with Guitars" from *Skatetunes* by Dave Metty
"Pemulwuy Returns" from *Feet in the Soil* by James Asher

Meditation and Relaxation

"Aad Guray Nameh" from *Prem* by Snatam Kaur
"Death Theme from *The Untouchables*" from *Yo-Yo Ma Plays Ennio Morricone* by Yo-Yo Ma

Chakra 2: Water

Wake Up/Early Morning

"Dreaming by the Stream" from *Forest Piano* by Dan Gibson
"Slow Belly Dance Drums" from *Drums of the World* by Various Artists

Yoga and Personal Time

"Gopinatha" from *Devotion* by Rasa

"Arati" from *Devotion* by Rasa

"Jaya Radhe" from *Temple of Love* by Rasa

"Quiet 3" from *Quiet* by Sheila Chandra

"Guajira Bonita" from *Music from the Coffee Lands* by Various Artists

Meditation and Relaxation

"Water 01" from *Waterscapes* by Dan Gibson

"Om Shanti" from *Jala* by Daphne Tse and Matt Pszonak

"Children (Lake)" from *The Harmony of Feng Shui* by Corciolli

For Belly Dancing

"Hips Don't Lie" from *Oral Fixation vol. 2* by Shakira

"Aaj Mera Jee Kardaa (Today My Heart Desires)" from the sound-track of the film *Monsoon Wedding* by Mychael Danna

For Your Daily Meditation (Loop the Following Three Songs Consecutively)

"Hold Me, I'm Falling" from the soundtrack of the film *Monsoon Wedding* by Mychael Danna

"Love and Marigolds" from the soundtrack of the film *Monsoon Wedding* by Mychael Danna

"Good Indian Girls" from the soundtrack of the film *Monsoon Wedding* by Mychael Danna

Chakra 3: Fire

Wake Up/Early Morning

"Iyawo" from *Mulatos* by Omar Sosa

"Bolo Ram" from *Jai Jai Jai* by Wah!

Yoga and Personal Time

"Lovers of Light" from *Volume 2: Release* by Afro-Celt Sound System

"Kakou" from *Music from the Coffee Lands* by Various Artists

"Wassiye" from *Ma Ya* by Habib Koite and Bamada

Meditation and Relaxation

"My Three Notes" from *Omar Omar* by Omar Sosa

Chakra 4: All Elements Are Contained Within— and Indeed Sourced from—the Heart

Wake Up/Early Morning

"Suite" from the soundtrack of the film *Mona Lisa Smile* by Rachel Portman

"Morning Arrival in Goa" from *Santa Fe Sessions* by Ottmar Liebert

Yoga and Personal Time

"Suni-ai (Listening Celebration)" from *Shanti* by Snatam Kaur

"Ong Sohung (I am Thou, I am Peace)" from *Shanti* by Snatam Kaur

Meditation and Relaxation

"Opening" from *The Best of Wah!* by Wah!

"Desire" (instrumental version) from *A Gift of Love* by Deepak Chopra and Friends

"Lovers Passion" from *A Gift of Love* by Deepak Chopra and Friends

"Intoxicated by Love" from *A Gift of Love* by Deepak Chopra and Friends

Chakra 5: Air

Wake Up/Early Morning

"Prelude in E Minor" by Chopin (available on various recordings)

"Concerto in A Minor for Recorder" by Vivaldi (from *Vivaldi: 14 Concertos for Mandolin, Flute, Trumpet, etc.* by Phillip Picket and New London Consort)

"Concerto in G Minor for Recorder" by Vivaldi (from *Vivaldi: 14 Concertos for Mandolin, Flute, Trumpet, etc.* by Phillip Picket and New London Consort)

Yoga and Personal Time

"Truth" from *Sapphire Skies* by Mick Rossi and Dr. Jeffrey Thompson

"American Beauty" from the soundtrack of the film *American Beauty* by Thomas Newman

For Kirtan (Call-and-Response)

"Govinda Hare" from *Pilgrim Heart* by Krishna Das

"Om Nama Shivaya" from *Pilgrim Heart* by Krishna Das

"Gobinda Gobinda Hari Hari" from *Prem* by Snatam Kaur

Meditation and Relaxation

"Children" from *Cello Blue* by David Darling

For Silent Practice

"Sounds of Perfection: Ocean Waves" from *Music for Deep Sleep* from Inner Splendor Media

"Three Buddahs" from *Singing Bowls* by Xumantra

Chakra 6: Ether

Wake Up/Early Morning

"Little Sparrow Reprise" from *Little Sparrow* by Dolly Parton (This short but gorgeous instrumental version of the song "Little Sparrow" is only one minute and thirty-seven seconds long; you will want to set your player to repeat this at least three to five times.)

Yoga and Personal Time

"Rag Shivarangani" from *Luminous Ragas* by Steve Gorn

"Rag Desh" from *Luminous Ragas* by Steve Gorn

"Rag Chandrakauns" from *Luminous Ragas* by Steve Gorn

"Indian Nights" from *Luminous Ragas* by Steve Gorn

Meditation and Relaxation

"Rain Forest" from *Spirits in the Wind* by Tsa'Ne Do'se

Chakra 7: Higher Consciousness

Wake Up/Early Morning

"Prayer" from *Sapphire Skies* by Mick Rossi and Dr. Jeffrey
  Thompson

Yoga and Personal Time

"Singing Winds Crying Beasts" from *Abraxas* by Santana
"Samba Pa'Ti" from *Ultimate Santana* by Santana

Meditation and Relaxation

"Ritual Movement" from *Tibetan Gongs and Atmospheres* by Tibetan
  Gongs

Index

Seventh Gate (juice), 211–12
Sexuality, thoughts and fears about,
 74–75, 76
Shakira, 73
Shirodhara hair conditioning
 experience, 150–52
 materials, 140
Shower meditation, 165
 experience, 170–72
 materials, 158–60
Siddhartha, 150
Sitali pranayam. See Breath of Fire
Sixth (brow) chakra, 137–53
 bedtime ritual, 153
 characteristics of, 8, 137
 cleansing events, 140–41
 creative inspiration (constructing),
  147–48
 creative inspiration (materials), 139
 external beauty indulgence
  (experience), 150–52
 external beauty indulgence (materials),
  140
 free time, 149
 grocery list and juice recipe,
  138–39
 yoga and meditation for, 142–47
Skin (cleansing events), 30–31
Slippery elm tea, 121
Smooth Move tea, 179
Smoothies (recipes), 215–19
 Deep Blue Break-Fast, 139
 E3Live® Cubes, 216
 Frosty Joy, 217–18
 Green Glow, 216–17
 Pink Spring, 219
 Pure Love, 217
 Super Human, 218–19
 Superfood Breakfast, 223
 Trinity Ice Cubes, 216
 Violet Brazil Nut, 157
 Wild Abandon, 218
Solar plexus chakra. *See* Third (solar
 plexus) chakra
Solé, 38
 cleansing with, 122, 132, 133
 in daily ritual, 58, 74, 91, 106, 123, 141,
  161
 preparation and administration of,
  41–42
Solid foods, incorporating, 137–38,
 155–56

Soup(s), 231–36
 Butternut Squash Chestnut, 232
 Carrot Lemon, 233–34
 Cauliflower, with Truffle Oil, 234
 Cucumber and Avocado, 231
 Miso, Break-Fast, 235–36
 Vegetable, Break-Fast, 236
 Vegetable, with Quinoa, 234–35
Soy sauce, raw, 188
Space, creating, 11, 14
Spaghetti Squash Several Ways, 224
Spelt flour, 188
Spiderweb
 constructing, 147–48
 materials, 139
Spontaneity (juice), 203
Squash
 Butternut, Soup, Chestnut and, 232
 Spaghetti, Several Ways, 224
Squatting poses, 59–60
Stability (juice), 196
Stafford, William, 148
Stevia, 44
Subtle body, 13
Sucanat®, 188
Suffering, diminishing, 4–5
Sugar, eliminating, 37, 38, 44, 178
Super Human (smoothie), 218–19
Superfood Breakfast Smoothie, 223
Survival (juice), 197
Sweet Potato and Chickpea Curry,
 226–27
Symptoms of cleansing. *See* Cleansing
 events

Tabletop pose, 109–10
Tadasana, 142
Tapas, 4
Tarragon Lemon Shallot Dressing, 243
Tartar, Tomato and Avocado, 225
Tea(s), 44, 56, 73, 89, 105, 121, 139, 158
Tea tree oil, 31
Teeccino brand grain beverage, 178
Television, avoiding, 68, 132, 152, 175
Thai Half-Cup Dressing, 241–42
Third eye, 137, 138, 146
Third (solar plexus) chakra, 87–102
 bedtime ritual, 102
 characteristics of, 8, 87
 cleansing events, 90–91
 creative inspiration (materials), 89
 creative inspiration (writing), 98

About the Author

MARY MCGUIRE-WIEN IS A yogini, dancer, and businesswoman. A classically trained ballet dancer, she spent her teens and early twenties dancing professionally. After the birth of her children, she retired from dance. Searching for a way to reclaim her fitness and reconnect with her body through movement, she was drawn to Pilates, which at the time was a little-known form of strength training used mainly by dancers as a method of rehabilitation. For three years she studied intensively with Ramona Kryzanowska, a former Balanchine dancer who is considered the "high priestess" of Pilates. With Kryzanowska's encouragement, McGuire-Wien became a certified Pilates instructor and opened the first Pilates studio in West Hampton, New York. Her timing was perfect: Pilates became an exercise craze and the studio flourished.

When the demands of teaching and running a studio drove her to the edge of mental and physical burnout, McGuire-Wien once again found herself on the cutting edge of fitness. Searching for a way to recharge her mind, body, and spirit, she discovered the benefits of Kundalini yoga. The movement, music, and spiritual and physical connection of this most ancient practice, brought to the United States by Yogi Bhajan, resonated deeply with McGuire-Wien and inspired her to explore other styles of yoga as well. She went on to study with noted instructors Alan Finger, Shiva Rhea, and Twee Merrigan. McGuire-Wien completed her teacher training in both Kundalini and vinyasa yoga. Believing that "what's true in your body is true in your life," she began teaching students a unique practice of yoga focused on the joy of connecting body and spirit by incorporating elements of dance, Pilates, and traditional yoga.

McGuire-Wien now leads luxurious juice cleansing retreats, creating a safe, supportive, nurturing environment for clients at her Green renovated retreat center in Jamesport, New York, on the bucolic North Fork of Long Island. She has personally guided hundreds of students from as far away as Japan and India and as close to home as Manhattan as they experience the life-changing results of her unique program, which combines yoga, movement, meditation, art, and gently guided self-insight to create physical, mental, emotional, and spiritual rituals of purification. Students at American Yogini's luxurious retreat are able to ease into a *lifestyle* that seamlessly incorporates the cleanse treatments in a private, supportive, custom-tailored environment. It is an experience they choose to return to again and again, and it is this experience McGuire-Wien has re-created for the readers of this book.

For more information on retreats, juice delivery services, and high-quality products to support juicing, visit McGuire-Wien's website: www.americanyogini.com.